BLACK LEGACY PRESS™
WWW.BLACKLEGACYPRESS.ORG

SLAVE NARRATIVES

VOLUME XIV
SOUTH CAROLINA NARRATIVES
PART 3

By
United States.
Work Projects Administration

Copyright © 2024 by BLACKLEGACYPRESS.ORG

All rights reserved. No part of this publication may be reproduced or transmitted in any form or by any means electronic or mechanical, including information storage and retrieval systems without permission in writing from the publisher, except for student research using the appropriate citations.

ISBN: 978-1-63652-214-2

SLAVE NARRATIVES

A Folk History of Slavery in the United States.
From Interviews with Former Slaves

**UNITED STATES.
WORK PROJECTS ADMINISTRATION**

TYPEWRITTEN RECORDS PREPARED BY
THE FEDERAL WRITERS' PROJECT
1936-1938
ASSEMBLED BY
THE LIBRARY OF CONGRESS PROJECT
WORK PROJECTS ADMINISTRATION
FOR THE DISTRICT OF COLUMBIA
SPONSORED BY THE LIBRARY OF
CONGRESS

WASHINGTON 1941

VOLUME XIV

SOUTH CAROLINA NARRATIVES
PART 3

Prepared by
The Federal Writers' Project of
The Works Progress Administration
For the State of Alabama

CONTENTS

Adeline Jackson ... 1
Cordelia Anderson Jackson ... 5
Agnes James ... 9
Fred James ... 15
Isiah Jeffries ... 19
Thomas Jefferson ... 23
Henry D. Jenkins ... 27
Maria Jenkins ... 33
Paul Jenkins ... 37
Emma Jeter ... 41
Adeline Hall Johnson ... 45
Anna Johnson ... 51
Jack Johnson ... 53
James Johnson ... 55
Rev. James H. Johnson ... 59
Jane Johnson ... 63
Jimmie Johnson ... 69
Mary Johnson ... 73
Miemy Johnson ... 79
Tom Johnson ... 83
Richard (Look-up) Jones ... 85
Wesley Jones ... 93
Sallie Layton Keenan ... 95
Ella Kelly ... 101

Martha Kelly	105
Mary Jane Kelley	111
Gabe Lance	113
Ephriam (Mike) Lawrence	115
Ben Leitner	123
Mary Ann Lipscomb	127
Govan Littlejohn	129
Easter Lockhart	133
Gable Locklier	139
Walter Long	145
Gillam Lowden	151
Emma Lowran	153
Nellie Loyd	155
Amie Lumpkin	161
Ballam Lyles	165
Eison Lyles	167
Moses Lyles	171
George McAlilley	175
Ed McCrorey (Mack)	181
Richard Mack	187
Jake McLeod	193
Bill McNeil	199
Andy Marion	203
Milton Marshall	209
Charlie Meadow	215
Albert Means	221
Andrew Means	223

Jason Miller	227
Lucinda Miller	231
Cureton Milling	235
Abbey Mishow	239
Sam Mitchell	243
Charity Moore	247
Sena Moore	251
Silas Nelson	255
Susan Nelson	257
William Oliver	261
Albert Oxner	265
Ann Palmer	267
George Patterson	271
Sallie Paul	279
Lina Anne Pendergrass	293
Amy Perry	297
Rob Perry	303
Victoria Perry	307
John Petty	311
Sarah Poindexter	315
Sam Polite	319
William Pratt	325
Henry Pristell	329
Junius Quattlebaum	333

ADELINE JACKSON

Interview with Adeline Jackson, 88 years old
—*W.W. Dixon, Winnsboro, S.C.*

"I was born four miles southwest of where I is now, on de other side of Woodward Station. I was a slave of old Marster John Mobley, de richest man, de larges' land owner, and wid more niggers than any other white man in de county. He was de seventh son of de seventh son, so he allowed, and you knows dat's a sign of a big family, lots of cows, mules, horses, money, chillun and everything dat's worth havin'. He had a good wife too; dis de way he got her, he say. She de daughter of old Maj. Andy McLean, who got a body full of bullets in de Revolution; he didn't want Katie to marry Marster John. Marster John git on a mule and ride up in de night. Miss Katie runned out, jump up behin' him, run away and marry Marster John. They had de same birthday, March 27th, but Marster John two years older than Miss Katie. Dat day was looked to, same as Christmas, every year dat come. Big times then, I tell you!

"My mistress had long hair, techin' de floor and could dance, so Marster John said, wid a glass of water on top of her head. Marster John got 'ligion and went all de way lak de jailer in de Bible. All de house jined wid him and mos' of de slaves. It was Baptist and he built a spankin' good church buildin' down de road, all out of his own money, and de cemetery dere yet. He called it 'Fellowship.' Some fine tombstones in dere yet. De finest cost two thousand dollars, dat's his daughter Nancy's tomb. Marster John and my old mistress buried in dere.

"When my younges' mistress, name Marion Rebecca, married her second cousin, Marster Edward P. Mobley, I was give to her and went wid them to de June place. It was called dat because old Doctor June built it and sold it to Marster Ed. I nussed her first chillun: Edward, Moses Hill, John and Katie. It was a large, two-story frame house, with chimneys at each gable end. Marster Edward got to be as rich as old marster; he owned de June place, de Rochelle plantation, de Peay place and de Roebuck place. Yes sir, course us had overseers for so many slaves and plantations. I 'member Mr. Oze Brown, Mr. Neely and Mr. Tim Gladney. In course of time I was took off de nussin' and put to de field. I drapped cotton seed, hoed some, and picked cotton.

"I don't 'member no poor buckra, outside de overeeers, 'cept a Mr. Reed dat lived down on wateroe, passin' our house sometime. He was a Godforsaken lookin' man dat marster or mistress always give somethin'.

"Our neighbors was de Pearys, de Durhams, de Picketts, de Barbers and Boulwares. Doctor Henry Gibson was our doctor. All dese folks kep' a pack of hounds to run deer and foxes. Yes, I has eat many pieces of deer. Good? I wouldn't fool you, taste it and you'll hunger for it ever afterward.

"Yes sir, at certain times we worked long and hard, and you had to be 'ticular. De only whipping I got was for chopping down a good corn stalk near a stump in a new ground. Marster never sold a slave but swaps were made wid kin people to advantage, slaves' wives and husbands sometimes. I never learned to read or write. I went to White Poplar Springs Church, de Baptist church my mistress 'tended. De preacher was Mr. Cartledge. He allowed Miss Marion was de flower of his flock.

"Slaves lived in quarters, a stretch of small houses off from de White House. Patrollers often come to search for stray slaves; wouldn't take your word for it. They would search de house. If they ketch one widout a pass, they whipped him. We got most our outside news Sunday at church. When farm work was not pressing, we got all of Saturday to clean up 'round de houses, and wash and iron our clothes.

"Everything lively at Christmas time, dances wid fiddles, pattin' and stick rattlin', but when I jined de church, I quit dancin'.

"After de war, a man came along on a red horse; he was dressed in a blue uniform and told us we was free. De Yankees dat I 'members was not gentlefolks. They stole everything they could take and de meanest thing I ever see was shoats they half killed, cut off de hams, and left de other parts quiverin' on de ground.

"I married Mose Jackson, after freedom, and had a boy, Henry. Last I heard, he was at Shelby, North Carolina. We had a daughter, Mary, she married Eph Brown. She had ten chillun, many gran' chillun, they's my great-gran' chillun. My mistress was a good Christian woman, she give me a big supper when I was married. Her house, durin' de war, always had some sick or wounded soldier. I 'member her brother, Zed, come home wid a leg gone. Her cousin, Theodore, was dere wid a part of his jaw gone.

My mistress could play de piano and sing de old songs. I 'members Marster Theodore had trouble wid de words. Dere was a song called 'Jaunita', 'bout a fountain. Marster Theodore would try hard, but would say, everytime, 'Jawneeta', and de folks would laugh but mistress never would crack a smile but just go on wid another song. I thinks everybody should jine de church and then live right. Have prayers in de family befo' gitting in de bed. It would have good change, 'specially in de towns I thinks.

"Yes, women in family way worked up to near de time, but guess Doctor Gibson knowed his business. Just befo' de time, they was took out and put in de cardin' and spinnin' rooms.

"Yes, I see folks put irons in de fire and some throw a big chunk of fire into de yard to make de screech owl stop his scary sounds.

"Befo' I forgits, Marster Edward bought a slave in Tennessee just 'cause he could play de fiddle. Named him 'Tennessee Ike' and he played 'long wid Ben Murray, another fiddler. Sometime all of us would be called up into de front yard to play and dance and sing for Miss Marion, de chillun and visitors. I was much happier them days than now. Maybe it won't be so bad when I gits my old age pension."

CORDELIA ANDERSON JACKSON

Interview with Cordelia Anderson Jackson, 78 years old
157 Kings St. Spartanburg, S.C.
—Caldwell Sims, Union, S.C.

Cordelia lives in a small shack with some friends. She is quite an actor and a tireless teller of yarns. She still ties her head up in a white rag and has large eyes set far apart and a very flat nose. She is ebony colored. She is a firm believer in her religion and she enjoys shouting on any occasion for joy or for sorrow.

"White folks tells stories 'bout 'ligion. Dey tells stories 'bout it kaise dey's 'fraid of it. I stays independent of what white folks tells me when I shouts. De Spirit moves me every day, dat's how I stays in. White folks don't feel sech as I does; so dey stays out. Can't serve God all de time; allus something getting in de way. Dey tries me and den I suddenly draps back to serving de Holy God. Never does it make no difference how I's tossed about. Jesus, He comes and saves me everytime. I's had a hard time, but I's blessed now—no mo' mountains.

"Ever since I a child I is liked white folks. Dey's good and dey does not know why dey tells stories 'bout Jesus. I got a heap mo' in slavery dan I does now; was sorry when Freedom got here. I 'specks I is nigh to a hundred, but dat's so old. I jest calls myself any whars twixt seventy-five and a hundred. I recollects slavery, though. Ma was Charlotte Anderson and she lived in Union County wid de Tuckers, jest across from de Richards Quarter.

"Biggest sight I ever see'd was dat balloon when it come down on Pea Ridge. De man in it everybody addressed as Professor (Prof. Lowe—1861). He let uncle Jerry git in it. Mr. McKissick helped uncle Jerry up in it. It was de first balloon ever come to Union county, and 'til dis day I don't like no balloons.

"Airplanes jest tickles, I cannot tell you how come, but dey jest does. I went out dar (throwing her arm in the direction of the landing field) and see'd 'em light. Dressed-up white folks hopped down out'n it from a little do' dat a man wid leg'uns and a cap on opened. Thing gwine on wid lots of burring and all like dat. When dem folks got out, some mo' clam'ned in. Dat same man opened de do', shot (shut) it, and de plane tuck off. White folks 'lowed dat it was gwine to 'lanta, Ga.

"Right dar I 'low'd, when I goes up like dat, I sho ain't gwine up wid no man—I'se gwine up wid Jesus.

"Dat white woman [HW: Amelia Earhardt] went up and ain't nobody found her yet and it been two months. Lawd, she looking fer de world's end. God don't mean fer womens to do nothing like dat. Womens is stumbling blocks at times.

"I got a boy dat been through school. He stays off, but he treats me so good and talks to me like white folks does; so I calls him, 'white child'. I 'longs to de church club. He tries to larn me to talk proper when I goes out to dem meetings, but I fergits how befo' I reaches de meeting. Us named it de 'Mothers' Club'. 'White child' pays fer me to 'long dar, and when I is down wid spells, dey nurses me. 'White child' pays fer my 'onsurance' so dat I does not have no worriment to aggravate my soul.

"White child birthed one Sunday morning jest a year atter de big earthquake. It was also Christmas morning, kaise my child drapped a year to de day atter dat earthquake and I feared dat he was not gwinter have no sense. But My God, how he can read!

"One night, Aug. 30th, our house started rocking. We thought a panther was a-rocking it, kaise my old man had see'd one. He run out wid a gun and went to de wood pile; den he hollered to me and said, 'Delia, come out here, de whole world is shaking'. God sho showed his power dat night. Ever since dat I been fixed wid God. It won't long atter dat, us heard a noise in our other room. Old man went in dar and see'd a panther climbing up fer our rations. He grabbed his gun from over de do' and shot dat panther in de corner.

"I used to think dat niggers was fools dat called me a nigger. I go and tell Miss Nellie Tucker. She 'low, 'No, you ain't no nigger when other niggers calls you one.' Marse William whistle like a partridge; den Miss Nellie play her pianny. I dance and Marse send fer me a sugar and butter biscuit. Marse git his banjo and he pick it fer me to sing 'Oh, Bob white, is your wheat ripe? No, no, not quite.' Dat when I lived as a little gal on Marse William's home tract, called Musgrove Tract.

VISION: "Was traveling in a gold chariot to Heaven. De overseer had come to bleed me, but I went up. Something say to look back and see whar you been. I looked back and said, 'Lawd, take me whar no rent won't bother me!' Lawd answer, 'Do not pray dat way. Pray fer Him to do His will'. Den I axed de Lawd whar is I. He say, 'Did you look down on dem chimneys?' Den I see'd dat I was in de chariot wid water all under me. It looked like de sky.

"To-day, I am so glad to walk about in Jesus' care. I wish people could see my faith. I am a Christian."

AGNES JAMES

Interview with Mom Agnes James, 80 years old
Claussens, S.C.
—*Annie Ruth Davis*

"Yes'um, I used to live in slavery time, but de Lord above know, I sho don' really recollect nothin much to tell you 'bout slavery time. I don' know exactly how old I is. Think I 'bout 80 some odd. Think dat 'bout de age Bubba Gregg say I is. I tell you, I was so chillunfied in slavery time, I ain' had no time to study 'bout no age. I say, I was so chillunfied. Yes'um, dat it. Dat somethin dat I ought to had ax my grandmammy 'bout how old I is, so den I might could call it up to you right sharp. Oh, I wishes now I had ax my grandmammy dat word fore she die.

"Us belong to Mr. Hector Cameron fore freedom come here. Right down dere to Salem Church, dat whe' I was born. You hear talk of Miss Janie Little over dere to Marion, ain' you? Dat who used to be my mittie in dem days. Yes, mam, boss had pick me out to tend to Miss Janie. You see, he give all his daughters one of us to have a care for dem.

"My white folks, dey had a right smart of colored people dey own en far as I can reckon, dey been spend mighty good treatment to dem all de time. I know 'bout old Miss used to love to feed us, my mercy! White folks would send for all us chillun to go up to de big house en get somethin to eat twixt meals. Yes'um, dey had a colored people quarter dat been settin way back up on de hill. Had to have a quarter 'cause dat whe' us been stay all de time old Miss won' stuffin' somethin down we mouth. I remember, dere used to was de most pretty flowers in de lane gwine through dem woods from us house right up to old Massa's yard en my Lord, honey, I did love to be de first one long dere on a mornin to see could I find a blossom to fetch to old Miss. Look like old Miss would be so please to see my granny marchin all we chillun up dat path 'cause when we would go dere on a mornin, she would set right down on de steps en talk wid us. Would set dere in listen to see could all us say dat prayin blessin she had learned us to speak fore she would hand us anything to eat. Den she would give us everyone a spoonful of dis here worm cure. Great Jerusalem! Miss would make dat herself out dese black lookin seed mixed up in molasses. I remember, she would bring a big bowl of dat out dere en would make Pickle tote it round for her while she put it in us mouth. Yes, mam, Miss would give us all a spoonful of dat every mornin en den she would ax us de next mornin if any us had any worms. No, mam, she never didn' give us any other kind of medicine as I can remember. Just give us dat en den feed us some milk en bread. Dat all she give us, but I tell you, I was as proud of dat milk en bread as I is of de rations I get dese days 'cause I never know no different den. No'um, didn' nobody eat den like dey do now. All de people would make dey own gardens in dem days en would fix soup en fry meat. I used to been so glad to get me a 'tatoe en a piece of bread. I thought I was eatin cake.

"I never didn' work in no field or nothin like dat no time. When I was a little small girl, I would stay dere home en play 'bout de yard en nurse my mammy's baby while she was workin in de field. Yes'um, old Massa would give her task to pick cotton en hoe cotton en pick peas or somethin another like dat 'bout all de time. Don' know whe' she work all day or no, but I know she would always let up at 12 o'clock en come to de house to get her somethin to eat. Can remember dat good as anything. Oh, she would have to cook herself when she come home bein' dere wasn' none of we chillun big enough to cook nothin. I recollects, I used to get chips en pile dem up for her 'cause she always been tell me, if de baby go to sleep, to get up some chips en put dem on de steps for her to hurry en start fire wid. She would cook us meat en bread like corn hoecake en fry meat de most of de time. Den another time, she would bake a big round loaf like dat en break it in two en give me half en my brother Charlie de other part. Would lay a piece of meat on de top of it. No'um, I reckon 'bout all de people used to cook in de chimney. I know my mammy used to cook in de chimney en I don' think she thought nothin 'bout no stove in dem days. Cose if she did, I know we chillun didn' get it.

"Yes, Lord, I been married 'bout 16 years fore my husband died. Yes'um, I had a tolerable good size weddin over dere to Mr. Elija Gregg's house. Been married in a white dress trimmed wid blue ribbon. You is hear talk of a cream of tartar dress, ain' you? Oh, my Lord of mercy, dere was a crowd of people dere dat night to get dey eye full en deyself full, too, I say. Yes'um, I had four waiters in my ceremony. En had cake en rice en 'tatoe custard en a yearlin pig wid a red apple stuck in he mouth, so dey tell me. Dat what was for de refreshments. De old man Charles Reynolds, he was de preacher dere dat night en, say, he eat so much pig till you could see pig in he face, so dey tell me. Cose I never had no mind to know nothin 'bout it. Oh, yes Lord, I got seven chillun dat come here fore my old man die, but dey all done gone en get married en left me by myself. Dat how-come I stays over here wid Miss Bertie 'cause she ain' have nobody to stay wid her neither en I tries to help her out somehow. Yes'um, me en Miss Bertie does rest right well together, I say.

"Oh, great jumpin mercy, de shake! I sho knows all 'bout dat 'cause I was stayin right up dere to old man Elija Gregg's place den. I tellin you, it was a time, honey. I was gwine down side de road to prayer meetin dat night wid my baby in my arms en dere come such a roarin' en a rockin' in de elements till I thought my baby had got out my arms en I was just a hollerin for somebody to come en help me get my baby back. Been so crazy dat I was lookin in all de ditches for my baby. My husband, he come a runnin to see what ailed me en say, 'Agnes, what de matter wid you?' I say, 'My baby lost. Do Lord, whe' my baby gone?' He say, 'Agnes, you must be ailin in de head. Dere de baby on your arm.' Yes'um, I was crazy 'cause I had my baby in my arms en didn' know it. Oh, de people done a piece of hollerin dat night. Everybody was a hollerin en a prayin. I hear talk three or four of dem got converted in de spirit dat night. I tellin you, it been a long time fore I got over dat thing, too, 'cause I was scared most to death.

"No'um, I never didn' believe in nothin like dat. Never didn' believe in no conjurin. Don' care what dey say 'bout it, I never didn' believe in it. Yes'um, I hear people talk 'bout somebody had hurt dem, but dey make a wrong mistake to say somebody do somethin to dem. Ain' nobody but de Lord do nothin, I say. I know dere ain' nobody never do nothin to me. Hear people say dey wear money round dey ankle to keep folks from hurtin dem, but ain' nobody never bother me, I tell dem. If dey live right, ain' nobody gwine trouble dem neither. No, Lord, ain' nobody never speak no harm word to me en I ain' got no mind to harness up myself.

"Well, it just seems like de world growin wilder for de young folks. Dey don' never think 'bout nothin 'cept gwine right head first all de time. I know when I been comin up, I never see no such livin like de people makin dese days. Dey just gwine head over heels to de worser. Don' never think near a day dey got to stop some of dese days.

"I tell de truth, it ain' make no difference which time I think de best time to live in. Everything went well en good wid me in de old days en everything still gwine dat way, Thank de Lord, too."

United States. Work Projects Administration

FRED JAMES

> Interview with Fred James (81)
> Newberry, S.C. RFD
> —G.L. Summer, Newberry, S.C.

"Yes, I 'member slavery time and de war. I was about 7 or 8 years old. I belonged to Marse Tom Price. My father, John James, belonged to Madison Brooks and my mammy belonged to Tom Price. When dey married dey lived wid Madison Brooks awhile, but dey was wid Tom Price when I was a boy.

"Of cose I 'member de war. Us chaps, both niggers and white, was made to go up-stairs in de big house and look out de window to see de soldiers when dey come. We heard de Yankees marching befo' dey got dar, but dey come from de other side of de house, facing south towards Caldwells, and we didn't see dem marching in. Dey stopped at our house and looked around and asked if marster was at home. We told him dat he wasn't dar. We was eating apples, and dey asked us whar we got 'em. We told dem dat we got de apples on de place, and dey asked us for some. We give dem some apples; den dey left. Marse had carried his fine stock about a mile off in de woods so de soldiers couldn't find dem; but we didn't tell de soldiers.

"We lived in a little log cabin made wid mud between de logs, dat was de kind of houses Marse had for his slaves. We slept on wood beds wid ropes stretched tight across in place of slats. Dis held our straw mattress.

"My father's daddy come from Africa. His name was Emmanuel James. Atter freedom come he give me a little yearling. We wasn't allowed to have anything befo' freedom come; and we wasn't allowed to learn to read and write. Dey whipped us if dey caught us wid a book trying to read or write. Ma said dey cut off a hand if dey caught you.

"We raised hogs, sheep, goats, cows and plenty chickens; raised everything at home, and had a good garden with plenty vegetables. Dem cows and hogs and other cattle were branded and allowed to graze around in bottoms of de lowlands whar dar was no fence.

"My clothes was made from yarn spun by my mammy, and she made my clothes, too. Marse had my mammy to spin and weave for all de slaves on de place. But marse and mistress was good to us. He had a nigger overseer who sometimes brought a nigger to marse when he misbehaved; den marse would have de nigger overseer to whip him. He had 8 to 10 slaves all de time.

"Some slaves dat lived on places close to us would run off sometimes and hide in de woods, and live dar in a den which dey dug. At night they would go out and hunt food, like hogs; den kill 'em at night and dress 'em. Most of de day dey would stay in de den.

"I 'member when freedom come, old marse said, 'You is all free, but you can work on and make dis crop of corn and cotton; den I will divide up wid you when Christmas comes.' Dey all worked, and when Christmas come, marse told us we could get on and shuffle for ourselves, and he didn't give us anything. We had to steal corn out of de crib. We prized de ears out between de cracks and took dem home and parched dem. We would have to eat on dese for several days.

"We had to work, all day, sun up to dark, and never had Saturday afternoons off anytime. My mammy had to wash clothes on Saturday nights for us to wear on Sundays.

"We chaps played marbles most all de time. Marse used to try to scare us by telling us dar was spooks. Some of de old folks did believe in spooks, but I don't know much about dem. We never used much medicine den but quinine. Folks had lots of chills den, but dey never had any kind of strokes or things like dat as dey do dese days.

"We had to get a pass from marse if we went out. If de patrollers caught us widout a pass dey would whip us.

"Right atter de war de Ku Klux started. I 'member dem when dey would march up and down de road. Dey marched most at night, and we could hear de horses for a long distance as deir feet struck de ground.

"I married Nellie Wilson, and had 12 children. I got now 6 children; my wife is dead. I got five grandchildren and eight great-grandchildren.

"I think Abraham Lincoln and Jeff Davis was good men in deir way, as dey thought. Booker T. Washington is a great man, and he is done lots of good for de niggers. I think slavery was good in some ways and bad in others. I was better off den dan I am now.

"I jined de church when I was 20 years old, because it was de law—to trust in de Lawd, you got to belong to de church.

"I member something 'bout 40 acres of land and a mule dat de slaves would get, but never come anything about it. When freedom come most of de slaves hired out as wage hands, cutting wood and working on farms or any odd jobs dey could get. Dar was lots of new ground, and many of de niggers got work clearing it up.

"We didn't get any money in slavery time, but got plenty to eat; and atter de war, we got a little money and a little to eat. I 'member dat old Mr. Brown hired me out once about 45 years ago at 30¢ a day and my meals. I think de younger generation ain't so good. Dey have deir own way and don't respect old folks. Dat's de way it is wid both whites and blacks."

ISIAH JEFFRIES

> Interview with Isiah Jefferies, (age 86)
> Gaffney, S.C. Rt. 6.
> —*Caldwell Sims, Union, S.C.*

"I is what is known as a outside child. My Ma went to Hamlet. I lived on de Jefferies plantation, below Wilkinsville in Cherokee County. My father was Henry Jefferies. My mother was Jane Jefferies. My mother's husband was named Ned. Before her marriage she was a Davis. She was sold in slavery to Henry Jefferies. I allus lived with my mother, and Ned was as good to me as he was to his own chillun. My mother had three outside chilluns, and we each had a different father. Atter she married Ned; den he jest come to be our Pa, dat is he let her give us his name. She and Ned had four chillun.

"My first wife is dead and my second wife is named Alice Jefferies. I got one child by my first wife, and I ain't got no outside chilluns. Dat works out bad, at best. None of my folks is living. All of dem is done dead now; jest me, my wife and my sister's daughter, Emma, who is grown now. Her Pa and her Ma took and went crazy befo' dey died. Both of dem died in de asylum. We took Emma, and she ain't jest 'zactly right; but she ain't no bother to us.

"First thing I had to do as a child was to mind my Ma's other chilluns as I was de first outside one dat she had. Dis I did until I was about twelve years old. My Ma and Ned was working one day and I was minding her chilluns as usual when I looked up and seed de top of our house on fire. I hollered and dey come running from de field. De other hands come with dem kaise I made such a noise hollering. Soon de big folks got de fire out. Atter dat, Marse Henry had me to leave de house and go to work fer him.

"It was spring and I started in chopping cotton. 'Peers dat I got on pretty well, and dat de overseer liked me from de start. From dar on I was broke into field work of all kinds and den I did work around de lot as well. It was not long befo' everybody started calling me 'uncle Zery', why—I did not know; but anyway dat name still sticks to me by dem dat knows me well. My grandpa never called me dat, kaise I was named atter him, and he too proud of dat fact to call me any nickname. I stayed wid him at his house lots atter I started working fer de marster, kaise he showed me how to do things. I worked fer him to git my first money and he would give me a quarter fer a whole day's work. Dat made me feel good and I thought I was a man kaise I made a quarter. In dem days a quarter was a lot of money. I spent it fer chawing tobacco, and dat made me sick at first. Dats all men had to spend money fer in dem days. Everything was give you on de plantation and you did not need much money. Sometimes we cooked out in de field and I have cooked bread in de field in a lid.

"Ma teached me how to cook befo' I was twelve years old. We had good things to eat den; more dan my chilluns has dese times. All de slaves had dere gardens on my marster's plantation. He made dem do it, and dey liked it. Niggers do not seem to take no pains wid gardens now. Land ain't soft and mellow like it used to be. In cold weather we had to bank out 'taters, rutabegas, beets, carrots and pumpkins. De pumpkins and carrots was fer de hogs and cows.

"In warm weather we had cotton clothes and in cold weather we had woolen clothes dat our marster had made fer us by de old ladies on de plantation. But we did go barefooted all winter until we was grown and married. We had all de wood we wanted fer fire. We kept fire all day and all night. We sot by de fire in winter and popped corn, parched pinders [HW: peanuts] and roasted corn ears.

"Marster and Mistress had six chilluns. Her name was Ellen and her house was three stories high. Dere overseers allus lived wid dem. Dere was a lot of slaves and dey all loved de white folks. De whole plantation was allus up at sunup. But we did not work very late. I remember de Patter-rollers, de Ku Klux and de Yankees. Niggers dreaded all three. Dere was no jail fer us; de Patter-rollers kept us straight.

"When I got to be a big boy, my Ma got religion at de Camp meeting at El-Bethel. She shouted and sung fer three days, going all over de plantation and de neighboring ones, inviting her friends to come to see her baptized and shouting and praying fer dem. She went around to all de people dat she had done wrong and begged dere forgiveness. She sent fer dem dat had wronged her, and told dem dat she was born again and a new woman, and dat she would forgive dem. She wanted everybody dat was not saved to go up wid her.

"De white folks was baptized in de pool first, and den dere darkies. When de darkies time come, dey sung and shouted so loud dat de Patter-rollers come from somewhar, but Marster and Missus made dem go away and let us shout and rejoice to de fullest. Missus had all her darkies to wear white calico in de pool dat was a-gwine in fer baptizing. In de sewing-room she had calico robes made fer everybody. My Ma took me wid her to see her baptized, and I was so happy dat I sung and shouted wid her. All de niggers jined in singing. De white folks stayed and saw us baptize our folks, and dey liked our singing."

Slave Narratives

THOMAS JEFFERSON

Interview with Thomas Jefferson, 102 years old
Shiloh Church, Highway 29
—*Ellie S. Rice, Anderson, S.C.*

It is not often that a person 102 years old is seen doing manual labor, and especially as hard a job as picking cotton. Yet that is just what Thomas Jefferson was doing, who, as he himself stated, is, "102 years and 18 days old today." Asked why he was doing this, he replied, "Just to take a little exercise."

Thomas lives with his daughter, Florence Humphreys, on a small farm, out near Shiloh Church, on Highway 29. Until recently, he slept in a little shack nearby, taking his meals with his daughter. He is too feeble to live alone now, however.

Thomas Jefferson was born on the farm of Mr. Jenkins Hammond, on the old Hammond place, out on the Williamston road, on November 1, 1834. When Mr. Hammond's daughter, Mary Amanda Pauline, married Elias John Earle, son of Samuel Girard Earle, who was one of the very first citizens of Anderson county, Mr. Hammond gave her, as a wedding gift, Thomas Jefferson's mother and five children, of which Thomas was one. And here he lived with the Earles on "Evergreen" plantation, for many, many years.

During the War Between the States, Mr. Earle operated a corn and flour mill, and Thomas Jefferson was his miller. Asked if he remembered this, he replied, "Well,

I do remember it. I remember one time we worked all night Saturday night, all day Sunday and Sunday night, and Monday morning had ten barrels of flour to send the Confederate army."

Shiloh (Baptist) Church, nearby, Thomas said, was being constructed at the time the war started, and was not finished until after the war was over. The first person buried in the Shiloh graveyard was Elijah Herring, who was in the Confederate army and became ill and died, and was brought home to be buried.

When Samuel Girard Earle died in 1848, and his wife in 1865, they were buried under a large apple tree at "Evergreen" plantation. Later, their bodies were removed to the Shiloh graveyard, by their grand-daughter, Miss Betty Earle. Thomas says he helped to move and rebury the bodies.

Thomas was at one time a member of Shiloh, but is now a member of the Mt. Sinai colored church.

Thomas is remarkably well for a person one hundred and two years old. His eyes are dim, his steps tottering, but his hearing is good and his mind is as clear as it ever was. Asked about his appetite, he said, "I eat anything I can get, I can eat anything." Many people much younger than he is, and certainly with more money than he has, would envy him for his splendid digestion.

Thomas has been on the relief rolls now for several years. It is a peculiar pleasure for Mrs. A.M. Mitchell, County Director of Temporary State Department of Public Welfare, to look after Thomas personally, because her grandmother was the bride to whom he was given, with his mother and brothers and sisters. The old man eagerly anticipates Mrs. Mitchell's coming each month, to bring his check and to look after his comfort. He is very humble and exceedingly grateful for everything done for him, and says he is expecting to live many more years, with the good care he is getting.

United States. Work Projects Administration

HENRY D. JENKINS

Interview with Henry D. Jenkins, 87 years old
—W.W. Dixon, Winnsboro, S.C.

Henry D. Jenkins lives in a four-room frame house, which he owns. His wife, two single daughters, his son and his son's wife and three small children live with him. The house is constructed on a tract of land containing four hundred and eighty (480) acres, which Henry also owns.

He does not suffer with an inferiority complex. He is self-reliant and thrifty, with a pardonable pride in his farm and his rise from slavery to a position of respectibility as a church member, citizen, and tax payer. He is well preserved physically, for his age, 87 years, alert in his movements and animated in conversation.

His plantation and home is in the south western part of Fairfield County, six or seven hundred yards east of State highway #215.

"Yes sir, tho' I am a 'spectable colored citizen, as you see me; I pays taxes and owns my own plantation. I was once a slave on de Reese place, in Sumter County, below Columbia. Just when I come to b'long to Mr. Joseph Howell, I don't know. I recollects dat Marse Joe had 'bout twenty families of slaves and dere was six hundred acres in his plantation.

"My mistress was his wife, Miss Sara. They had four chillun. Miss Mattie, married Oscar Chappell. Johnnie, married a Miss Lever. Thomas, married some lady in Columbia, disremember de fam'ly name. Miss Jessie, married Rev. Huggins, a Baptist preacher, though her folks wasn't of dat 'suasion; they was Methodist. Us niggers was 'structed early in 'ligion. Took to Cedar Creek and camp meetin'. My white folks had a fine carriage. A mulatto boy, Adam, was de driver. Sometime I'd go wid him to meet visitors from de low country at de station, and look after de baggage and sich.

"Yes sir, I doesn't deny it, I got many whuppins. Dere's not much to a boy, white or black, dat don't need a whuppin' sometime on de way up. When you break a wild spirited colt, they make de best hoss or mule. I can do more work today, than most of dese triflin', cigaret young mens. You sees me today, as straight as a arrow and like a wild cat on my foots.

"You bet yo' life, my white folks was de bestest in de land. They wasn't mealy mouthed; they made everybody work, sun to sun, seven days in de week. But didn't de good Lord set de 'zample? Yes sir, he made us all work, women in de perils of child birth, drapped cotton seed and corn kernels. Dr. Turnipseed, dat was our doctor, 'low dat light labor lak dat good for them.

"Farm hands got a peck of meal, three pounds bacon, quart of 'lasses, cup of salt, and two cups middlin' flour, no white flour. Had good warm clothes in winter, one-piece cotton suit in summer, and de little niggers went dressed in deir shirt tails from fust of June, to fust of October. They sho' did, and was as happy over it as de day was long.

"My mother named Emma. Never married to my daddy, 'cause they didn't live on de same place and b'long to same master. Daddy b'long to de Halls. I have a brother by dis same mammy. Daddy go by de name of Dinkins. He took up wid another woman after freedom, and my brother and me was 'shame of him. Us 'cided to take Jenkins for our name but keep a 'D' in de middle, so if anything come up, de 'D' could 'cite 'membrance of who us really is. You see what I mean?

"Our shoes for de winter was made on de place, out of leather from our own tan-yard and from our own cow hides. Marster had a good fish pond. He had a four-hoss gin, though mules pulled it. De lint cotton was packed in a bale and a screw pit. Baggin' was any old thing, like old sacks or canvas sheetin'.

"My mother jined de Baptis' church, and I followed in her foot steps. Everybody ought to b'long to some church, 'cause it's 'spectable, and membership in de church is both a fire and a life insurance. It 'sures you 'ginst hell fire, and gives you at death, an eternal estate in Hebben. What you laughin' at? It's de gospel truth I'm givin' you right now. Wish everybody could hear it and believe it.

"My marster, Joe Howell, went off to de old war. His niggers was so well trained, dat they carried on for him whilst he was gone and dere was no trouble. Everything went on just de same as if he was dere.

"Pat-a-rollers (patrollers) would come often and ketch niggers sometime; caught my daddy once and whup him good. Ours was a fine body of slaves and loyal to de mistress and her chillun.

"Dances? Yes sir, I can hear them fiddles and de pattin' now. Dis de way de dance was called: 'Balance all; sashshay to your partners; swing her 'round and promenade all; forward on de head; ladies change;' and all dat. Then de jigs went on. Believe me, them was times!

"The main drawback on Marster Joe's plantation was, de water on de place was no 'count. Us had to haul water on a sled, wid a mule, from de Friday place; dat's de oniliest trouble us had. Sometime us had to tie up fodder and 'tend to de hay in de field on Sunday.

"I married fust a girl name Sarah, in 1878. Got three chillun by her. She died. Not good for a man to live alone, de Lord say. I picked out another Sarah, but called her Sallie. Us has had nine chillun. Three of dese [TR: are] Sailor, Tera, and Monroe. Monroe lives on my place and farms 'long side of me. Sam is in Detroit, Michigan; Henry in Flurida (Florida).

"When de Yankees come, what they do? They did them things they ought not to have done and they left undone de things they ought to have done. Yes, dat just 'bout tells it. One thing you might like to hear. Mistress got all de money, de silver, de gold and de jewels, and got de well digger to hide them in de bottom of de well. Them Yankees smart. When they got dere, they asked for de ve'y things at de bottom of de well. Mistress wouldn't tell. They held a court of 'quiry in de yard; called slaves up, one by one, good many. Must have been a Judas 'mongst us. Soon a Yankee was let down in de well, and all dat money, silver, gold, jewelry, watches, rings, brooches, knives and forks, butter-dishes, waters, goblets, and cups was took and carried 'way by a army dat seemed more concerned 'bout stealin', than they was 'bout de Holy War for de liberation of de poor African slave people. They took off all de hosses, sheeps, cows, chickens, and geese, took de seine and de fishes they caught, corn in crib, meat in smoke house, and everything. Marse General Sherman said war was hell. It sho' was. Mebbe it was hell for some of them Yankees when they come to die and give account of de deeds they done in Sumter and Richland Counties."

United States. Work Projects Administration

MARIA JENKINS

> Interview with Maria Jenkins, about 90 years old
> 64 Montague Street, Charleston, S.C.
> —Martha S. Pinckney, Charleston, S.C.

Maria Jenkins, who is about ninety, is very nearly blind, and only by quiet persistence can she be made to hear; once started, her mind is clear. She shows no bitterness. Occasionally there are flashes of humor. Her body is brawny, sturdy and well carried, considering her age.

Maria Jenkins was a daughter of Aaron Grant; her mother's name is Ellen Grant, all of whom were owned by Mr. Hugh Wilson of Wadmalaw Island.

"I b'long Wadmalaw. When de Yankee come I ole 'nuf for mind chillun, and take um to de field. I go up to Maussa' house ebery day for de milk for we; and dey give we clabba (clabber) and cow peas and ting out de garden. We git ebery evening a bushel ob corn grind and hand ober to de nurse, and him sift out de flour. Yes Mam. He done grind in de hand mill in de barn yard—de stone mill. Dat been uh big mill too. And dey gib we uh big piece ob meat—so—(measuring with hands) and sometime chicken. Rachel cook in de big pot for we chillun, and he dip um out. (She here explained the big ladle or dipper.) You know dem big ladle. We put um in we pan. Yes, Ma'am, he name Rachel, and he lick we. We haffa love um or she lick we." Her huge mouth was illumined by a humorous smile.

"He teach me to wash de baby clean and put on he dipa (diaper), and if I ain't do um good he konk my head. When de wah come, my pa put heself free off to New Orleans; I dunno how he look. I dunno if he libbin or dead now. My ma dead fust year ob de wah, I hab twelve chillun, and all dead; I got two grand chillun left—de one in New York—I raise him from baby atter he ma and pa dead."

"Your grand son helps you?"

"Wat dat?", leaning forward with her hand back of her ear. The question was repeated.

"Him ain't no man, him my grand daughter, Ellen Jenkins. I raise him from baby yes, she name Ellen. Him good to me; him help me ebery minute."

"Are all your people dead?"

"De whole nation dead," reflectively, "De whole nation dead—Peggy dead—Toby dead—all leaning on de Lord."

"When dem boat come up de ribber, and he shoot, and shoot, de big gun, dat been de awful time. My ma dead de fust year ob de wah—I dunno if dem big gun kill um. He kill 'nuf people.

"Maussa come and he say: 'Who-na (all of you) nigger take care ob yourself, I must leab to take my fambly away. Will is here; and de cow, and de pig in de pen, and de chicken all ober de place—I gib you your freedom for take care ob yourself.' W'en he gone, dem nigger break for the thick woods. Some dead and some ain't dead."

Later a camp was established for this plantation of

Negroes, back in the pine woods. When asked what they did after the war, Maria raised her hands and said:

"After de wah we all come home, tank de Lord! tank de Lord!"

"But your master didn't have any money to care for you."

"Haffa scrabble for yo'self." Said she.

PAUL JENKINS

> Interview with Paul Jenkins, 70 years old
> 18 Belser's Alley, Columbia, S.C.
> —*Stiles M. Scruggs, Columbia, S.C.*

SON OF A SLAVE TELLS OF HIS FATHER'S POLITICAL EXPERIENCES

Paul Jenkins, age seventy, living at 18 Belser's Alley, Columbia, S.C., is a son of Paul Jenkins, a former slave, who decided to endure the burdens he had in Colleton County, South Carolina, after he was set free in 1865, rather than to fly to other places he knew nothing of. There he won the respect of the white folks and Negroes alike, was repeatedly elected to office, and lived there happily to the end of his life.

Here the present Paul Jenkins takes up the story, with:

"I was born in Colleton County in 1867. My daddy was in office when I begin to recall things, and he keep in office, by the will of the people, until I was nearly grown. My mammy, too, was a slave, when she and daddy marry. She die when I was 'bout twelve years old, and my only brother, Edgar, was goin' on ten. My daddy never marry again.

"One day some white men come to see daddy long after mammy was gone, and they say to daddy: 'Paul, when you gwine to jump the broomstick again?' My daddy was the only one who not laugh when they say that. He reply: 'I has no women in view and no weddin' dream in the back of my head. I has decided a wicked woman am a big bother and a good woman am a bore. To my way of thinkin', that is the only difference between them.' The white folks not smile, but say: 'You'll see! Just wait 'til the right girl come along.'

"Daddy just seem to make friends of all the people 'bout him, and our house, close to Smoak, was a big meetin' place most of the time. Sometimes the visitors are all white men. But at other days the niggers come and talk, tell funny tales, and laugh. Most of the meetin's at the house was late at night, 'cause my daddy always go to his office at Walterboro, on week days. People comin' and goin' there, all the time. Daddy was sho' popular with the people, generally speakin'.

"The biggest crowd I ever seen up to that time, was when General M.C. Butler come to Walterboro in 1882, to speak. He had been United States Senator since 1876, and was a candidate for re-election. General Butler much pleased, that day, when many white leaders and daddy call at his hotel and tell him that daddy had been asked by his neighbors to introduce him. He say: 'Well, from what I hears, Paul Jenkins can do that job as well as anybody in the State.' Then he pat daddy on the shoulder.

"At the speakin', daddy gets up, and the big crowd claps its hands for joy, and laughs, too. Daddy not laugh much, just smile. Then he throw back his shoulders and say:

> General Butler, lak Moses, led us forth at last,
> The barren wilderness he pass'd

> Did on the very border stand
> Of the bless'd Promise Land,
> And from the misty mountain tops of his exalted wit,
> Saw it himself and showed us it!

"'That's why we am sendin' him back——'. That was all I hear. Daddy not allowed to finish. The people riot with pleasure, and General Butler say the tribute am de finest he ever hear, and smile at daddy sittin' there on the platform with the other big folks. At another time, daddy has a nigger lawyer runnin' 'gainst him for County Commissioner. The lawyer's name was Amphibious McIver. They begin the campaign at Cottageville. McIver speak first. Daddy follow, and begin with:

> A bullfrog tied by its tail to a stump,
> It rear and it croak, but it couldn't make a jump!

"The white folks and the niggers clap, stamp, throw hats, and laugh; finally, marchin' up to the table to grab daddy and carry him up the street on their shoulders. He keep sayin': 'Boys, why don't you let me finish my speech?' They would laugh and say: 'Paul, you done made de best speech in de world!' Daddy win at the 'lection, in a big way.

"My daddy learn to read, write, and cipher while he was a slave. The Jenkins family help him, he say, 'cause he always keep the peace, and work as he was told to do. When he's set free, that white family help him get settled and loaned him books. He go to Charleston 'bout 1868 and buy an armful of books and studied at night or whenever he had the chance. That is why he was able to make the political races which he make and profit by. He send me and my brother, Edgar, to school, so that we learn a good deal in books. Edgar, he fidgitty lak, and decide he go to Pennsylvania and make a fortune!

"Edgar got work in a steel mill at Johnstown, soon after he got there, and had considerable money, when he was sent to the hospital with pneumonia. He pull through that sickness and go back to his job, but the big flood come (May 31, 1889) and the girl he was to marry was among the 2,000 unknown people who was drowned, and he never has married—peculiar lak our daddy, don't you think? I just been married to one. She is 68 and I's 70 and I may say we's through, too!

"I specialized on bridge-buildin'. I has helped build a sight of bridges in my time, travelin' as far as Memphis, Tenn., in that work. I has made oodles of money, but my dollars always has wings and, one way or the other, they get away from me. Still me and my old woman not sufferin' much and we hopes, when we goes away for good, we goes together."

EMMA JETER

> Interview with "Aunt" Emma Jeter
> 21 Long Twelve, Union, S.C.
> —*Caldwell Sims, Union, S.C.*

"Lordy, Honey, I sho was born in slavery and I is proud o' it too. Ole Marse Cole Lawson was my ole marster. When I axed him how old I was, he allus 'lowed something like dis, 'you is older than you is good', and dat all he ever said 'bout my age. Sweet Dreams (her grand daughter), come here and fetch me a drink from de well to wet my mouth! My grand-daughter stay wid me at night. When she doan stay, some o' de other grand uns stays. Sometime it's jest me and Sago here all alone. I jes' sets and looks at him at night while he sleep. He work de rich white folks' flower yards fer 'em, and dat brings him in at night real tired. My grand-daughter's real name is Marguerite Porter, but nobody don't hardly know dat; kaise everybody call her Sweet Dream, her lil baby name. She my oldest daughter's fifth chile. My feelings tells me I is ole, and my white folks 'll tell you I was born in slavery, 'cept dey is all dead.

"Light furs' struck me on de large plantation o' Ole Marse Cole Lawson, de paw o' Mr. Victor Lawson. Mr. Victor ain't no spring chicken no mo' hisself. Dat over in Sedalia in de Minter Section. You kno's 'bout de large plantation o' Marse James E. Minter, dat gib de section its name? (CHS show boundaries of Minter lands). Way back over dar whar I was born.

"Paw stay in Union County. Maw was sold to a man name Marse Bailey Suber over in Fairfield, while I still a suckling. At dat time, my paw was bought by a widder woman, Miss Sarah Barnett, in Union Cnty. Lawd Jesus! Dat separate my maw and paw. Maw tuck me 'long wid her. Maw name Clara Sims. When Me and maw went to Fairfield, us didn't stay dar long 'fo ole man Harrison Sartor of Santuck, bought my maw. Us glad to git back to Union. I was a big size gal by dis time and I start to be de waiting gal in my new Marse's house fer his wife, Miss Betsy. Miss Betsy had one sister, Miss Nancy Wilson, dat live wid her. Her missus and old Marster and dere son, Willie, was all dat I had to wait on, kaise dat was all dar was in de household.

"God-A-Mighty! Is you gwine to fill up dat book wid all dat I says? Well, Marse Harrison didn't 'low paw to see maw 'cept twice a year—laying-by time and Christmas. My paw still 'longed to Miss Sarah Barnett. Dat's 'zactly why I is got five half-sisters and one-half brother. Paw got him another wife at Miss Sarah's. Miss Sarah want young healthy slaves. Maw had jes' me and Ann. Ann been daed, Oh, Lord, forty years. Dis all to my recollections.

"Is you gwine to fix fer me and Sago to git some pension? Gawd naw, some dese lil babies whats 'er sucking de maw's titties is gwine to git dat pension. Us all gwine to be daed 'fo it even come out. You ain't gwine to even sho' dat to no Gov'ment man; no Lawd, ain't never thought I's gwine to git it.

"Yes, Honey, I was in Fairfield den, but I 'members when crowds o' men come in from de war. All us chilluns seed mens coming and us run and tuck off fas' as us could fer de nearest woods, kaise us wuz dat scared, dat dem mens gwine to git us. Atter dat, us found out dey was our own folks. Us had done tuck and run from dem den.

"Chile, you come back when Sago here, and us tell you dat book full, sho nuff."

United States. Work Projects Administration

ADELINE HALL JOHNSON

Interview with Adeline Hall Johnson, 93 Years old
—W.W. Dixon, Winnsboro, S.C.

Adeline Hall's husband was Tom Johnson but she prefers to be called "Hall", the name of her old master. Adeline lives with her daughter, Emma, and Emma's six children, about ten miles southeast of Winnsboro, S.C., in a three-room frame house on the Durham place, a plantation owned by Mr. A.M. Owens of Winnsboro. The plantation contains 1,500 acres, populated by over sixty Negroes, run as a diversified farm, under the supervision of a white overseer in the employ of Mr. Owens.

The wide expanse of cotton and corn fields, the large number of dusky Negro laborers working along side by side in the fields and singing Negro spirituals as they work, give a fair presentation or picture of what slavery was like on a well conducted Southern plantation before the Civil War. Adeline fits into this picture as the old Negro "Mauma" of the plantation, respected by all, white and black, and tenderly cared for. She has her clay pipe and stick ever with and about her. There is a spacious pocket in her dress underneath an apron. In that pocket is a miscellany of broken pieces of china, crumbs of tobacco, a biscuit, a bit of wire, numerous strings of various colors, and from time to time the pipe becomes the warm individual member of the varied assortment.

Her eyes are bright and undimmed by age and the vigor with which she can telegraph her wants to the household by the rappings of that stick on the plank floor is interesting and amusing.

She is confident that she will round out a century of years, because: "Marse Arthur Owens done tell me I'll live to be a hundred, if I stay on his place and never 'lope away wid any strange young buck nigger.

"I's not so feeble as I might 'pear, white folks. Long time I suffer for sight, but dese last years I see just as good as I ever did. Dats a blessin' from de Lord!

"Who I b'long to in slavery time? Where I born? I born on what is now called de Jesse Gladden place but it all b'long to my old marster, William Hall, then.

"My old marster was one of de richest man in de world. Him have lands in Chester and Fairfield counties, Georgia and Florida, and one place on de Red River in Arkansas. He also had a plantation, to raise brown suger on, in old Louisiana. Then him and his brudder, Daniel, built and give Bethesda Church, dats standin' yet, to de white Methodis' of Mitford, for them to 'tend and worship at. He 'membered de Lord, you see, in all his ways and de Lord guide his steps.

"I never have to do no field work; just stayed 'round de house and wait on de mistress, and de chillun. I was whupped just one time. Dat was for markin' de mantel-piece wid a dead coal of fire. They make mammy do de lashin'. Hadn't hit me three licks befo' Miss Dorcas, Miss Jemima, Miss Julia, and Marse Johnnie run dere, ketch de switch, and say: 'Dat enough Mauma Ann! Addie won't do it agin'. Dats all de beatin' I ever 'ceived in slavery time.

"Now does you wanna know what I do when I was a child, from de time I git up in de mornin' to de time I go to bed? I was 'bout raised up in de house. Well, in de evenin', I fill them boxes wid chips and fat splinters. When mornin' come, I go in dere and make a fire for my young mistresses to git up by. I help dress them and comb deir hair. Then I goes down stairs and put flowers on de breakfas' table and lay de Bible by Marse William's chair. Then I bring in de breakfas'. (Table have to be set de night befo') When everything was on de table, I ring de bell. White folks come down and I wait on de table.

"After de meal finish, Marse William read de Bible and pray. I clear de table and help wash de dishes. When dat finish, I cleans up de rooms. Then I acts as maid and waitress at dinner and supper. I warms up de girls' room, where they sleep, after supper. Then go home to poppy John and Mauma Anne. Dat was a happy time, wid happy days!

"Dat was a happy family. Marse William have no trouble, 'cept once when him brudder, Daniel, come over one mornin' and closet wid Marse William. When Marse Daniel go, Marse William come in dere where me and de mistress was and say: 'Tom's run away from school'. (Dats one of Marse Daniel's boys dat 'tended school at Mt. Zion, in Winnsboro) Her 'low: 'What him run away for?' 'Had a fool duel wid a Caldwell boy,' him say. I hear no more 'bout dat 'til Marse Tom come home and then I hear plenty. White folks been laughin' 'bout it ever since. Special talk 'bout it since Marse Tom's grandson b'come a United State Judge. Bet Marse Dan Hall told you 'bout it.

Want me to go ahead and tell you it my way? Well, 'twas dis a way: Marse Tom and Marse Joe Caldwell fell out 'bout a piece of soap when they was roomin' together at school. Boys crowd 'round them and say: 'Fight it out!' They hit a lick or two, and was parted. Then de older boys say dere must be a duel. Marse Joe git seconds. Marse Tom git seconds. They load guns wid powder but put no bullets in them. Tell Marse Joe 'bout it but don't tell Marse Tom. Then they go down town, fix up a bag of pokeberry juice, and have it inside Marse Joe's westcoat, on his breast. Took them out in a field, face them, and say: 'One, two, three, fire!' Guns went off, Marse Joe slap his hand on his chest, and de bag bust. Red juice run all over him. Older boys say: 'Run Tom and git out de way.' Marse Tom never stop 'til him git to Liverpool, England. Marse William and Marse Daniel find him dere, sent money for to fetch him home and him laugh 'bout it when he git back. Yes sir, dat is de grandpappy of Marse Lyle Glenn, a big judge right now.

"De white folks near, was de Mellichamps, de Gladdens, de Mobleys, Lumpkins, Boulwares, Fords, Picketts, and Johnsons.

"When de Yankees come, they was struck dumb wid de way marster acted. They took things, wid a beg your pardon kind of way, but they never burnt a single thing, and went off wid deir tails twixt deir legs, kinda 'shame lak.

"After freedom I marry a preacher, Tom Johnson. Him die when in his sixties, thirty years ago. Our chillun was Emma, Mansell, Tom, and Grover. Bad white folks didn't lak my husband. Dere was a whiskey still, near our house where you could git three gallons of liquor for a silver dollar. Him preach agin' it. Dat gall both makers and drinkers. Him 'dured persecution for de Lord's sake, and have gone home to his awards.

"In slavery, us have all de clothes us need, all de food us want, and work all de harder 'cause us love de white folks dat cared for us. No sirree, none of our slaves ever run 'way. Us have a week off, Christmas. Go widout a pass to Marse Daniel's quarters and they come to our'n.

"Dr. Scott and Dr. Douglas 'tend sick slaves. I don't set myself up to judge Marse Abe Lincoln. Dere is sinners, black and white, but I hope and prays to git to hebben. Whether I's white or black when I git dere, I'll be satisfied to see my Savior dat my old marster worshipped and my husband preach 'bout. I wants to be in hebben wid all my white folks, just to wait on them, and love them and serve them, sorta lak I did in slavery time. Dat will be 'nough hebben for Adeline."

ANNA JOHNSON

Interview with Anna Johnson (75)
Rt.4, Gaffney, S.C.
—*Caldwell Sims, Union, S.C.*

"I sho is spry, kaise I sho is done took care of myself and I done dat good, too. I know Will Evans who is 72 and he is all bent over and wrinkled and all stewed up. Dat's de way folks wants to see you befo' dey calls you old, but dey ain't gwine to see me like dat, 'deed dey ain't. Most folks calls me de youngest, but I was born on de 30th day of July, and I is passed by 75 Julys and still gitting around better dan some dat is seed but 60 Julys.

"Well does I remember when my young marster, John Kitchens, went to de 'Federate War. He was a big fat feller, and jolly. De morning he left, he come through de yard leading a fine bay. All of us was dar to see him off. We had fetched him things, but he say dat you couldn't carry nothing to war but a pack on your back and he laid dem all down and wiped his eyes and rode off wid a big yell to us. Dat was de rebel yell and we answered back.

"One morning de very next week we heard our young missus hollering and we went to see what de trouble was. She had got word dat he had done gone and got kil't by a Yankee. We all cried. De little chilluns, John, Will, Ella and Bob cried, too. Missus went to her ma and pa, Mr. Green and Miss Sallie Mitchel, near Trough Shoals. Frankie

Brown and Malissa Chalk went wid her to her pa's. Our plantation was awful big. It was sold and us wid it.

"Wasn't long till young Missus married again and went to Virginia to live. Frankie and Malissa come back to our plantation. Den slavery was over and dat is de last dat I ever heard of our Missus."

JACK JOHNSON

> Interview with Jack Johnson, 84 years old
> —W.W. Dixon, Winnsboro, S.C.

"You see me right here, de sin of both races in my face, or was it just de sin of one? My Marster was my father, his name was Tom Reed, and he lived six miles from Lancaster Court House. Dats where I was born. My mammy name Jane, don't know where she come from. My marster was kind to us. I done no work much, just picked peas and sich like during de war. I was my mammy's only child, and when de war was over, and I grow up, I left dere and come to Cedar Creek, low part of Fairfield County. I marry a gal, Bella Cook, and us had sixteen chillun, thirteen of them is a livin' now. I then marry Hannah Dubard, a widow. She and me have had no child.

"I b'long to de Sanctified Church, and you have to go down into de water and come up straight way out of de water to b'long to dat church. Where is it? Its on Little Cedar Creek in dis county. Who de preacher? His name is the Reverend Edmunds. Us sings spirituals, one is, 'Dat Heavenly Railroad Train', another is 'Dere is a Rock in my Heart', another, 'So glad I'm here, but I'd rather be up yonder Lord'. Some colored churches 'sinuate a child born out of wedlock can't enter de kingdom of heaven. Our church say he can if he ain't a drunkard, and is de husband of one wife and to believe on, and trust in de Lord as your Savior, and live a right kind of life dat he proves of. Dat seem reason to me, and I jine and find peace as long as I does right.

"Never was sick a day in my life, can plow yet, eat three meals a day, but can't sleep as much as I use to, six hours plenty for me now. I's just here today findin' out 'bout dat old age pension dats a comin'. Will you kinda keep a eye on it for me and let me tend to de ox and de grass at my home on Little Cedar Creek? A short hoss is soon curried, so dats 'bout all I kin 'member to tell you now."

JAMES JOHNSON

> Interview with James Johnson, 79 years old
> —Henry Grant, Columbia, S.C.

THE COTTON MAN

James Johnson lives with a sister at 1045 Barron Street, College Place, [HW: Columbia], S.C. He is incapable of self support on account of age, ill health, and impaired feet. One of his feet was mashed off and the other badly damaged by handling bales of cotton several years ago. He subsists on what his sister and other people are able to give him.

"I has been livin' right here in Columbia for the past thirty-six years. I has worked in de cotton business, first as ginner and then wid cotton buyers, ever since I has been here. I knows all de grades of lint cotton and can name them right now. (He ran through the different grades fairly correctly.)

"I learned all I knows 'bout cotton and de grades from Mr. M.C. Heath and Mr. W.E. Smith, cotton buyers in Columbia for thirty years or more. They thought so much of my knowledge of cotton, dat they sent me many times to settle claims wid big men and big buyers.1

"It ain't what a nigger knows dat keeps him down. No, sir. It is what he don't know, dat keeps de black man in de background. White folks dat is business folks, pays no 'tention to our color as much as they does to dat money makin' power us has. Of course, de white man sticks to his color and you can't blame him for dat. If de nigger shows dat he is willin' to work and to learn to be business lak, make money and walk straight wid his boss and fellowman, de better class of de white people is gwine to treat him right. I knows what I's tellin' you is so, from my own 'sperience wid Mr. Heath and Mr. Smith. They always treated me better than I deserved and even now in my old age, deir folks and deir friends gives me money, dat keeps me out de poorhouse.

"No, sir, I don't 'member de Civil War a-tall myself but I has heard all 'bout it from my own folks and de white folks I has worked wid. It seems lak I knows too much 'bout them awful times. I sho' am glad I didn't come 'long then. I feels and knows dat de years after de war was worser than befo'. Befo' de war, niggers did have a place to lie down at night and somewhere to eat, when they got hungry in slavery time. Since them times, a many a nigger has had it tough to make a livin'. I knows dat is so, too, 'cause I has been all 'long dere.

"Many niggers have gone north to live, since freedom, but de most of them either comes back south again or they wants to come back. De north don't suit de nigger. Cold climate lak they has up dere is too hard on him. He has thin blood and you knows dat a thin pan gwine to git hot quicker than a thick one and cold de same way. You see a heap of niggers is lak wild animals, in a way. He laks to eat a heap, sleep a heap, and move 'bout slow. When he goes up north he has to step 'round fas', 'cause if he don't, he gits in de way of them Yankees dat move 'bout quick.

"De black man is natchally lazy, you knows dat. De reason he talks lak he does, is 'cause he don't want to go to de trouble to 'nounce his words lak they ought to be. When he says 'dat' he saves a letter, same way wid 'dis' and nearly all other words. It ain't after savin' so much; he is just too careless and lazy to care 'bout it. A nigger wants what is in sight and not dat what he can't see; it can look out for itself. I is sorry I has to say all dis 'bout my own color but it is de truth. De truth makes you free and runs de devil. I is a nigger myself and I knows what they is and what they does.

"Is de nigger 'ligious? Yes, sir, many of them is very 'ligious widout 'ligion. He takes all dat from white folks. So many think 'ligion is gwine to git them somethin' widout workin' for it and fool people by makin' them think they is good and can be trusted and all dat. But I 'spects some of them is right, even at dat, 'cause if they ain't got 'ligion they sho' ain't got nothin' in dis world. I pays no 'tention to all dis 'gwine on' lak I see some 'ligious folks does. Maybe I wouldn't be in de fix I is, if I paid more 'tention to churches and all dat. I believes in churches and good folks but I don't practice them good things lak I ought to. Boss, if you take de dollar out of 'ligion and de churches, you sho' would have to hunt for them. I believes dat. I don't see no 'ciples gwine 'bout a preachin' and doin' good, lak I has heard they once done, barefooted and askin' no pay. De preachers dese days is a ridin' in de finest automobiles and you sho' better look out for yourself, if you don't, you is gwine to git run over.

"I has been a good man, in body, all de time since I got grown. For many years I didn't know my own strength. I never seen a bale of cotton I couldn't pick up and tote where I wanted to, by myself. You see dese foots of mine? They was mashed off, from drappin' bales of cotton on them, back yonder many years ago.

"I 'members mighty well, when de fust skyscraper was built in Columbia. My bosses was one of de fust to have a office in dere. Dat was de Loan and Exchange Bank Building, on de corner of Washington and Main streets. I has been here and seen dis city grow from a small place to what you see 'tis now.

"My mammy and daddy b'long to Mr. Andrew Johnson of Orangeburg County, of dis State. They said dat they was treated mighty good by deir marster all de time they was slaves. My daddy took his old marster's name. I was born a slave but all I knows is what I has heard. Some of it might be right and some might be wrong."

REV. JAMES H. JOHNSON

Interview with James H. Johnson, 82 years old
—*Stiles M. Scruggs, Columbia, S.C.*

"My name is James H. Johnson. I was born December 20, 1855, at the town servants' quarters of Alfred Brevort at Camden, South Carolina, and that was home until I was turning into twelve years of age. I was nearly ten years old, when the army of General Sherman came to Camden. I talked to some of the soldiers, soon after they arrived."

Such was the greeting of the Rev. James H. Johnson; a retired, and well educated Methodist Episcopal minister, when a WPA reporter called at his residence, 2029 Marion Street, Columbia, South Carolina, and asked for an interview. He sat in his study, furnished for comfort and equipped about as well as any study, of this kind, in Columbia.

"My mother," he explained, "was one of the maids at the Brevort home, and my father was one of the overseers of the plantation. We did not hear about President Lincoln's freedom proclamation in 1863, but the status quo of slavery kept right on as it had been until Sherman's army came through. You know General Lee surrendered the same spring, and we learned we were free.

"In 1866 my father bought four acres in the vicinity of Camden and improved it with a house and barn, and we lived there for several years. My father went into the mercantile business in Camden and prospered. There I went to the public schools. We had teachers from the North, and I finished all the grades. There were no high schools in the state at that time.

"We had our own home-raised hams and plenty of food products in our quarters, when my mother and I heard shooting nearby. We stepped into the yard and saw a big number of soldiers shooting at a running white man of the community. They did not hit him. In a moment or two five soldiers strode into our yard and we were scared at first, but they told us they were friends, and one of them spied the hams and asked if they belonged to the big house. When told that they were ours, they said they were hungry, and mother fixed them a dinner of ham and eggs and plenty of other things. They thanked us and left, doing no harm.

"Before they left, I noticed a crowd of soldiers at the Brevort home. I ran there, and told the troops, please, to do no damage to the premises, as the mistress, then in charge, was the best friend my mother and I had ever had. They left soon afterward, showing no animus toward the Brevort family and taking nothing away.

"We never received any aid from the Freedmen's bureau, for we did not need it. After I finished the public school work at Camden and helped my father in his store for a time, I entered the University of South Carolina, in October, 1874 and stayed there until 1877. You know there was a change in government in 1876, and Negroes were excluded from the university in 1877. I was in my junior year, when I left.

"I returned to Camden and taught school in Kershaw

County for ten years. During that time I opened school in the Browning Home, which still stands in Camden. In the meantime, I had been an interested member of the Methodist Episcopal Church since my early years, and I was made an elder in that denomination in 1888, and sent to Columbia as pastor of the Wesley Methodist Church.

"When I came here as pastor, that church stood on the corner of Sumter and Gervais streets, on the site where the United States post-office now stands. The congregation sold that corner in 1910 and built the brick church at Barnwell and Gervais streets. I was the pastor all that time, retiring in 1930 due to physical feebleness. The congregation of that church has always been rather small. This accounts for my doing other work. I was a clerk in the internal revenue office in Columbia for eighteen years.

"Now, I am a notary public and make some income from that. The church gives me a small pension, and I advise and do literary work for a large number of Negro residents. In that way, I keep fairly busy and my family has never gone hungry. I did preach some, a few years ago. I am now too feeble to undertake that task, and have to be content, mostly at home."

(Reporter's Note: The Rev. James H. Johnson speaks no dialect. He speaks choice, grammatical diction and has a most pleasing personality. His is one of the very few Methodist Episcopal Churches in South Carolina for Negroes. He says he is glad the church is now seeking to void the split over slavery in 1860. He resides in a comfortable home at 2029 Marion Street, Columbia, S.C.)

United States. Work Projects Administration

JANE JOHNSON

> Interview with Jane Johnson, 90 years old
> —Henry Grant, Columbia, S.C.

Jane Johnson is living with her niece at 1430 Harden Street, Columbia, S.C. She is of small statue, dark, not black, plump and apparently well cared for. On account of her age and bodily afflictions she is incapable of self-support. Her niece is unmarried, owns a comfortable home, works and provides for her grandmother in a good and satisfactory manner.

"Come in, white folks, take dat chair and set down. I hears dat you wants to talk to me 'bout myself and my master in slavery time. My name is Jane Johnson and I's 'bout ninety years old, from de best 'membrance I has from my white folks friends and my own people. One thing I does know, I's been here so long, dat I sometimes think I's near 'bout a hundred years old.

"I b'long to Master Tom Robertson. My mistress' name was Ophelia. I didn't see her much in slavery time, 'cause she stayed in de big house on Arsenal Hill, Columbia, S.C. De onliest time I see her a-tall, was when I was sent to de big house for somethin' and dat wasn't often. Master and mistress had heaps of chillun, 'mong them was twins, all dead now, if I 'members right, 'cept Master Tom Robertson, a grandson and a rich man too; he living right here in Columbia. My old master lived in Columbia but his plantation, where us slaves lived, was 'bout four or five miles from Columbia on de Sumter road, just beyond de soldiers hospital (Veterans Hospital), dat's right.

"Master Tom come to de plantation every day 'cept Sundays and sometimes he come dat day, 'specially in crop season. He never talked to us slaves much, just talked to de overseer 'bout us all, I reckon. De overseer was a nigger and de meanest man, white or black, I ever see. Dat nigger would strut 'round wid a leather strap on his shoulder and would whip de other slaves unmerciful. He worked us hard from sunrise to sunset every day in de week, 'cept some Saturday evenin's. 'Most of de grown slave women knocked off from field work at dinner time on Saturdays and done de washin' for de rest of de slaves.

"Yes sir, us had a plenty of rations to eat; no fancy vittles, just plain corn bread, meat and vegetables. Dere was no flour bread or any kind of sweet stuff for de slaves to eat. Master say sweet things 'fected de stomach and teeth in a bad way. He wanted us to stay well and healthy so us could work hard.

"Master Tom was good to us, course he was, 'cause he didn't see us much no way. But dat nigger overseer was de devil settin' cross-legged for de rest of us on de plantation all de time. I never has believed dat master 'tended for dat nigger to treat us like he did. He took 'vantage of his bein' 'way and talk soft talk when he come again. Yes sir, he sho' did.

"Not very long after de Yankees come, us was told dat de niggers was free. You might think dat was a happy day for us slaves, but I didn't think lak dat. I was kinda lonesome and sad lak. Us slaves was lost, didn't know what to do or where to go. Don't you think dat was a sad time?

"How old was I when I done my courtin'? What's dat? Dat courtin' stuff is what white folks does, no nigger knows what dat fancy thing is. Us just natchally lives together; men and women mates lak de animals out dere. Colored people don't pay no 'tention to what white folks call love, they just 'sires de woman they wants, dat's all. I married dat man of mine, Tilghman Thompson, and us got 'long right smart, 'til he die. I got 'nother one, Anderson Johnson, and he die too, so here I is, left here yit.

"You knows de black man has had a long, hard road to travel since he was first brought to this country. From de first, he b'long to de white man to be took care of and to work. Some colored folks 'pear to be doin' right well dese days but back yonder long befo' I was born, I's been told, they didn't know how to provide for themselves. What I wants to know, what de nigger gwine to do widout de 'sistance of de white man? What they has got come from them, you knows dat. I hear some of them growlin' 'round, dat they is gwine to do dis and gwine do dat and they don't do nothin', 'cept talk too much. They sho' better do right; live in peace and git somethin' dat will stay with them.

"Maybe I's wrong to say dis but you knows, white man, de nigger is a far way back of de white man; his time ain't come yit, leastwise dat's de way it 'pear to me. De nigger come from Africa and other hot places, so he takes after de hot country he come from and has a short temper, hard head, and not 'nough sense to keep him out of trouble when he gits mad or 'cited. When he come here, de white man made him work, and he didn't like dat. He is natchally lazy and when he had to work, then he began to get huffy and to conjure up in he mind hate and other bad things against de whites. Ever since the first time de nigger found out he had to work, he has silently despised the white man. If he had lived and done nothin', then he would be a 'tirely different person to dis very day, I knows dat.

"Does I 'member President Lincoln? I sho' does, but not so much, 'cause I was too young to have much sense. I has heard my mammy and daddy say he was a good man and wanted everybody to be free, both white and black. Dere was a heap of poor white folks in slavery time, and some of them lived mighty hard, worse than the slaves sometimes. You knows blood is thick and it is gwine to turn to its kind befo' helpin' de others. They say slavery was wrong but what 'bout hard times? Dat is de worse kind of slavery, I thinks. All dis hollerin' 'round 'bout freedom they has, shucks, all dat kind of talk ain't nothin'. When you has work and some money in your pocket so you can go to de store and buy some meat and bread, then you has de best freedom there is, don't tell me.

"President Roosevelt is 'nother good man. He has looked down on de poor and 'tressed in dis land wid mercy; has give work and food to de poor people when nobody else would. He sho' has turnt dis country 'round and tried so hard to make things right wid de people. When he turn dis way and turn dat way, them men up there where he is, try to stop him from helpin' us, but de Blessed Master is gwine to hold his hands up. They ain't gwine to be able to stop him, 'cause he has done so much good in de world. Dat man is gwine to be 'membered by de people always, but them dat has fought him and worked against him is sho' gwine to be forgot. Nobody wants to 'member them for de evil they has done. You knows dat if you sows evil you is sho' gwine to gather evil in time. They ain't gwine sow much longer; their harvest time is right out dere in sight, but de President is gwine to live on wid us.

"I's gettin' old now, I has to draw on de 'membrance of de past, tottle 'long in de present and stare wid dese old eyes out dere into what is to come (future). I has rheumatism and high blood pressure, so you see I's in for a troublesome time from now on to dat last day. I's livin' wid my niece now, in her own home, dat is some pleasure to me in my old age."

JIMMIE JOHNSON

> Interview with "Uncle" Jimmie Johnson (90)
> 172 E. Park Ave., Spartanburg, S.C.
> —F.S. DuPre, Spartanburg, S.C.

"I was born in Virginia, but Dr. L.C. Kennedy bought me, my mother and brothers and we moved to Spartanburg. My father stayed in Virginia. Dr. Kennedy lived near where North Church Street and Kennedy Place now is, and I lived in a two-room house in his back yard. I was just a baby at the time. My old masser was as good and kind to me as he could be, so was my missus. My mother died when I was ten years old, and Missus was just like a mother to me all the time. When I got old enough I used to do some things around the yard for Masser and Missus.

"Masser was an Episcopalian, and I went to Sunday School where the rock church now stands (Church of the Advent). Miss Mary Legg was my teacher, and she was a saintly woman. She was a niece of old Masser. Old Missus used to come to the house where I lived and teach me my alphabet. After I got older, I used to take care of Masser's horse and buggy for him; used to hitch-up the horse for him and go with him on his ways to see a patient. Bless his heart, he let me take my Webster's blue back speller and my history with me when I would drive with him. I would study those books and Masser would tell me how to pronounce the hard words. That is the way I got my education. Masser would tell Missus that Jimmie was a smart boy, that he had no father nor mother and that they must be good to him. They sure was. I never wanted for a thing. Sometimes on our drives Masser would tell me some Latin words, but I never did study Latin—just English.

"My masser would say that Jimmie had sense, was a good boy, so Missus would let me practice on her organ or her piano in the house. I got pretty good on these, so when I got to be a young man, I taught lessons on both the reed organ and the melodian, then on the piano. I taught the rudiments of music and piano for about 25 years.

"When the Yankee soldiers come to Spartanburg it scared me. They kept telling me that they were not going to hurt me, but I got a pile of brick-bats and put them under the house. I told Missus I wasn't going to let any of the soldiers hurt her. The Yankee soldiers did not bother me. They came all around our house, but every one of them was quiet and orderly. They took some of Missus' sugar and hams, but did not kill any of the chickens. I told them not to take the sugar, but they took it and the hams anyhow.

"Missus told me that I was free, but I told her I was going to stay on where I was and protect her until I died. And when Masser died, I grieved and grieved about him. I loved him dearly and I know he loved me. He was good and kind to me always. He never whipped me, not once. I grieve about my masser to this day. He was a kind gentleman.

"No, I never married, and I haven't got anybody kin to me now. My brothers all died and I am the only one left. I adopted four children. I taught them music and we got on pretty well after Missus died. I stayed with her until she died. I told Masser I was going to stay with them even if I was free, and I did. When Masser died, I had no one to love but Missus. I taught music and gave piano lessons, but I can't do that now, as I am too old. Lately I tried to cut some wood. I would cut a lick, then rest; cut a lick, then rest, so I gave it up.

"Lord bless your soul! I am so glad you told who you are, and you talk like Masser Dan. You know he and I used to play together as boys. He would give me anything he had. Honey, come around and see me again. I is sure glad to see you. What did you say your name was?" Upon being told, his face would light up with a smile, and he would repeat just what he had said before. He was then asked when he got to be a poet. "Law' chile, my old missus told me I was going to be a poet."

This ninety-year-old ex-slave then sat down at the piano and played for the writer.

MARY JOHNSON

I

Interview with Mary Johnson (85)
Newberry, S.C.
—*G.L. Summer, Newberry, S.C.*

"I was born seven miles from Newberry, near Jalapa. I was a slave of John Johnson and his wife, Polly (Dorroh) Johnson. They was good to dere slaves. My daddy was Daniel and my mudder Elisa Johnson who was slaves of marster John Johnson. My mudder come from Georgia when she was 14 years old, bought by Marse Johnson. We lived in a little one-room house in dere yard. The mistress learned me to card and spin, and to weave when I was a child. When I was old enough, dey put me in de field to work, hoe and pick cotton. We got no money for working, but got our place to live, some victuals and a few clothes to wear. We had no garden, but helped de mistress in her garden and she give us something to eat from it. We had homespun dresses; we made not much underclothes, but sometimes in awful cold weather, we had red flannel underskirts.

"Nigger boys in slavery when dere work was done in evening, sometime went hunting and caught rabbits, squirrels or 'possums.

"We got up at sun-up in mornings and worked 'till sun-down. We had Saturday afternoon off to do anything we wanted to do. At Christmas time, we got dat day off, and de master would have a big dinner wid all kinds good things to eat, spread out in de yard.

"We never did learn to read and write—had no nigger school and had no nigger church, but sometimes de white folks would have us go to dere church and set in back seat or gallery.

"The white folks had cotton pickings and corn shuckings often and we helped. Dey had good dinners for them coming to it. De childrens, white and black played marbles sometimes, and played base. Us slave children played base and jumped from one base to another before could be caught; and we sing: 'Can I git to Molly's bright? Three course and ten. Can I get there by candle-light? yes, if your legs are long and light.'

"Marse John's youngest son got to be a doctor. He was a good man and helped us when we was sick. He did not gibe herbs much, but some of de ole folks used 'life everlasting', now called rabbit tobacco, for cure of bad colds or pneumonia. Dey boiled it and make a plaster and put it on sore places of chest. Dey used holly bush or spice bush bark, boiled to a tea and drunk for sickness.

"De padderrollers come in dat section, they rode at night and if caught, a nigger, when he was out of his place, would be took in and told dat he would get 25 lashes if he was caught again. When de war was over, de Yankees went through but didn't bother us; but dey stold horses, mules, cows and supplies. When freedom come, we left the place, 'cause marse Johnson and some his folks went to Mississippi. We hired out to Kirk Richards nearby.

"De Ku Klux was not a bother. Dey jus marched sometimes at night, wid long white sheets over dem and all over de horses. Dere heads were covered with small holes for eyes, nose and mouth, and had long white ears like a horses ears.

"I think Abe Lincoln was a fine man, and Jeff Davis was good too. Slaver did good to nigger, made him careful and know how to work."

United States. Work Projects Administration

II

Interview with Mary Johnson (85)
Newberry, S.C.
—G.L. Summer, Newberry, S.C.

"I live in town in a little two-room house wid some of my grandchilluns. We rent de house. I am too old to work, but do what I can.

"I was de slave of John Johnson. His wife was Miss Polly. Dey was good to de slaves, and I had no trouble. My mother was Eliza Johnson and my pa was Daniel Johnson. Dey was both slaves to Marse John Johnson. My mother was from Georgia. We always lived in de yard behind de house in a small one-room cabin, a pretty good place to live, I reckon.

"We didn't git no money fer our work. We got something to eat, but not much clothes to wear. We worked hard dem days; got up at sun-up and worked all day till sun-down or as long as we could see. We didn't git much time off, 'cept maybe a day at Christmas.

"No, de white folks didn't learn us to read and write. We had no school and no church in slavery time, but some of de niggers was made to go to de white folks' church and sit in de back seat.

"Yes, de Yankees was bad. Dey burn't everything in deir way, and stole cattle; but dey didn't come near our place."

MIEMY JOHNSON

Interview with Miemy Johnson, 82 years old
—W.W. Dixon, Winnsboro, S.C.

Miemy Johnson has no particular place of abode. She is a transient among her children, kin people, and friends. In whatever home she may be temporarily an occupant, she does the cooking and family washing.

"I knowed when dat bunty rooster hopped in de door, flap his wings and crowed, dis mornin', dat us gonna have company today. I told Sam so befo' he left here. Him laugh and say: 'Ma, dat bunty rooster is a big liar sometime. Maybe him just wanna recommend hisself to you and beat de pig to de slop bucket dat you ain't carried out to de pen yet.' I's sure glad dat you come, for it'll show Sam dat dat chicken never told a lie.

"Set down dere and let me fetch you a plate of boil peanuts, which I just is set off de fire. You lak them? Glad you do, honey. Most white folks love them dat way, 'stead of parched. How you been? You sure is growed since de last day I clap my eyes on you. How's I been? Poorly. I's just a waitin' for de chariot to carry me home!

"Well, us done cut down de underbrush, now let us git into de new ground. You just wanna talk 'bout me and what happen to me all 'long de last eighty years? Dat's some big field to go over.

"My pappy was name Henry. My mammy name Ceily.

They both b'long to old Marse Johnnie Mobley, but my pappy's pappy b'long to de Johnson's; they's big white folks on de Catawba River side of de county. They sold deir plantation and some of de slaves, to old marster and his daughter, Miss Nancy. She was de widow Thompson befo' her marry dat Kentucky hoss drover, Marse Jim Jones.

"Freedom come. My pappy 'membered de Johnson's and took dat for his name. I never been able to git 'way from dat name. I marry little Phil Johnson. My brudder was Adam Johnson and my sister was Easter. Her marry Allan Foster.

"My husband and me live in de old Mobley quarter, three miles southwest of Woodward and just 'bout a quarter of a mile from where you settin' dere a writin' right now. Long as him live, him was de carriage driver for de Mobleys. He 'tend Fellowship Church. All de Mobleys done dead or moved 'way. Dere is nothin' left to tell de tale but dat cemetery you passed, comin' 'long down here and de ghosts dat shiver 'round dere in de nighttime. Whenever it snow, them ghosts have been seen travelin' down de road and up de avenue to Cedar Shades. You know dat's 'bout a quarter of a mile farther down de road from where Marse Johnnie's brudder, James Mobley, lived. Fine old house dere yet, but just colored folks live in it.

"Our chillun was Roxanna, Malinda, Ben, Mary, Waddell, Queen Elizabeth, Russell, Pearly, Thomasine, Helen, Alberta, Maggie, Mary Jane, Willie, Sam and Roy. Had de easiest birth pains when, to my big surprise, de twins, Sam and Roy come. Dat been forty years ago last July. I 'members well, dat de twins was born on a Wednesday and I walk to Red Hill Church de very nex' Sunday. Rev. Richard Cook was de preacher. Him didn't see me a settin' in de church and he pray for me by name, as bein' in de perils of childbirth. And bless God, me right dere in dat church a goin' 'long wid de rest of them a singin': 'Amazin' Grace How Sweet De Sound Dat Saved A Wretch Lak Me'. I was a proud wretch dat day as sure's you born!

"Does I 'member anything 'bout de earthquake? Jesus my Lord, yes! Us was holdin' a revival meetin' in Red Hill dat night! It was a moonlight Tuesday night. Brother Stevenson and Brother Moore was a helpin' Brother Richard Cook carry on de meetin'. It was de last day of August, in '86. Brother Moore had preached, de choir had sung a hymn, and Brother Stevenson was in de middle of a prayer. Him said sumpin' 'bout de devil goin' 'round lak a roarin' lion a seekin' folks for to devour. Then de roarin' was heard. De church commence to crack and shake and rock. Then all de folks holler: 'Oh Lordy.' They run out dat church and some took up de big road to de depot at Woodward. Some fell down in de moonlight and cry and pray. Brother Cook say de Bible says: 'Bow down, or kneel or fall on your face befo' de Lord'. Then he say: 'Let us all fall on our faces dis time.' Us did and each one of them preachers pray. 'Bout time they git through, us see a rider on a milk white hoss a gallopin' up to de church wid de white mane and tail of dat hoss a wavin' and shinin' in de moonlight. De people went wild wid fear and scream at de top of deir voices; 'It's de white hoss wid his rider of de book of Revelations goin' forth, conquerin' and to conquer.' They bust forth in dat mighty spiritual 'Oh Run Here, Believer, Run Here, Oh Sinner Your House On Fire! Oh Sinner Your House On Fire!' They run and surround de white hoss and his rider and what you reckon? Us find out it was just Marse Ed Woodward on his white hoss, John, comin' back from courtin' my young mistress, Tillie Mobley, dat him marry de nex' Christmas.

"Marse Ed got down off dat hoss when us beg him to stay wid us. It's a pow'ful comfort to have a brave white man 'round at sich a time 'mongst a passle of terrified niggers, I tells you! And to think Marse Ed done dead.

"You goin' now? You ain't eat all your peanuts. Put them in your pocket and eat them on de way to de Boro. Goodbye—I 'spect I'll git to glory befo' you does. If I does, I'll be dere a waitin' wid a glad hand and a glad voice to welcome you to de everlastin' home."

TOM JOHNSON

Interview with Tom Johnson (83)
Newberry, S.C.
—*G. Leland Summer, Newberry, S.C.*

"I was born on the Gilliam place, I reckon about 1854. My father died when I was little; I don't remember him. My mother was Lucy Gilliam who belonged to Reuben Gilliam. Reuben Gilliam was a big farmer and slave-owner. He was good to de nigger chaps but whipped de big ones every day or two. I was too little to learn to read and write, but dey never learned any slaved to do dat. Dey never paid us any money wages, just give us eats and a place to sleep, and a little clothes. I worked in de field when I got bigger. Never had school in de place, and never had a church, either.

"Us children played lots of games, like rolly-hole. There are two holes and you try to roll a ball in one hole. The white folks had corn-shuckings, lots of them, as they raised lots of corn on de farms. Dey had cotton pickings, too, and carding and spinning bees, quilting bees. I used to feed de shippers when women folks spin de yarn, when I was a small boy. We raised plenty corn, cotton, and other things. We had a big garden, too.

"When freedom come all of us left and went off. I went back to get something to eat. I married Mattie Kinard who belonged to old Maj. John Kinard. We had nine children.

"I 'member de red shirts when dey come through our place. I like it better now dan in slavery times."

United States. Work Projects Administration

RICHARD (LOOK-UP) JONES

Interview with Richard Jones (Dick Look-up), age 93 [HW: 125?]
County Home, Union, S.C.
—*Caldwell Sims, Union, S.C.*

Dick has an upward stare all the time, and holds his head as if he were always looking up into the sky, consequently he has won the sobriquet, 'Look-Up'.

"Everybody dat knows me knows dat I was born on de Jim Gist plantation, and it used to jine Mr. Winsmith's and de Glenn Peak plantations. Mr. Winsmith was a doctor. Marse Jim sho was a good man to his darkies.

"My father was named Ned Jones and he belonged to Marse Berry Jones. His plantation was across de forest, next to West Springs. Mother was Lucy Gist, belonging to Marse Jim. My parents had de following chilluns: Esther, Bella, Ephriam, Griggs, John, Penfield, me and Richard. Dey married and so we was all Jones.

"De slaves in de Gist Quarter lived well. All nigger chilluns in dat quarter had very small tasks until dey was seventeen or eighteen years old. De quarter had nine houses. Dere was seventeen hundred acres in our plantation; or dat is, de part where we lived and worked. We lived in one-room log cabins dat had to be well kept all of de time.

"All de chilluns in de Quarter was well fed, clothed, housed and doctored until dey was strong and well developed younguns. Den dey was give tasks and learnt to do what de master and de mistress thought dey would do well at.

"In de houses we had comfortable home-made beds and chairs. We had nice tables and plenty to eat. Our clothes was kept mended by a seamstress, and dese things was looked after by one of de mammies on de plantation dat was too old to work.

"Ah yes, well does I 'member my Granny from Africa, and straight from dere, too; Judith Gist, dey named her. Dat ole lady could not work when she died, fer she was a hundred and ten years old. Dey had in de paper dat I was 125 [HW: 93?]. It gives me notice to say dat I is de oldest man in Union County. Can't 'member any of my grandfathers. Millie Gist was my mother, and aunt Judith was her mother.

"Granny Judith said dat in Africa dey had very few pretty things, and dat dey had no red colors in cloth, in fact, dey had no cloth at all. Some strangers wid pale faces come one day and drapped a small piece of red flannel down on de ground. All de black folks grabbed fer it. Den a larger piece was drapped a little further on, and on until de river was reached. Den a large piece was drapped in de river and on de other side. Dey was led on, each one trying to git a piece as it was drapped. Finally, when de ship was reached, dey drapped large pieces on de plank and up into de ship 'till dey got as many blacks on board as dey wanted. Den de gate was chained up and dey could not get back. Dat is de way Granny Judith say dey got her to America. Of course she did not even know dat de pieces was red flannel, or dat she was being enticed away.

Dey just drapped red flannel to dem like us draps corn to chickens to git dem on de roost at night.

"When dey got on board de ship dey were tied until de ship got to sea; den dey was let loose to walk about 'cause dey couldn't jump overboard. On de ship dey had many strange things to eat, and dey liked dat. Dey was give enough red flannel to wrap around demselves. She liked it on de boat. Granny Judith born Millie, and Millie born me. No, I ain't never had no desire to go to Africa, kaise I gwine to stay whar I is.

"Uncle Tom come 'long wid Granny Judith. Two womenfolks come wid dem, aunt Chany and Daphne. Aunt Chany and aunt Daphne was bought by de Frees dat had a plantation near Jonesville. Uncle Tom and 'Granny' was bought by Marse Jim Gist, but dere marsters allus 'lowed dem to visit on July 4th and Christmas. When dey talk, nobody didn't know what dey was talking about. My granny never could speak good like I can. She talk half African, and all African when she git bothered. No, I can't talk no African.

"After I was seventeen I did all kinds of hoeing and plowing and other farm work fer my marster. He said dat by dis time, his little niggers' bones had done got hard enough fer dem to work. We had a 'driver', a older person, dat showed us how to do everything right. Marse never let him over-work or hurry us. We liked him—'Uncle July Gist', we called him and dat was his real name, too. His wife, Aunty Sara, was good to us; dey both buried at Woodson's Chapel Baptist Church.

"Fer my first task I had 1/4 of an acre in taters, 'bacca and watermelons de first year. Some of de boys had 'pinders, cantloupes and matises (tomatoes) in dere task of a 1/4 acre.

"De next year, we made corn and sold it to our master fer whatever he give us fer it. All de use we had fer money was to buy fish hooks, barlows, juice harps and marbles. Boys did not use 'bacca den until dey got twenty-one or over. Marse allus carried a roll of money as big as my arm. He would come to de quarter on Christmas, July 4th and Thanksgiving, and get up on a stump and call all the chilluns out. Den he would throw money to 'em. De chilluns git dimes, nickles, quarters, half-dollars and dollars. At Christmas he would throw ten dollar bills. De parents would take de five and ten dollar bills in charge, but Marse made de let de chilluns keep de small change. I tell you, I ain't never seed so much money since my marster been gone. He buried at Fairforest Presbyterian Cemetery as white folks calls it, but we calls it Cedar Grove.

"When he died, he had sixteen plantations, you can see dat at de courthouse in Union. All his darkies went in a drove of wagons to his burying. He was killed by dem Yankees in Virginny. Uncle Wylie Smith, his bodyguard, come back wid his body and told us dat Marse was kilt by a Yankee. Marse Jim was a sentinel, and dat Yankee shot him in his nose, but strange to say, it never tore his face up none. Miss Sara buried him in his uniform and she wrapped a Confederate flag over de top of de coffin. Uncle Wylie put Master's watch around Miss Sara's neck like he had done told him to do when he got home. Miss Sara cried and us cried, too. Jim never married and dat's why Miss Sara to do everything, kaise she was his sister what lived wid him.

"Mr., I run on Broad River fer over 24 years as boatman, carrying Marse Jim's cotton to Columbia fer him. Us had de excitement on dem trips. Lots times water was deeper dan a tree is high. Sometimes I was throwed and fell in de water. I rise up every time, though, and float and swim back to de boat and git on again. If de weather be hot, I never think of changing no clothes, but just keep on what I got wet. Five niggers allus went on Marse's boat. One man steer de boat and of course he was de steerman, and dat what he went by. I recollects two steermans, Bradley Kennedy and Andy McCluny. Charlie Gilliam was de second steerman, by dat I means dat he de young nigger dat Bradley and Andy had to break in.

"Sometimes Marster have three flat boats a-gwine down at one time, and I has recollections of as many as five a-gwine from our plantation; dat was not so often, though. Us had long poles to steer de boats wid; den dere was some paddles, and some of de niggers was called privates dat handled de cotton and used de paddles when dey had to be used. You knows dat batteaus was what dey always used de paddles wid. Privates did de shoving and other heavy work. De seconds and de privates allus shoved wid de poles when de water was rough, and de steerman give orders. I was allus a boatman.

"Charlie Gilliam acted as boatman, some; and den de other boatmen was: Bill Hughes, Warren Worthy, Green Stokes and John Glenn. Dey made de poles to suit de job. Some of de poles was longer dan others was. Some of dem was broad and flat at de end; others was blunt and others was made sharp. When de Broad River rose, sometimes de waves got higher dan my house dar. Den it was a real job to handle one of Marse's boats. Fact is, it was five men's jobs. Wid water a-roaring and a-foaming and a-gwine round you like a mad tiger a-blowing his breath, so dat you was feer'd (scared) dat all your marster's cotton gwine to be spilt, you had to be up and a-doing something real fast. Sometimes dat river take your boat round and round like a merry-go-round, 'til you git so swimmy-headed dat you have to puke up all de victuals dat you done eat. Den it swing from dat whirl into a swift stream dat take you a mile a minute, yes sir, a mile a minute fer I don't know how fer.

"Den you see a tree a-coming right straight to you. If de boat hit dat tree, you knowed dat you be busted into a million pieces. You had to git your poles and somebody had to let a pole hit dat tree ahead of de boat. Of course dat change de boat's course from de tree and you went sailing on by. Once in a freshet us raced twenty-five miles in twenty-five minutes. Marse Jim was wid us dat time, and he tole us so by his watch. De water a-jumping real high and dat boat a-jumping still wusser made me so skeer't dat I just shake in my knees and all de way up and down my legs.

"On dis trip we had went plumb up in North Carolina. Us never had been dat fer up befo'. I ain't never seed North carolina befo'; neither is I seed it since. Broad River was real narrow when we went up and she look like a lamb; but when we come down it had done and tuck and rained and dem banks was vanished ... but dat water sho did rare up dar to git back in its regular channel. De rocks up dar was mo' scary looking dat dey is whar it run through Union to Columbia. Dat night we run into a nine-mile shoal. Couldn't none de niggers keep dat boat off'n dat shoal it was so powerful ... dat is, de water just tuck dat boat plumb smack out'n our hands. But it throwed our boat in shallow water and of course dat made it drag. Good dat it never drug over no sharp rocks—and dey was setting all around us—but it happened dat it hit sand. We camped dar fer de night. By morning we had done go a quarter mile from de channel.

"When we et (ate), we worked de boat out into de main channel again. Den we staked her to a tree and tuck a look around befo' we started down stream fer Union; dat seemed fer off right den. Finally de master boatman give de order, 'Shove off, boys!' We shoved and we fell into a clear open channel and our boat went a-skeeting down stream. We never had to hit a lick, but she went so fast dat we was all skeer'd to take a long breath. Finally Marster said, 'Boys, see dem willow trees down yonder; well, steer her to run over dem so dat she will slack her speed.' Us did, but it never deadened our speed a mite, dat us could see. Marster shake his head and 'low, 'Bound fer hell, maybe, boys'.

"Got to Cherokee Falls, wid water so high couldn't tell no falls dar. Marster say, 'Lay her to de right, we can't wreck dis boat widout putting up a honest man's fight.' Den he say, 'If us does, us'll sho go to hell.' We tried to swing her by grabbing to a big willow, and we broke a lot of limbs in trying, but we did swing her and she run a 100 yards widout steering, and de boat landed on a little mountain of land. Marse 'low, 'Ain't never seed sech a ocean of water since I was eighteen years old, damn if I have.' He look at me and say, 'Don't know whether Dick scared or not, but he sho is a brave man.' I was a-setting my feets on land den, and I look at him and 'low, 'No sir, I ain't skeer't, why I could come over dat little place in my bateau.' Truth is, dat I was so skeer't dat I wasn't skeert. We lay over a day and a half. De water had done receded back some, and we come 27 miles down to Lockhart Shoals in dat one day. De water was still so high dat we run over de shoals widout a tremor. Come sailing on down to Fish Dam and went over de Fish Dam and never knowed dat it was dar. Den we landed at de road wid everybody safe but still scar't.

"Dar was two Charlie Gilmores ... one was kil't right below Fish Dam. He was hit in de head by a private. When de private was cutting de boat, Charlie got in de way of de pole and it hit him in one of his temples and he fell over in de water dead. When dey got him, wasn't narry drap of water in his lungs, dat's how-come us knowed dat he was kil't straight out. Some says dat he was hit in de y'er (ear), but anyway it was on a tender spot and de lick sho done him up. Nothing wasn't done to de private, kaise it was all accidental and Marse and everybody felt sorry fer him.

"On river trips, we took rations sech as meat, bread and cabbage, and us cotch all de fish dat we wanted and had coffee. We each took day in and day out to cook, dat is, all dem dat could half-way cook did dat."

WESLEY JONES

Interview with Wesley Jones
Rt. 2, Union, S.C.
—*Caldwell Sims, Union, S.C.*

"Yes sir, I drinks jes' a leetle likker, and I drinks it—I don't let it drink me. One call fer another. Dar it goes 'till you be's drunk. I is 97 years old and I ain't never been drunk in my life. No siree, nobody ain't never saw me drunk. It sho drink some of 'em though.

"Heep o' stars fell when I was young. Dey fell regular fer a minute er so. I laid down fer a nap and de niggers woke me up a hollering. Ev'y darky was scared, but it sho was a pretty sight.

"I 'members de earthquake, too. De earth shake and tremble so hard dat some loose bricks fell out my chimney and de pitcher fell off de winder-sill down on de flo'. I was 'bout 50 years old den, if I 'members correct. Dat come 'long in 1886.

"I also 'members Gen. Wade Hampton, when I was a building up de breastworks to keep de Yankees from shooting us. Dem was scary times, but de Ku Klux days was scary times de most.

"My young marster, Dr. Johnny Hill, used to have me drive him to Padgett's Creek Church. Sometime us go to de Quaker church, den agin, us go to church over in Goshen Hill.

"'Bout fus' thing my white folks had me a-doing, was gwine fer de papers up to de sto' at Sardis. I would git a lot o' letters, fer in dem days, de white folks rit letters to one another mo' dan dey does now. I guess dese days de mos' writing dat is done is business writing. At de Sardis sto' dey used to give big barbecues. Dem days barbecues was de mos' source of amusement fer ev'ybody, all de white folks and de darkies de whole day long. All de fiddlers from ev'ywhars come to Sardis and fiddle fer de dances at de barbecues. Dey had a platform built not fer from de barbecue table to dance on. Any darky dat could cut de buck and de pigeon wing was called up to de platform to perform fer ev'ybody.

"Night befo' dem barbecues, I used to stay up all night a-cooking and basting de meats wid barbecue sass (sauce). It made of vinegar, black and red pepper, salt, butter, a little sage, coriander, basil, onion, and garlic. Some folks drop a little sugar in it. On a long pronged stick I wraps a soft rag or cotton fer a swab, and all de night long I swabs dat meat 'till it drip into de fire. Dem drippings change de smoke into seasoned fumes dat smoke de meat. We turn de meat over and swab it dat way all night long 'till it ooze seasoning and bake all through.

"Lawyer McKissick and Lawyer A.W. Thompson come out and make speeches at dem barbecues. Both was young men den. Dey dead now, I living. I is 97 and still gwine good. Dey looked at my 'karpets' (pit stakes). On dem I had whole goats, whole hogs, sheep and de side of a cow. Dem lawyers liked to watch me 'nint' dat meat. Dey 'lowed I had a turn fer ninting it (annointing it)."

SALLIE LAYTON KEENAN

>Interview with Sallie Layton Keenan, 80 yrs. old
>20 Calhoun St., Union, S.C.
>—*Caldwell Sims, Union, S.C.*

'Aunt' Sallie (80 yrs. old) and 'Uncle' Robert live with their grandson. A daughter lives nearby. They like to tell of the days when they were children:

"Land o' de libbin, my maw, she wuz one o' de Hughes and Giles niggers. She used to lob to set down by de fire an' tell us younguns 'bout de times what de had down dar on de big ribber (Broad River). Our plantation, she used to say, wuz de one what de white folks called Mt. Drury. But when maw wuz rael young, jus big enough to wait on de fine white ladies, she wuz put on de 'block', you nos what dat wuz, and sold to Marse 'Matt' Wallace. Marse Matt took it into his haed dat he wuz a gwine to a place what dey calls Arkansas. His white folks, specially his wife's, dem wuz de Mengs, dey riz up an put forth mighty powferul objections. Fer a long time he wuz jus onsettled in he mind 'bout zactly what he really wuz a gwine to do.

"Peers to me like my maw 'lowed dat he sorter kept his intentions secret when he had rightly make up he mind 'bout de whole business. In dem days, dere wo'nt no trains like dare is now. Everbody had to ride in waggons, and de white ladies, dey allus rid in fine carriages. De chilluns, dey rid wid de wimmen folks. Our Marster, he rid high steppin' horse, cept on de Sabbath, when he rid wid de missus to meetin' house out on de creek. (Brown's Creek).

"Anyhow, one cold mornin' not long fore Christmas and jus atter Thanksgivin' us sot out fore day, or dat is, my maw and pa did, kaise I wuz not born till we got to Mississippi River. Dar wuz fo' in de white folks carriage—I is heered Maw tell it a thousand times, over and over—In de carriage dar wuz Missus; and de fo' chilluns, Jeanette, Clough, Winter and Ida. Marse Matt, he rid de horse right by de side o' de carriage. Paw—de call him 'Obie', he driv a waggin wid all de little nigger chaps in it dat wuz too little to walk. De big nigger boys and gals dat wuz strong, dey walked. De roads wuz jus narrow little trails wide enough fer de carriage and de waggin to git through de lims o' de trees. Dey would hit you in de face iffin you didn't duck 'em, so maw allus 'lowed. Dey had pack mules dat fetched along de supplies, fer dey had to spen' de night in de thick woods what nebber had been cut. All kinds er varmints used to git atter dem and maw 'lowed dat dey wuz scared when dey sot camp, and she used to tremble mo' den she slep. When she did sleep, she 'lowed dat she drempt de awful varmints wuz a gittin' atter her. De missus, she wuz scared at night too. Marse Matt, he 'lowed he warn't one bit scared, but maw sat dat Missus say he jump powerful in he sleep sometimes.

"Marse Matt had done sot a task of so many miles fer dem to travel from sun-up to sundown, but maw 'lowed dat dey nebber did hardly git dat fer. De pack mules would git short winded, and sometime de carriage horses, dey would git lame; or one o' de waggin wheels would take and break; or it wuz allus some bad luck er follerin atter dem. Den Marse Matt, he 'lowed dat he didn't believe in no travelin' signs, and 'cause o' dat, maw 'lowed dat dey had de worsest kind o' luck. Dat is de reason dat de train did not git no further than 'Promoter' County, Miss. (Mr. Wallace really went to Como, Desoto County, Miss., verified by Mrs. J. Clough Wallace). It took dem fo' weeks to reach 'Promotor'. Dar dey set up de new home. Maw 'lowed dat dey wuz called tender feeted poineers by dem what had got dar ahead of dem. Peers like maw 'lowed dat dey stayed dar five year. Anyway de fus year, a lot o' de niggers tuck all manner o' ailiments and dey died. De Missus, she kept full o' cold in dat log house. Dey had a fine house here, you nos de house what Miss Roberta Wallace libs in, well, dat wuz de one, cepin it wuz not as fine as Miss Roberta got it now. Anyway, maw and paw, dey didn't like it no better dan missus, cepin dey wuz skeered to speak dere minds. Finally, de Marster, he tuck down sick, and in spite o' all dat Missus do fer him, maw 'lowed he kept a growin' worser and worser till he tuck and died one bad night. Missus, 'Dandy' de Marster allus called her, had got so broke down wid worry and sorrow, dat she wuz nigh to death's door, herself, when de Marster died, maw said. Fer dat reason, dey kept it from her fer two weeks. Dey thought dat she wuz gwine to have de pneumonia, like him, but she started to gittin' well fore she tuck de pneumonia. Maw said dat dey used all o' de ole nigger remedies on de Missus dat dey knowed and fer dat reason dey brung her through. Maw is told me dem remedies but I is so ole now, dat I jus remembers dem. If Bob wuz at hisself he could give you some. You come by here some day when de moon is right and den Bob'll be in his right mind to tell you some o' dem.

"De Missus, she come back powerful slow, and it wuz mi' nigh Thanksgiving when she got strong. It wuz so cold dat she used to 'low how she wish fer her paws big warm fire, and de Carolina sunshine. So one bad morning, she took and got a letter from her paw in Union. He axed her to fetch us all back here to Union. It had done tuck de letter over three weeks to git to her. Long fore de Marster had died he had gib up hope er gwine to Arkansas. When dat letter rive, maw 'lowed dat de Missus she tuck and started to cryin'. All dat day she cry and read it over an over. De very next morning she called up all us, I wuz born den, and maw 'lowed dat I wuz a carrin' a sugar tit in my mouf and dat I had de cooter bones round my neck. Course I disremembers all cept dat what I is been told over and over. When maw and paw went out dar, dey had one little chile. He wuz six years ole when dey got back here. One had done tuck and died fore dey lef here. Den me and my sister, we wuz born in Miss.

"Dat wuz one glad day fer us, kaise Missus 'lowed dat she wuz a gwine back to her paw in Union. All de niggers, dey started to dancing and a hollerin' like dey wuz wile. Maw 'lowed dat some folks dat libbed three miles away tuck and come to see us. Some o' dem called us slackers, er sometin' kaise we wuz a leavin'; but others, maw 'lowed, dat dey wished dey could go as fer as Georgia wid us. But I is nebber liked Georgia myself. Missus gib de orders fer us to begin packin' and maw said dat de way dem niggers worked wuz a dyin' sin. De Missus, she sell her mules and other stock, kaise we wuz a gwine to ride all de way back on de railroad train. It had jus broke through to Miss. Some o' de ole niggers 'lowed dat dey wuz feered to ride on dem things, bein' as dey wuz drawed by fire. Dey thought de debbil, he wuz a workin' in de inside of dem. Maw 'lowed dat if de Missus wuz not feered she would not be. De Missus was feered 'bout dem dat wuz not gwine to ride on de train, but when she 'lowed dat dey could jus stay in Miss. Maw said dat dey nebber did hear no mo' 'bout dem bein' feered o' de train.

"Maw and paw allus tole me 'bout de things what I did on de train. I wuz so young dat I jus remembers anything about dat. She 'lowed dat she tuck de cooter bones from my neck fore we started to de train. Maw 'lowed dat when de train come up, dey wuz so scairt dat we did not want to git on till she did. All de niggers wuz looked up to when dey got back here, maw 'lowed, kaise no niggers in Union had ebber rid on de train ceptin dem dat had rid fer as Alston, and dey wuz so few dat you could count dem on your hand.

"Missus 'Dandy' come right back to her paw's house. He wuz Mr. Clough Meng. Missus Dandy's little boy, Clough, wuz big enough to go to school when dey got back. It wuz Christmas when dey got to 'Promotor' County, and it wuz Christmas when us rive back.

"When my paw, 'Obie', wuz a courtin, a nigger put a spell on him kaise he was a wantin' my maw too. De nigger got a conjure bag and drapped it in de spring what my paw drunk water from. He wuz laid up on a bed o' rheumatiz fer six weeks. Dey all knowed dat he wuz conjured. He could not even set up when his victuals wuz fetched to him. So his brother knowed who had put de spell on him. He tuck and went to another old conjure man and axed him to take dat spell off'n paw. De conjure man 'lowed to paw's brother dat a grapevine growed over de spring, and fer him to go dar and cut a piece of it six feet long and fetch it to his house at night. When he tuck it to de conjure man's house, de conjure man, he took de vine in a dark place and done somethin to it—de Lawd knows what. Den he tole my paw's brother to take it home and give it to paw. De man what put de spell on paw, I mean de nigger what had it done, he come often and set down by paw and ax him what was ailen him. Our conjure man, he tole paw dat de nex time de man come an' set down by his bed, fer him to raise up on his lef elbow and rech down by his bed and take dat piece o' grapevine and hit de nigger over de head and face. Den atter he had done dat, our conjure man 'lowed dat paw could den rise up from his bed o' rheumatiz.

"It wont long before de nigger come to visit my paw. My paw, he axed him real nice like to have a seat. His maw had done put a chair by de bed, so dat he would set down wid his face toward paw. Atter he and paw got to talkin, paw reched down an' axed him to have a look at de grapevine dat he was gwine to smoke fer his ailment. Dat nigger, he 'lowed to my paw dat it wuz not a goin to do his rheumatiz no good. Jus as he 'lowed dat, paw, he riz up on his lef shoulder and elbow and wid his right han' he let loose and come down over dat nigger's face and forehead wid dat grapevine. Dat nigger, he jump up and run out o' dat house a hollerin' kaise he knowed dat paw and done got de spell offin him. My paw got up de next day and dey 'lows dat he nebber did have no mo' rheumatiz."

ELLA KELLY

Interview with Ella Kelly, 81 years old
—W.W. Dixon, Winnsboro, S.C.

"Yas sir, I was born a slave of Mr. Tom Rabb, they call him black Tom Rabb, 'cause dere was two other Tom Rabbs. Marster Tom's hair was jet black and even when he shave, whisker roots so black face 'pear black. Yas sir, I come to birth on his place two or three miles from Monticello in de country, so I did. They say de year was de year President Buchanan was president, though I dunno nuttin' 'bout dat.

"My pappy name Henry Woodward, and b'long to old preacher Beelie Woodward's son, John. But all dis was just what I heard them say 'bout it. My mammy name Ella. She was de cook. I too little to work in slavery time, just hang 'round kitchen wid mammy, tote water and pick up chips, is all de work I done I 'members.

"Money? Help me Jesus, No. How could I ever see it? In de kitchen I see none, and how I see money any where else, your honor? Nigger never had none! I ain't got any money now, long time since I see any money.

"What did us eat? Dat's somethin' I knows 'bout. My mammy de cook for de white folks, wasn't I right dere at her apron strings all de time? Eat what de white folks eat, all de time, sho' I did! Too little to 'member much what slavery was like; can't tell nothin' 'bout clothes, never had no shoes. Us went to church some Sundays. Funny, them dat had not been good or done somethin' bad was kept at home by de white overseer, and some of them played wid de white chillun. Sorry I can't answer every question.

"One story I 'member 'bout is de pa'tridges and de Savior. My pappy allowed de reason pa'tridges couldn't fly over trees was: One day de Savior was a-riding long on a colt to de Mount of Olive Trees, and de drove flewed up, make sich a fuss they scared de colt and he run away wid him. De marster put a cuss on de pa'tridges for dat, and ever since, they can't fly over tree tops. You reckon dat so boss? They say they never does fly over trees!

"I had a good marster and mistress. When de slaves git sick, they 'tend to them same as one of their own chillun. Doctor come quick. They set up and fan you and keep de flies off. They wouldn't let de slaves do dis, 'cause certain times you got to take medicine 'cordin' to doctors orders, and a slave might make a mistake. Oh, they was 'ticular 'bout sickness. They has a hard time wid some nigger chillun and dat cast' oil bottle, I tell you!

"One of my young marsters was name Charlie. After freedom he marry one of Colonel Province's daughters and me and my mammy moved and lived wid them a while. Then I got married to Wates Kelly, and went to live and work for a white man 'bove White Oak. His name was Long John Cameron, de best white man to work for, but when Sat'day come and all de hands paid off, he git dat red hoss and turn and gallop to Winnsboro and bring back a passel of low down white trash wid him to de disturbment of all de good colored person on de place.

"Yas sir, Klu Klux was a terror to certain colored persons. I 'members they come dressed up in white and false faces, passed on to de Richardson place and whipped somebody one night.

"My husban' been dead twelve years. I's got thirteen chillun and Minnie is de onliest one livin' wid me in dis house. Her name Minnie Martin. Got whole lot of gran' chillun; they cover de earth from Charlotte to Jacksonville, and from Frisco to Harlem, New York; but never see them, just three, Franklin, Masie and Marie Martin.

"I heard 'bout Lincoln and Booker T. Washington. De President now in de White House, Mr. Roosevelt, have done more good for de nigger in four years than all de other presidents since Lincoln, done in fifty years. You say its been seventy-two years? Well, than all de rest in seventy-two years. Don't you know dat is so? Yas sir, dats de gospel truth.

"I's a member of de Baptist Church. Been buried wid my Lord in baptism and hope for a resurrection wid him in Beulah Land.

"Yes, de overseer was de poor buckra, he was what you calls dis poor white trash. You know boss, dese days dere is three kind of people. Lowest down is a layer of white folks, then in de middle is a layer of colored folks and on top is de cream, a layer of good white folks. 'Spect it'll be dat way 'till Jedgement day.

"I got one boy name Ben Tillman, livin' in dis town. White folks calls him Blossom, but he don't bloom 'round here wid any money, though he is on de relief roll by sayin' he got a poor old mammy nigh a hundred years old and he have to keep her up. 'Spect when I gits my old age pension my chillun will pay me some little 'tention, thank God. Don't you know they will, sure they will."

MARTHA KELLY

Interview with Martha Kelly (age between 70 and 75)
Marion, S.C.
—*Annie Ruth Davis*

"All I can tell you, I come here de second year of freedom. Cose I had a lot of trouble en I can' hardly imagine how long it be dat I de age I is. My mother, she know my age good, but she been dead for de years come en gone from here. Ain' much I can remember to tell you 'cause I was small den. No, my mammy didn' tell we chillun nothin. Didn' have no time to tell we chillun nothin. She had to go out en work in de field in de day en she would be tired when night come.

"My mammy white people was name Charlie Law en his family en dey lived in Britton's Neck till dey come up here to Marion. We lived in a rice country down in dat place call Britton's Neck. Ain' you hear talk of it? My mammy en her chillun stayed right dere on old man Law's place till long time after dey tell dem dey was free to leave dere. Stayed to de nigger quarter in my mammy house 'cause we was learn to be field hands.—Harold, I told you hold off me 'cause I don' feel like you layin on me dis mornin.—(Harold—small grandson). Didn' know 'bout nothin much to eat in dat day en time, but bread en meat en rice en all such as dat. Oh, de peoples in dat country made plenty rice. Dey would plant it on dis here black lookin dirt en when dey would see dat it was right ripe, dey would cut it en thrash it out. Den dey would have one of dem pestle en mortar to beat it wid. My blessed, child, dat been turn out de nicest kind of rice. No, mam, don' see no such rice dese days dat been eat like dat rice eat.

"I recollects I used to be right much of a hand to pull fodder en pick cotton en all such like dat 'cause all my work was in de field mostly till I got to de place dat I couldn' work no longer. You see, when I was married, I moved out dere on Dr. Miles' place over next Pee Dee en 'bout all my days was spent in de country. Lived out dere on Dr. Miles' place till I come here to town to live 'bout seven or eight years ago. You is hear talk of Dr. Miles, ain' you? I used to do what you might say a right good size washin, but I ain' able to get 'bout to do nothin dese days much. Just washes out a piece or two like a apron every now en den.

"Some of de peoples used to sing dere, but I wouldn' never bear much along dat line. Didn' have no voice much to sing. Is you got dis one?

> Lord, I wonder,
> Lord, I wonder,
> Lord, I wonder,
>
> (Repeat 3 Times)
>
> When de lighthouse
> Gwine shine on me.

"Dat all dere be to dat one. I don' know whe' if I could remember dat other one or no. Seem like it go somethin like dis:

> Oh, didn' it rain?
> It rain 40 days,

En it rain 40 nights,
It ain' never stop a droppin yet,
En I heard de angel in de mornin sing,
Oh, didn' it rain?

But down by de graveyard,
Me en my Lord gwine stand en talk.
Up on de mountain fire en smoke,
I wouldn' be so busy 'bout de fire en smoke.
I heard de angel in de mornin sing,
Oh, didn' it rain?

Oh, didn' it rain?
It rain 40 days,
En it rain 40 nights,
Widout still a droppin yet,
I heard de voice of de angel in de mornin sing,
Oh, didn' it rain?

Oh, didn' it rain?
Down by de graveyard,
Me en my Lord gwine stand en talk.
Chillun, my good Lord,
I heard de voice of de moanin angel,
Oh, didn' it rain?

Oh, didn' it rain?
It rain 40 days,
En it rain 40 nights,
Widout still a droppin yet,
En I heard de voice of de angel in de mornin,
Oh, didn' it rain?

"Well, dere ain' been so much dat I remember dat happen when I come along but what been happen in a way dis day en time. Cose dere been a difference 'cause de people ain' used to live fast like dey do dese days. Dere been de shake dat come here in '86 dat I ain' never see de like since en ain' want to see nothin like dat no more neither. I remember it come here on a night en when I get in bed dat night, I ain' been expectin nothin had been de matter. Den dere somethin been rouse me up en all de dishes was a rattlin'. When I get up en go out in de yard, de house en all de elements was a rockin'. Yes, mam, I was scared. Didn' know what was de matter. Thought it was de Jedgment comin when I wake up en hear all de people round 'bout dere screamin en a hollerin, Jedgment! Oh, Jedgment! Say dem what ain' right better get right. I tell de people dat dere won' no need to run to de church den 'cause we was all gwine be destroyed dere together. Child, I give myself up den en I get just as happy as I could be.

"Oh, dey had slavery time doctors to tend de people when dey was sick in dat day en time. Yes, mam, had dey plantation doctor right dere dat would go from one plantation to de other en doctor dem what was ailin. De doctor would come dere to my white folks plantation en tell my grandmother what to feed dem on en she would give dem de remedy dey tell her. Dey would use all kind of different herbs in dat day en time dat dey would get out de old fields en de woods for dey cures. Honey, dey was good too en dey good yet. I couldn' tell you half de herbs dey use, but I recollects dere was boneset dat was good for fever, sage for de baby, pennyroyal dat was good for girls dat catch cold, mint for sick stomach, catnip to hope a cold, horehound to strike a fever en dat 'bout all I recollect. No, mam, I can' remember half de herbs dere was in de field, but I know we got some of dat sage growin dere in de garden now.

"I hear talk of dem Yankees plenty times, but I don' know much to speak 'bout dem. Couldn' tell de first word 'bout dem. I dis kind of person, I don' pay much mind to nothin like dat. Dey was white people, I think.

"Seems like it was better livin long time ago den dere be now. Seems like times so tight dese days. Reckon it 'cause I ain' able to work, but dey tell me de people don' get nothin much to speak 'bout for dey work dis day en time. Seems like I got along good when I was able to whip round en 'bout.

"I hear de people say dere such a thing as ghost, but I don' know en I ain' de kind to speak 'bout de devil business. I hear talk dey could be walkin right along wid you en dere some people could see dem en den dere others could look wid all de eyes dey got en couldn' see dem. No, I ain' never see dem. I has seen people wear one of dese dime round dey ankle, but I never didn' ax dem nothin 'bout what dey wear it for 'cause some people is curious en don' like for you to be axin dem 'bout things. I did always keep out of fuss en I still keepin out it. Never did bother none wid it. When I see anybody fussin, I shuns dem. My mammy didn' raise me to do dat."

MARY JANE KELLEY

>Interview with Mary Jane Kelley (85)
>Newberry, S.C.
>—G.L. Summer, Newberry, S.C.

"I live in a rented house wid my daughter who takes care of me. I was born in de Santuc section. My pa and ma was Richard Dawkins and Marsha Shelton Dawkins. I think dey lived wid de Hendersons in de Maybinton section near Broad River, but dey lived wid Marse Bill Jeter near Santuc when I was born. My husband was Ike Kelley, he been dead good many years.

"Marse whipped me once or twice. We had to work in de cotton fields, and I have split rails and ditched like men, too.

"We had home-raised meat, lots of hogs and cattle. Marse had a big garden and we got lots of vegetables. Marse fed slaves in a trough in de yard. He had his own smokehouse whar he cured his meat. His flour was ground in de neighborhood. Sometimes he give a slave family a small patch to plant watermelons in.

"We wore heavy brogans wid brass toes. Sometimes Marse would make his own leather and have shoes made in de neighborhood and dese would have wooden bottoms. He never let us learn to read and write. He never allowed us to go from one place to another unless it was on his place. De patrollers would git us if we didn't have a pass; even if we went to church wid white folks we had to have a pass. Niggers didn't have no church till atter de war; den dey built brush arbors in de woods.

"I married at my house. We is Baptists, and I used to go and see dem baptize sinners.

"We used to go home at night when de work was over and go to bed and rest. We worked all day on Saturdays, but never worked on Sundays. On Christmas Days we had off, and Marse would give us good things to eat and some whiskey to drink.

"My mother worked around de house in slavery time, she helped cook, clean up and wash dishes, and sometimes she would card, spin and weave.

"Dey used to make a yellowish dye from mud, a grayish dye from maple tree bark and a brownish dye from walnut tree bark. We allus planted by de signs or de scales. Irish potatoes, turnips and sweet potatoes we planted in de dark of de moon; while beans was planted in de sign of de craw-fish.

"I remember when de Yankees come through atter de war. Dey stole everything and burned up everything dey couldn't steal. De Ku Klux was in our section. Dey killed lots of niggers around dar.

"I don't remember anything about Abraham Lincoln nor Jefferson Davis, only heard about dem. I don't know much about Booker Washington, either."

GABE LANCE

> Interview with Uncle Gabe Lance, age 77
> Sandy Island, Murrells Inlet, S.C.
> —*Genevieve W. Chandler*

BORN AND LIVING ON SANDY ISLAND

"Great Peace! Missus, have to study up that!"

Uncle Gabe had just arrived from Sandy Island at the country post-office, having rowed over for his month's supply of sugar and coffee and things he cannot raise. After the five or six mile row he must needs walk three miles to the office.

"I could remember when the Yankee boats come to Montarena—gun-boats. 'Bout ten o'clock in the morning. Soldier all muster out and scatter all over the island. You know that cause-er-way? Gone over that two by two, gun on shoulder glisten gainst the sun! Blue-coats, blue pants, hat all blue. Come back to landing 'bout five o'clock. Have hog, geese, duck! Broke in barn. Stole rations from poor people. My Grandfather the Driver—slave Driver. Name Nelson. Maussa—Frank Harriott. Maussa gone in swamp. Hid in woods. My Grandfather take old Miss Sally—Miss Sally Harriott—count she couldn't walk with rheumatism—Grandfather took old Miss Sally on he back to hid 'em in the woods where Maussa. Yankee stay but the one day. Ravage all over us island. All goat, hog, chicken, duck, geese—all the animal but the cow been take on the Yankee gun boat. They broke in Maussa big rice barn and share all that out to the colored folks.

"Some my people run away from Sandy Islant. Go Oaks sea-shore and Magnolia Beach and take row-boat and gone out and join with the Yankee. Dem crowd never didn't come back.

"Any slave run way or didn't done task, put 'em in barn and least cut they give 'em (with lash) been twenty-five to fifty. Simply 'cause them weak and couldn't done task—couldn't done task! 'Give 'em less rations to boot! Cut 'em down to

> 1 qt. molasses
> 1 lb. meat
> 1 pk. corn for a week

"Good Master all right. Give plenty to eat. Reasonable task. Task dem time one-fourth to one half acre. Ditching man ten compass. Got to slush 'em out. Got to bail that water out till you kin see track.

"All dem rice-field been nothing but swamp. Slavery people cut kennel (canal) and dig ditch and cut down woods—and dig ditch through the raw woods. All been clear up for plant rice by slavery people.

"Beat my Pa and Ma to death and turn me loose! Ought to take care 'o me! I send off my 35 ct. fust (first) time, next time twenty-five cents I put what little I have in it. Ain't hear no answer. Some ten or fifteen head round here send off blank and don't get no hearing! Take what little I have and don't send me nothing 'TALL! I tired with that now! Ain't had a hearing!" (Referring to 'old age compensation').

EPHRIAM (MIKE) LAWRENCE

I

Interview with Ephriam Lawrence
Edisto Island, S.C.
—*C.S. Murray*

"I don't 'member much 'bout slavery time 'cause I been lee (little) boy when war declare. I raise up under de Murray—all my generation belong to de Murray. Dey know how to treat slave. Ain't lick um much, hardly any. Chillun hab easy time. All I been require to do was tote coal to Mosser when he ready fer light. Adam Mack and me, we been de fire boy. Mosser gib Adam to Mister Eberson. I ain't gib to nobody—'specially.

"All white people ain't treat slave good. Some make um wuk haa'd all day, and 'cuss um plenty. De slave who been live near Steamboat Landing had rough time when dere old Miss git in tantrum. She been 'nuse to trabbel all over de world, and when she come back, she call all de slave together, and say: 'When I come, de debbil come.'

"We family ain't had all dat to worry 'bout. Behave yourself and you all right. Plenty to eat, plenty to drink. Run 'round and enjoy yourself if you got uh mind to. Wuk when you wuk, play when you play. Ole Miss 'nuse to 'tend all de sick nigger. Go from house to house, wid lee pair of scale and bottle ram jam pack of calomel. Give lee nigger big dose of castor oil, and dey git well quick, mighty quick.

"Old Mosser 'nuse to keep all de likker in de world on hand. Had to keep plenty, 'cause he friend drink lot and nigger drink lot too. He ain't drink so much heself. Old nigger been live on de place call John Fraser, same one I tell you 'bout, dat cut all dem tree down. John sure been slick. When Mosser call fer he fine likker to hand 'round, John come back and tell him all gone. Mosser want to know why. John make reply: 'Why, Mosser you know you hab Mister Binyard to supper last night and he finish all dat good stuff. You know how Mr. Binyard drink. Sometime he drink when your back t'un (turned). How you 'speck um to last?' Mosser scratch he haid, and say, yes he know how Mr. Binyard drink, and mebbe dats why de last bottle empty. He ain't satisfy, but he can't prove dat John drink um.

"Mosser 'nuse to keep de whiskey down in de cellar by de barrel, and he draw um off in bottle when he need um and take um upstair to de wine room. De nigger dat wuk 'round de house and de yaa'd, help dem self out de barrel when dey feel tired. Mosser 'spect dem to do dat—dey 'title (entitle) to um. Whiskey been kinder ration in dem day.

"Nigger jest know haa'd time now. Ain't been dat way when I been lee boy. You ain't lacking fer nutting den dat you really need. No tussling 'bout fer yourself and knock 'round from pillar to post. If we need anything slavery time we ax (ask) fer um—make we want known. Any feeling ably white man who hab slave, gib we what we need. No puzzling 'tall (at all).

"Ain't I tell you 'bout dat time when John Fraser take overcoat from Mosser right on Meeting Street? No. Well, it been uh cold day, and Mosser tell John Fraser to meet him on de corner Meeting and Broad wid de overcoat, 'cause he going out dat night and he want 'um. John been wid Abel Wright, and de two of dem walk down de street to meet de Major. John say to Abel: 'I cold as de debbil, and I going to ax Mosser fer he coat.' Abel say: 'You crazy. He send for um and he sure ain't going, to gib you he good new coat anyhow.' John say: 'You wait and see.'

"Soon Mosser come in sight. When he see John he git mad right off 'cause John hab on he overcoat. Before he kin say uh wud (word) John speak up fast. He say: 'Yes, Mosser I got on your coat 'cause it mighty cold. Got to excuse old nigger. You hab 'nother coat. I ain't got nutting but dis here jumper. Go on home Mosser and git torrer (the other) coat. I going to keep dis. He jest fit me. Go on home.'

"Mosser study fer uh while, den he laugh. He see how keen de coat fit John, and he know it been cold sure 'nough. John look sekker (just like) dress up monkey in dat long tail overcoat, and dat make de Major laugh all de more. So he tu'n round and go home, and John hab dat coat till he die.

"Old Mosser scarcely going to deny you nutting, if he like you."

II

Interview with Ephriam (Mike) Lawrence, about 80, farmer and laborer
Edisto Island, S.C.
—*C.S. Murray*

Mike Lawrence belonged to what he calls "de Murray state" in slavery times. He was one of Major William Meggett Murray's "fire boys", who was charged with the specific duty of bringing live coals to the master whenever he wanted to light his pipe. Mike was only a small lad when war was declared, but he remembers numerous stories relating to "Maussa's niggers", some of which are worth recording. He speaks from first hand knowledge, he says, for the things that he tells about happened during his childhood and still stand out clearly in his mind.

Here is one of Mike's stories:

"Old John Drayton was de smaa'test of all de nigger de Maussa place. He wuk so haa'd some time dat Maussa jest got to stop him, or he kill heself. I nebber see sech uh man fer wuk in all my life. Maussa t'ink uh lot ob um, 'cause he been uh good field hand, beside know lot 'bout cutting 'ood (wood) and building fence. What been more old John play fer all de dance on de plantation. He fair (really) mek fiddle talk. When Maussa gib uh dance he always call 'pon John.

"Yas, suh dat man sure could play. W'en he saw down on de fiddle and pull out dat june (tune) 'Oh, de Monkey Marry to de Babboon Sister,' he mek paa'son (parson) dance.

"One day more dan all, Maussa Murray send wud (word) to John dat de cow der break out ob de pasture, and he got to mend de fence quick. But John done promise some nigger on Fenwick Island to play fer uh dance, and he steal paa't (path) and go. (This expression means to go away by stealth). Dat been Friday night and Maussa say John got to finish de fence by sundown the next day.

"W'en Old John ain't show up Saturday morning, Maussa ax eberybody where he been and de nigger all band togedder (together) and tell Maussa dat dey see him leabe in uh boat to go fish and he ain't seen since. Maussa been worry sure 'nough den 'cause he t'ink John might be drown'. He 'gage (engage) four man to shoot gun all ober creek to mek John body rise. Atter dat day drag all 'bout in de gutter.

"Maussa gone bed wid heaby haa't (heart) 'cause he been very fond ob Old John.

"John come back from Fenwick Island early Monday morning and 'fore day clean he in de 'odd der cut fence rail. Now, one hundred rail been call uh good day wuk, but Old John decide he going to do better den dat. He find fibe (five) tree grow close togedder, and he cut piece out ob every one. Den he chop at the biggest tree till he fall, and dat tree knock all de rest ober wid um.

"W'en all dem tree fall togedder, it make sech uh noise, dat ole Maussa hear um in he bed, and hasten to dress so he kin see w'at der go on in de woods.

"Maussa saddle de horse and ride 'till he git to de center ob de noise and dere he see Old John cutting 'way like he crazy. Maussa been mad sure 'nough, but den he glad to see John ain't drown'. He staa't to say some t'ing but Old John interrupt, and sing out: 'Go 'way Maussa, I ain't got time to talk wid you now.'

"Old John den gather up five ax, and go to de five tree laying down on de ground. He dribe uh ax in ebery tree and den grab uh neaby maul. W'en Maussa look on, he tek de maul and run from one tree to torrer (one to the other) and quick as he hit de ax, de tree split wide open. Maussa staa't to say some t'ing 'gain but John ain't let him talk. He say: 'Go on home to Missus, Maussa, I too 'shame, great God I too 'shame! Go on home.'

"Maussa tun (turn) 'round in he track and go home widout uh wud, 'cause he see de old nigger ain't going to gib him any satisfaction 'bout Saturday. W'en he go back in de 'ood dat evening he check up and find dat Old John done cut five hundred rail. Oh, dem been man in dose day, I tell you."

BEN LEITNER

Interview with Ben Leitner, 85 years old
—W.W. Dixon, Winnsboro, S.C.

"I see you go by de road de other day, on your way to old man Wade Jackson's house. 'Member de old fellow dat am paralyzed, de one dat lives beyond Fellowship graveyard? I was setten' in dat graveyard when you and Marse Thomas pass in de automobile. I 'quire nex' day where you was a goin', then Marse Thomas say you goin' 'round doin' sumpin' 'bout old slaves and 'spect you'd like to see me. So here I is.

"Well, I's knowed you since you was knee-high and Marse Thomas say, maybe you help me to get a pension. If you can't, nobody can.

"I was born a slave of old Marse Robin Brice, not far from New Hope A.R.P. Church. My mistress was name Miss Jennie. My young marsters' was: Marse John, Marse Chris, and Marse Tom. Marse Tom been a little runt; they call him Tom Shanty. Him got to be a member of de Legislature, after de war. All them went to de 'Federate War. Deir sister, Amanda, marry Marse Bill Kitchen. You 'member him, don't you? Course you does.

"'Member dat day baseball fust come out and they got up a team, not a team then; they called it a 'Nine', when de game fust come to woodward section? If you ketch a ball on de fust bounce, dat was a 'out'. No sich thing as a mask for de face, gloves for de hands, and mats to protect your belly. No curves was allowed, or swift balls throwed by de pitcher. Him have to pitch a slow dropball. De aim than was to see how far a batter could knock de ball, how fast a fellow could run, and how many tallies a side could make. Mighty poor game if de game didn't last half a day and one side or de other make forty tallies.

"Marse Bill Kitchen was workin' in de store of his brudder-in-law, Marse John A. Brice. Him was called out to make one of de 'Nines'. Him went to de bat, and de very fust lick, him knock de ball way over center field. Everybody holler: 'Run Kitchen! Run Kitchen! Run Kitchen!' Marse Bill stand right dere wid de bat; shake his head and long black whiskers and say: 'Why should I run? I got two more licks at dat ball!' They git de ball, tech him and de umpire say: 'Out'. Marse Bill throw de ball down and say; 'D—n sich a game!' Folks laugh 'bout dat 'til dis day.

"My daddy name Bill Leitner. Him never b'long to Marse Robin. Him b'long to Marse John Partook Brice. Mammy b'long to Marse Robin. Her name Sarah. Daddy have to have a pass to come to see mammy.

"My brudders and sisters was Eliza, Aleck, and Milton. Patrollers whup daddy one time when they come to de house and find him widout a pass. Marster have mammy whup us chillun, when us need a whuppen. Her milk de cows, churn, and 'tend to de milk, butter and dairy. I helped her wid de cows and calves, and churnin'.

"You ask me is I had plenty to eat? Sure I did, wid all dat milk 'round me all de time. Best thing I 'member right now was runnin' my finger 'round de jar where de cream cling, and suckin' it off my fingers.

"Marster took good care of his slaves. They never went hungry or cold.

"My marster and mistress live in a big two-story house. Us live in little log house, wid log chimneys. I 'members fightin' chinches in de summertime and fleas all de time. I wore a asafetida bag 'round my neck, when a child to keep off croup, measles, diphtheria, and whoopin' cough. Marster send for Dr. Walter Brice when any slave get very ill.

"De fust year of freedom I work for Marse Chris Brice. Been wid de Brices all my life. Now livin' on Marse Tom Brice's place.

"When de Yankees come, they ramsack de house for silver and gold. They burn de house and gin-house; carry off mules, hosses, and cows. They took de chickens, load all de provisions, put them in a four-hoss waggin, and leave us and de white folks cold and hungry. It was cold winter time then too.

"I marry a ginger cake lady, one-fourth white, daughter of Louis Grier. Tho' I ain't much on looks as you sees me today, dat gal often, befo' and after de weddin', put her arms 'bout me and say: 'Ben you is de han'somest man I ever have see in de world.'

"Us had three chillun. My wife led me to de light of de Lord. I jined de Red Hill Baptist Church, under de spell of Peter Cook's preachin' and my wife up in de choir a singin': 'Give me dat old time Religion.' Preacher Miller is my pastor now. Peter Cook dead and gone to glory long years ago. I 'members now dat old preacher's warm hand, when he took my hand dat night I jined. Him say:

'God give you a life to live. You have a soul to save. God give you His Son to save dat soul. Glory be His name!."

MARY ANN LIPSCOMB

> Interview with Mrs. Mary Ann Lipscomb
> Gaffney, S.C.
> —*Caldwell Sims, Union, S.C.*

REMINISCENCES

"My husband, Nathan Lipscomb, was over on Mt. Pleasant fighting, and I had been over there to see him. He was a private in the rear ranks. When we were coming back to Charleston on a rice steamer, an open boat, the Yankees were shelling the town. I played with my fingers in the water of the bay as the steamer went along. We landed at a different landing from the one where we had started from. When I got off the steamer I was very much frightened, for they had shot through the hotel where we were staying.

"We immediately left the city by train. I hated to leave my husband so far behind, but I could do nothing about it. In that day the train used only wood for fuel. Only two trains a day came from Columbia to Charleston. They made about 18 miles per hour, but that was good traveling at that time.

"My brother, Thomas Wilkins, went through the war. My father, Russell, and Richard were in training when the surrender came. I stayed with my father at White Plains while my husband was off to war. When we heard that the Yankees were coming, we had the Negroes to hide all the horses but two, and to hide the cows and turn the hogs loose to ramble in the woods.

"When the Yankees rode up to the yard and got off their horses, we could easily tell they had been drinking. We told them that our horses were in the stable and that the Negroes had fled in terror, which was true. They ate up everything they could find and ransacked the closets and pantry. They then caught the chickens, took the two horses in the stable and went away.

"The darkies came back with the cows and horses, and we got settled for the night. About nine o'clock, the Yankees came unexpectedly and took all the horses and cows. They killed the cows, and made our darkies help them to butcher them and barbecue them. The Yankees soon ate everything up and left with our horses.

"My grandmother, Agnes Wood, gave my mother, Elizabeth Wilkins, a beautiful young mare. The Yankee who took that mare, turned over a pot of fresh soap when my mother asked him not to take the mare. Our cook, Matilda, had the soap ready to cut in the pot, so we saved some of it.

"During the second year of the war I was making me a homespun dress, and while my father helped me with the weaving he told me of a dress that one of his friends made during the Nullification days. I carded and spun the filling for my new dress, wove it, made the dress and wore it to Charleston when I went to see my husband. It had broad, black stripes the width of my two fingers, and two green threads between the black stripes. It also had a little yellow stripe. It was really a beautiful dress and looked very much like silk."

GOVAN LITTLEJOHN

I

Interview with Govan Littlejohn
Park Ave. and Liberty St., Spartanburg, S.C.
—*Caldwell Sims, Union, S.C.*

"Capt. Sam Littlejohn whipped Miss Sallie H.'s slave. His name was Ambus H. Cap' tied him to a tree. Never had no corn-shuckings, us shucked de corn quick as us hauled it from de field.

"My marse kilt as many as twenty hogs every time he butchered, which be about fo' times every winter. Marse Richard Littlejohn never married. He lived wid his mother and seven brothers.

"Marse was one good man and he love his darkies. He never had no overseer, because he had only 'bout 80 slaves as I remembers. I de onliest chile dat my ma had and I be 88 if I live to see dis coming December. My ma teach me to fight nothing in dis world but de devil.

"My father was Peter Littlejohn. Lawyer Tommie Dawkins was his marster. I never was sold. I married, but never had no chilluns. My old lady been gone over de river dese many years, so many dat I cannot recall how many. Yes Sir, I used to light my ma's pipe and wear home-made clothes. Ole lady Rhoda was de seamstress. She died not long atter we was liberated.

"I lives in de Woods Funeral Home which is on de corner of Park Ave. and Liberty Street. Once I befriend a man in distress. He now own interest in de undertaking 'stablishment and dat is why I has a room dar in my old age."

II

**Interview with Govan Littlejohn
387 S. Liberty St., Spartanburg, S.C.**
—*F.S. DuPre, Spartanburg, S.C.*

Govan Littlejohn, of Spartanburg, told the writer he was 87 years old and that he remembered slavery times. He said he was born on the farm of Dicky Littlejohn, located near Grindal Shoals. He said Richard Littlejohn owned a mill on Pacolet River, though his brother, Jim Littlejohn, owned the land. This was a grist mill. Govan Littlejohn's father was a colored man from another farm and his name was Hawkins, but he took the name of Littlejohn. He remembers the Yankee Soldiers passing in the public road, but they did not bother any one there; didn't take or steal anything, and just passed on quietly. He says his master did not know how to whip anybody, though he remembers him catching hold of him one day and switching him with a small twig, saying "You little rascal, you." His master whipped some of the grown negroes but not hard enough to hurt them, though once or twice he saw a grown negro with bare back feel the switch. "But he did not know how to whip anybody."

"Yes, I been conjured," he said. "You see that left foot? Well, once when I was a young 'buck', I was setting up to a gal and there was another fellow setting up to her, too. I held a little bit the upper hand with the gal. But when my left foot began to swell up and pain me, I had to go to bed. I stayed there three months. Dr. Nott came to see me and treated me with corn poultices, but they would dry up and fall off and I didn't get any better. He lanced my foot three times, but nothing but blood would come. One day a herb doctor came to see me and said he could cure my foot. He took corn meal poultices, rhubarb roots and some other things, and it wasn't long before my foot got well. About that time, my mother found the 'conjuration' right in the front yard at the door-steps. I must have stepped over it, or got my foot caught in it some way. The 'conjuration' was, pins, feathers and something else all tied up in a bag. My mother heard that if it was put in running water, the conjurer would leave the country. So pretty soon after she put the stuff in running water, that fellow left the country. He got his arm caught in a cotton gin not long after he left, and got it chewed off right to his shoulder.

"Vegetables should be planted during the dark of the moon. One day, the man I was working for told me he wanted his Irish potatoes planted. I told him that wasn't the time to plant potatoes. He told me to plant some in one particular place that day and call them his potatoes, then when I thought the time was right, to plant the rest in another place. His potatoes came up and made prettier vines than mine, had pretty blooms on them and the vines grew very high. He ragged me about how fine his potatoes were. He told me to gather the potatoes under my vines for the house, but not to disturb his potatoes. For several days, the family ate potatoes from my vines, then I gathered up the potatoes left. I got five or six wheelbarrows full. I then dug his potatoes and got a little more than one wheelbarrow full. He told me to plant the garden when I thought the time was right, and not to say anything to him about when and what to plant. I always had plenty of vegetables for his family."

EASTER LOCKHART

> Interview with Easter Lockhart (80)
> 322 Hill Street, Gaffney, S.C.
> —*Caldwell Sims, Union, S.C.*

"Folks thinks that I was born round Easter, but that ain't so. March the 9th is what they always told me. The year I cannot recollect hearing, but by my count that I keep I am running close to eighty years. White folks give me my age to keep when I married, and I have kept it ever since, so I cannot be far wrong.

"It was the chief of police's grandpa that I knew and it was off his place that my old man come from. I was born Easter Norris and I married Nathan Lockhart when I was young, maybe fifteen, ain't sure about that. He was a little older than me. In slavery I was born and my mother was sold while I was a very young child, so they say. We then lived with Mr. Clayton Clark. Freedom broke when I was around thirteen, and we then went back to the Lockhart Plantation. There is where I nursed Henry, a little baby. He is now the chief of police. Miss Bessie, his mother, had me to clean up her yards for her.

"Miss Bessie fixed me up to be baptized at the Limestone Baptist church. It was then near Johnson Street and across from where Central school now stands. It was a Negro church. We had to go to the spring pond called Austin's Pond where all the baptizing took place in those days. Mr. Austin had a mill there run by a big water wheel.

The white folks carried on their baptizing there, too. The first warm Sunday in May was when I was baptized.

"All Saturday I prayed and Miss Bessie told me what I was going to do, and read to me from the Bible about baptizing and about John the Baptist baptizing Christ. Yes sir, the Bible say Christ went down in the water, in the waters of Jordan. Miss Bessie was telling my ma how to fix my clothes while she was reading the Bible to me. All my clothes was white but my shoes. In those days they did not have white shoes. I wore white cotton stockings. I had a white dress to wear to the pond and I took two pairs of white stockings. A crowd was to be baptized at 2:30 o'clock that evening. The sun was good and hot. I went with my folks. Miss Bessie went and all the white folks went to see their Negroes go under.

"The dress I wore to the baptizing was starched so stiff it stood out. I wore a white handkerchief over my head that Miss Bessie give me. On top of that I had a white bonnet that had frills and tucks all over it. When we got there the banks of Austin's Pond was lined with Negroes shouting and singing glory and praises. They sang all the songs they could think of and the preacher lined out songs to them. The people to be baptized congregated before the preacher, and he told them what to do. Then we went in and put on the clothes we was to go under in.

"I had a long white gown gathered from my shoulders and it had a big kind of sleeves. On my head I wore a white cap and kept on my white stockings, but I pulled off my black shoes. Never had no white shoes that I know of way back then. I felt so good that I seemed to walk real light. While we were getting in our baptizing clothes we shouted praises as the people on the banks sang. Some of us jumped up. When my time come I started to the pond and just before the preacher turned to take my hand, I shouted 'Lord have Mercy' and clapped my hands over my head. Somebody said, 'Dat child sho is gitting a new soul'.

"Down in the water I went. First it hit my ankles and then I felt the hem of my skirts getting wet. I looked down and my gown was floating on top the water. I took my hand and pushed it down. The preacher pulled me to him and I went in water to my waist. I said 'Oh Lordy' when that water hit my stomach. The preacher said, 'Now sister, you just hold your breath and shut your mouth; trust in the Lord and don't act like a grunting pig, but have faith'. Then the singing seemed far off and the preacher's voice got deep. He put his big hand over my mouth and told me to limber up my back. His other hand was under my back. He pushed me over, and down in the water I went; then up I come. The preacher put a towel over my face, and while I was getting water out of my eyes and mouth, he was saying about the Lord done reached down from Heaven and created a new soul. I felt real funny when I turned to walk up out of the water. I could hardly walk for I had on so many clothes and they were so heavy. As soon as I could I got into the clothes that I wore to the baptizing and put on my black shoes and the pair of white stockings that I had fetched with me. While aunt Kizie Lockhart was tying the handkerchief around my head that Miss Bessie give me, I told her about how I felt. She said, 'Why, sure child, ain't you done washed your sins away and got converted?'

"Then she grabbed me by the hand and we went out among the people shouting praises to the Lord. I ain't never felt the same since. Aunt Kizie took me round to say 'howdy' to Miss Bessie. When the preacher had got them all baptized, we went into the church and had services. The white folks went on home after the baptizing was over. At the church we shouted till we could not shout no more. Folks don't like that now. They don't feel good when they join the church no more, either. I ain't had nothing to come against me since I was baptized. My head loses lots of things, but not my religion.

"Lots of folks was at Mr. Henry's Pa's house for his infair dinner. Mr. Hiram and Miss Bessie give the infair after the wedding. Miss Agnes, his sister come back for the wedding. Mr. Henry had sharp snapping eyes and he was good looking then. His eyes can still snap. When he looked at Miss Mary his face would light up. Her name was Miss Mary Gilmer, and she lived up near the lead mine. She sure looked good in white. I did not see the wedding, so I had to look careful at them when they come in Miss Bessie's front door so I could take it all in.

"The infair sure was fine. The table was most breaking down with turkey, chicken, ham, salads, pies and cakes. All the things to eat, already fixed on the plates, was fetched in from the kitchen by the Negroes. The chickens and turkeys just set on the table for ornaments and was not touched until the next day.

"The infair started at three o'clock in the afternoon. There were three or four tables for the people to sit at. The dining room and one other room were used to seat the guests at the tables while they ate. I can still see Miss Bessie's white linen table cloth that reached nearly to the floor. Such a time as I had the week before, washing and ironing the big linen napkins and shining the silver.

"They all looked mighty fine at the tables in their fine clothes. I could not help looking often at Mr. Henry's wife. Miss Bessie had done studied everything out so as it all went off fine."

GABLE LOCKLIER

> Interview with Uncle Gable Locklier, age 86
> Gourdin, S.C.
> —H. Grady Davis and Mrs. Lucile Young, Florence, S.C.

"I born in Clarendon county, 50 yards of Davis Station. Massa Henry Bethune dat have big plantation dere was my first boss en after he died, Mrs. Bethune sold everything en moved to Summerton. Stayed dere till she married Mr. Thomas, de preacher, dat have big place in Summerton wid trees in long row right up to de door. He bought place three miles from Summerton called de Bashet place. Mrs. Bethune was a sport lady en was good to me en Mr. Thomas good man too, but he was a Yankee. He come to Summerton to be a school teacher en won' long fore he commence to escort my Missus en dey made up in a year or two, I hear ma say. I was in de kitchen en I hear dem. She told ma, 'Eliza, I gwine marry Mr. Thomas.' Ma say, 'You is.' 'Yes, you reckon he gwine be all right?' 'I reckon he is, he looks all right.' 'Well, I gwine marry him en try him.' Mr. Thomas, he Yankee, but he fought for de Confederates.

"Massa Henry Bethune had big plantation en had a right sharp of slaves dere. De boss house was here en my house next en all de other slave house was string along in row dat way. My white folks, dey didn' exactly treat you as most of dem did. Dey come round en examine you house en see what you needed. All us live in two room pole house dat have a wood floor. Old people sleep on some kind of bed prop wid rope wind up like cow yoke en have quilts en mattresses taking white homespun. De others sleep on de floor. Dey give us good clothes made out of blue denim cloth en some had checked or stripe goods. Den dey give us heavy woolen clothes to wear in de winter time en had Sunday clothes too. My Massa was good to his slaves all de time. Have own garden dat my mother en sister would work en my mother done all de cookin for de slaves 'cause our folks all eat out de same pot. Cook rice en fat meat en dese collard greens en corn bread en cabbage. Make plenty of de cabbage en eat heap of dem.

"I didn' never have to work hard, but dey work dem till dark come on some places. Dey blow horn en us go to work after daylight en sometimes get off in time to eat supper by sundown. I was so slow dat when de rest knock off, dey make me work on. Mr. Thomas, he stand en look at me. My hands just look like dey put on wrong. When I quit off, I eat supper en den I go to bed.

"I ain' never see any slaves punished but I hear tell 'bout it. Some of dem run away 'cause dey get tired of workin en if dey catch em, dey sho whip em. Used to have to get ticket from boss or Missus to go any place off de plantation widout you get punish for it. I hear tell 'bout de overseer en de driver whip plenty of de slaves en some of de time, dey would put em in de screw box over night. Sell em if dey didn' do like dey tell em to do. Speculator come dere to buy slaves en dey sell em to de highest bidder. I hear em say a certain one bring $1400 or $1500. I know a man offered my boss $1000 for my brother, Joe, but he wouldn' sell him.

"My Massa would give me money now en den. First money I remember he give me was 75¢ paper money. He tell me to check his horse en bring him up to de yard en give me 75¢ en said, 'I can' carry you wid me dis mornin.' I was 'bout 9 or 10 years old den. I stood up on de block en wondered why he couldn' carry me en when I go back to de house, I see my Missus cryin en she say, 'We won' see him no more.' When he come back, he shot through de foot. He tell me to go to de blacksmith shop en bring crutches. Den he went to de war again en when he come back, he was shot on de right side of de neck. Give me a quarter in silver money dat time. I ain' never been to de store fore den, but I go to de storekeeper en I say, 'Mr. King, half dis money mine en half Joes.' I thought it was his place to give me what I wanted en when I walk out, he say, 'Come back en get your money,' I carried it home en give it to brother Joe en he give it to pa en don' know what come of it after dat. Bought plug of tobacco for pa wid de other money I had.

"Our folks didn' get no learnin much nowhe' in dem days, but my Missus sister child learn me right sharp. Dey was boardin at our house en when I started to school, I didn' have no trouble. I remembers I found a little book one time en man say he pay me 10¢ for it. Ma give me a needle en thread en little sack en I sew my 10¢ in it. Put it in de rafter en it stay dere till next Christmas. Believe I took it down en tote it a long time fore man come by sellin tobacco en I bought piece en give it to pa. Man give my sister bigger piece for a dime den he give me.

"De slaves what belong to my white folks have frolicsome days all through de year. Go to frolic on Saturday en go to white folks church on Sunday en sit in portion of church in de gallery. Den on Christmas eat en drink de best liquor dere was en de Fourth of July de one day dat dey have to go to [HW: Eutaw] Springs. Dey go in buggies en wagons en have plenty of everything to eat dat day. I know dere was a battle up dere, although I didn' never go wid em. Cotton pickin en corn shuckin days won' no work times, dey was big frolics. De first one shuck red corn had to tell who his best girl was en all dem things. All dem come to cotton pickin dat want to en pick cotton en cook big dinner. Pick cotton till 'bout 5:30 in de evenin' en den knock off for de eats en de dancin. Go to all de slaves weddings too. Dey would mostly get married 'bout on a Sunday evenin'.

"I was 'bout 15 year old when freedom come, but I don' remember much 'bout dat day. I remembers de Yankees come to de house one day. De white folks had a bull dog tied in de smoke house en one Yankee hold de gun on de dog en another take de meat out de house. Den dey come out en set table en eat. Dog didn' try to bite em 'cause dog know when to bite. Somebody ask em to have some rice en dey say, 'I would cut my throat fore I eat dat thing.

"I tell you de truth wid de treatment I been gettin I don' see why I could fought slavery time. I lives here by myself en I used to get check but check don' come no more en I just lives on what people gets me. Government got woman bring me wood en bucket of water en niece give me dis house en acre of land to live on my lifetime. Cook only one meal a day 'cause I can' afford it. De water I got it ever since yesterday mornin. Sunday mornin I had hominy en salt water fish en dat de last time I had good meal. (Wednesday afternoon). Lady tell me dere ain' gwine be no more checks. It be two months since I get check en lady come en I tell her I hungry en she go to Gourdin en buy me two cans en loaf of bread. Had two big watermelons en was saving one for Miss Lanes. Girl come runnin in en say my niece house on fire en I go runnin to see 'bout fire en my biggest watermelon gone. Dat de one I been saving for Miss Lanes en den I wake up on Friday mornin en de other one gone. Next thing I know, dey started on my late ones. One night woman come in patch en thump en thump. I was standin at de peach tree in de patch en she have one en when she get near me, she stoop down en pick another. I say, 'You reckon dat one ripe?' She sho drop em en run dat time.

"Thank you, sir, your kindness will not be forgotten. Dis here dozen matches last me till next week.

"Good-by. Yunnah come back."

United States. Work Projects Administration

WALTER LONG

> Interview with Walter Long, 83 years old
> 2440 Sumter Street, Columbia, S.C.
> —Henry Grant, Columbia, S.C.

"I's a little bit stiff, when I tries to git up, and sometimes when I's walkin' I weaves and wobbles like a drunk person, but know all dat comes from old age. I has been healthy and strong all my life. De onliest trouble I has ever had in my life has been wid my teeth; they sho' has been bad a long time, and now I has only one or two old snags left. I don't want no store bought teeth nohow, 'cause they 'minds me of a hoss or mule wid a bit in their mouth floppin' up and down. No sir, I don't want them triflin' things botherin' me, I think I can take care of de little I gits to eat wid dese few snags I has left.

"Me and all my folks was slaves and b'longs to Master John Long, and his wife, Betsy Long. Their plantation was six miles north of Chapin, Lexington County, South Carolina. De plantation was a big one and lay 'long Saluda River. You know it had to be a big place 'cause master had over three hundred slaves in all. Everything de slaves needed was made right dere on de plantation; all de food 'cept sugar and coffee, and what us need to wear, 'cept buttons for de clothes.

"Master and mistress raised four fine boys, no girls I 'members 'bout. De boys names was: West, Mid, Gradon and Hill. Master West and Mid served as overseers on de plantation. Dese boys being de overseers, was de whole reason us slaves was treated good and kind. They knowed us slave would b'long to them some day, when old Master John died. De slaves never worked hard, and they was give every Saturday and Sunday to rest.

"Our food in slavery time was good and a lot of it. De food was cooked good and prepared for us by servants dat didn't do nothin' else but 'tend to de food dat de rest of de slaves had to eat. When us had beef us went to de pasture for it; when us had pork, us went to de hog lot. De cabbage and turnips come from de garden and field dere at home, and when us was eatin' them us knowed they didn't come from out yonder, like de stuff us has to eat dese days.

"De houses us slaves lived in was built of logs and then de logs was covered over inside and out wid plank, dat made them tight and warm. Every family was furnished plenty of covering, so they wouldn't suffer in cold weather but in summer de most of us slept on pallets on de floor.

"Master John was a business man, but he never got too busy to be polite and gentle to mistress. Both of them has good schoolin'. They knowed just how to treat both their slaves and their white friends. They was good to all, and they never turnt anybody down dat come to them for help. Many was de poor white folks dat 'most lived on Master John. They was what I calls, real white folks; no sich people is easy found dese days by de poor niggers.

"Mistress was mighty 'ticular 'bout our 'ligion, 'cause she knowed dere was no nigger any too good nohow. Us slaves 'sorbed all de good us had in us from our mistress,

I really believes. She was so kind and gentle, she moved 'mong us a livin' benediction. Many was de blessings dat fell from her hands for de sick and 'flicted. She got tired, but I has never seen her too weary to go to a cryin' child or a moanin' grown person on de place and 'quire what was de matter. Us was 'bliged to love her, 'cause she knowed us more better than us knowed ourselves. More than dat, she and her sons' wives teached us how to read, write and figure, 'nough to help us in small business.

"When did I git married? I wish you hadn't ask dat question. I sho' had a bad mixup wid my first gal. You see it was dis way: I was good grown befo' I left my daddy and mammy who was then farmin' for Master Mid Long, on the other side of Saluda River. My mammy had a heap of sense dat she got from de white folks. So, one day while me and she was pickin' cotton out in de field she all at once stopped pickin' cotton, straightened up, pointed her finger at me and said: 'Look here nigger, you knows I don't like for you to be gwine to see dat brown skin gal what lives over yonder on Cling Creek. After I has raised you up de best I knowed how and then for you to do like you is, foolin' your time 'way wid such sorry women makes your old mammy sick and mad all over. One other thing I wants to say to you is dat some of dese nights when you go to see dat gal, you is gwine to see something dat is sho' goin' to call to your mind what I's sayin' to you.' Well boss, you know how 'tis wid men. I knowed mammy could give good 'vice, and I knowed she sho' wouldn't do me no harm. But what 'bout dat I's gwine to see some nights when I go to see dat gal? So I thinks and thinks 'bout dat two or three days and never did satisfy my mind what dat something gwine look like.

"Late one evenin', close to sunset, several days after mammy said what she did to me, I kinda loafed off down to de cross-road store, 'tending I was gwine after some 'bacco. I fool 'round de store a good long while like I didn't have nothin' on my mind 'cept my 'bacco. I had a plenty on my mind, 'cause as dark come I headed up de Cling Creek road towards dat gal's house. When I got close to her house I seen her down at de fence in front of de house. Soon as she glimpsed me, she 'tended like she was lookin' for something dat wasn't dere. I knowed what she was lookin' for, 'cause women has got their own 'culiar way of foolin' men; keepin' them from knowin' what they are thinkin' 'bout. Dat gal knowed all de time in dat little kinky head of hers dat I was goin' to see her dat night. When I spoke to her she didn't 'pear to be de least bit frightened or surprised.

"Quick as a cat she climbed up and set down on top of de fence, while from de other side I leaned against it, close by. Dere she was smilin' just as shy and skittish as a squirrel. Us stayed right dere and talked and talked 'bout everything we knowed 'bout and a heap we didn't know 'bout, 'til de big yellow moon stood straight up, befo' I said farewell to her and begun makin' my way down de big road towards home.

"I went on down de road whistling wid nothin' on my mind 'cept dat gal. When I got 'bout a mile from home I seen a woman wid a basket on her arm, a little piece ahead, comin' towards me. Just as I turnt to let her pass I kinda raised my hand to my hat to speak. But bless your soul, I ain't seen dat woman no more. I stopped and looked everywhere and dere was nobody in dat road 'cept me. Well, dere you is. What does all dis mean nohow? So de more I thought de more a 'culiar feelin' crept over my body. Then I say: 'Here I is been lookin' for hants and spirits all my life and I ain't never seen one befo' dis one.' By dis time dat 'culiar feelin' had reached my foots and they got to movin' 'bout uneasy like. Dis ain't gwine to do I said and wid dat I tore off down de road faster than a wild hoss. White man, I believes I run de first hundred yards in nearly no time and after dat I kinda picked up a bit. I begun to feel dat I wasn't makin' as good time in de road as I ought to be makin' so I cut 'cross de field towards a narrow strip of woods close to home. When my foots hit de rough grass and corn stalks of de field they took holt then and got to bird-working2, smooth and nice like machinery. I thought I heard something back of me, I glanced back to see what it was and befo' I could git my head straight again I smacked head on into a pine tree as big as I is. Well, my runnin' ceasted right dere, de big yellow moon went dark, a breeze fanned my face, and then everything got still.

"De next mornin' when my mind come back to me, de sun was shinin' straight in my face. I lay dere on de ground blinkin' my eyes, wonderin' if I was still livin'. After a while I tried to move and sho' 'nough I was dere all right.

"After de war de most of us slaves stayed on de plantation and worked right on just like nothin' had happened. I lived with my mammy and daddy a long time after I was grown. Old master and mistress died soon after de war and then my family went to live wid young Master Mid on his plantation on de other side of Saluda River.

"When I got some over thirty years old I got married and then I left de farm, moved lower down in Lexington County and went to work at a sawmill. I worked in de sawmill business 'bout twenty-five years. Rollin' big logs to de saw wid a kanthook ain't no easy job, but it was better to do dat than nothin'. I made a pretty good livin' but didn't save no money, 'cause money was scarce in them days, nobody was paid much for their labor in them times.

"Soon after I quit working in de sawmill business I moved to Columbia and has been here every since. De white folks has been pretty good to me here, 'cause I has had work most all de time. I has always been able to pay my bills and support my family right good. I believes de reason of dat is, I has never bothered nobody, and attended to my own little business as best as I knowed. Even now, as old as I is, I can git work from my white friends 'most all de time, dat's right.

"Did I marry dat first gal what mammy fussed wid me 'bout? Listen at dat. No sir, I ain't seen dat gal in 'bout fifty years and I don't know if she is dead or not."

GILLAM LOWDEN

> Interview with Gillam Lowden (75)
> Greenwood, S.C.
> —G.L. Summer, Newberry, S.C.

"I was born at Greenwood, S.C. about 1862. I can't 'member anything 'bout de Confederate War or anything right after de war. I heard my mammy and daddy talk 'bout de patrollers but I don't know much. My daddy was Abram Lowden and my mammy was Sidney Williams dat married my daddy. Our marster in slavery was Dr. Davis, and his wife, our mistress, was Miss Martha Davis. Dey didn't learn us to read and write.

"Atter de war, my mammy always done washing on Sad'day atternoons, and us little chaps helped to tote water and bring her wood. I 'member de old brick oven our marster had. Dey cooked lots of bread on Sad'day atternoons to last several days. Den we had corn-shuckings, de women had quiltings.

"Us chaps didn't play many games 'cept marbles, rope-skipping, and jumping high rope. We didn't git to go to school.

"Some of de cures dey made was from gypsum weed, which was boiled into a tea and drunk. Thread-salve buds was picked and strung on thread like a necklace, den put around de neck to keep off chills.

"I jined de church when I was 31 years old, because I was seeking salvation. I wanted God to release me from my sins and dat was de way I had to do it. We can't git along widout Jesus.

"I never did think anything 'bout Jeff Davis or Abraham Lincoln, and don't know nothing 'bout Booker Washington."

EMMA LOWRAN

Interview with Emma Lowran
550 Horseshoe St., Spartanburg, S.C.
—*F.S. DuPre, Spartanburg, S.C.*

A colored woman who states she was about four years old during slavery times, states she doesn't remember much about those days, except what her mother told her. Her mother was a slave and was given to Bill Smith, otherwise known as "Big-eyed Smith", and they used to live on his plantation somewhere between Glenn Springs and Spartanburg. The actual possession of her mother was 'vested in Mrs. Bill Smith, as the mother was presented to Mrs. Smith by her father. Her mother's work was around the house, such as cleaning house, washing, milking the cows etc.; but she never had to do the cooking for the Smith family. The source states that she and the other children of slaves used to play in the sand and have a good time—just as all children do. Sometimes Mr. Smith would go to whip her mother for some reason, but Mrs. Smith wouldn't let him do so, for she told her husband that the woman belonged to her and she was not going to have her whipped. However, she stated she does not remember ever seeing Big Eyed Smith whipping any slave, for his wife would always stop him. As a whole, she and her mother were treated very kindly, though at times they did not have enough to eat. Mrs. Smith would always tell her mother who was milking to give the children plenty of milk. This woman was too young to remember anything about the Yankee soldiers coming to their place, but one day a black man came by the house and told her mother she was now free. She states her mother continued to work for Mr. Smith after she was set free. She was sent to school where she learned to read and write, but when she became older, she came to Spartanburg to live, because it looked like in the country, no one could get a doctor out there until he or she was about dead; so she wanted to be in town where she could get a doctor when she got sick.

NELLIE LOYD

I

Interview with Nellie Loyd
Newberry, S.C.
—G.L. Summer, Newberry, S.C.

"I was born in Union County, S.C., near Goshen Hill, about 91 years ago. I belonged to Mr. George Buchanan. He went to the war and got his right arm shot off. After the war, his sons moved to Oklahoma. He was good to his slaves, and never allowed any negro under 12 years of age to work in the fields. I helped around the house until I was 12 years old.

"The soldiers were called 'minute men'. They had wide hats with palmetto buttons in front. They sometimes mustered at Goshen Hill. Some of the slaves was hanged for stealing, but my master never hanged any.

"I married Nozby Loyd soon after the war, and had three children. I come to Newberry about thirty years ago, and have worked with white families or in the fields."

United States. Work Projects Administration

II

Interview with Nellie Loyd (91)
Newberry, S.C.
—*G.L. Summer, Newberry, S.C.*

"I lived wid Albert and Carrie Coleman. Dey is no kin, but dey give me a place to live. I am too old to work much, but I does what I can to help.

"I was born near Goshen Hill in Union County, and I was a slave of Marse George Buchanan. He give us good quarters to live in and plenty to eat. He was a good master. I believe he never whipped any slaves, for I never did hear of it if he did, and he never allowed anybody else to whip dem either.

"My grand-mother's mother come from Virginia. It was said she was kin to de Indians.

"I worked around de house most of de time. My mother cooked at de home of Marse George. She kept de keys to de smokehouse where dar was always plenty of home-raised smoked meat. Marse made his own flour, too. He made salt by digging a deep hole in de ground and getting de mud dat had salt in it. We never had our own gardens, but we had small watermelon patches. Marse had a big garden.

"Marse had a blacksmith shop and he used charcoal in it. To make de charcoal he would cut down pine trees and pile de big limbs up and put dirt over dem; den burn de limbs and dat would leave de charcoal. He would pour water over it den.

"Some of Marse Buchanan's boys went to war, and

some of dem got killed. Dey had patrollers den, and if dey caught you off de place dey would have twelve men to whip you.

"We never worked at night except sometimes when it rained and we had to get de corn shucked or de fodder hauled to de barn. Sometimes we picked cotton by de light of de moon. We worked on Saturday afternoons but not on Sundays. On Christmas we had a good time and good things to eat. De men would drink beer and whiskey. Beer was made from locusts and persimmons, and everybody would drink some of it.

"De slaves never learned to read and write. Dey never had any churches, but dey had to go to church and so dey went to de white folks' church and set in de back or de gallery. Niggers had lots of dancing and frolics. Dey danced de 'flat-foot'. Dat was when a nigger would slam his foot flat down on de floor. De wooden bottom shoes sho would make a loud noise. At weddings everybody would eat and frolic.

"We had our own leather made and tanned at home; den it was tacked to de wood soles to make shoes.

"When anybody got sick, de old folks made hot teas from herbs dat dey got out of de woods. One was a bitter herb called 'rhu'. It was put in whiskey and drunk to prevent sickness. Marse always give it to de nigger children, and to de grown ups, too. Dey hung asafetida bags around de necks of de kids to keep down sickness.

"When freedom come, Marse said we was free, but he kept us till dat crop was finished, and some of de niggers stayed on for several years and worked for wages.

"De yankees come through our section, and Marse hid his meat and things in deep holes dat he dug in de cemetery. He built a fence around de cemetery. De yankees took good horses and left poor ones. Dey made niggers cook for dem all night. De Ku Klux wore white clothes and white caps. Dey made out dey was ghosts from de cemetery, and dey would get a man and carry him off, and we never would see him again. De Red Shirts come in '76. I 'member my husband voted once or twice. He was a Republican; but dey soon put a stop to dat.

"I think Abraham Lincoln and Jefferson must have been all right; just heard about them. Dey said dat Jeff Davis surrendered under a June apple tree. Just heard about Booker Washington and dat is all I know. Reckon he is doing good work.

"I joined de church when I was quite young, because meningitis was in de neighborhood killing so many folks and I got scared.

"Atter de war de niggers started up hill; den went back. Since dat time up to now, dey has been working most on farms. Some rent small farms and some work as wage hands or share-croppers. Dem dat went to town have worked as carpenters and other such work.

"I can't 'member anything more, except dat marse had a still-house on his place, and other farmers did, too. Dey made brandy and whiskey from peaches, apples and grapes dat dey raised; den sold it to other farmers in de neighborhood who didn't have as much as dey did."

AMIE LUMPKIN

> Interview with Amie Lumpkin, 88 years old
> 1411 Pine St. Columbia, S.C.
> —*Stiles M. Scruggs, Columbia, S.C.*

"I was born on de plantation of Master John Mobley, in Fairfield County, South Carolina, in 1849. Both my parents was slaves on that plantation at that time. Master Mobley had a big farm and he had many slaves and chillun when I began to understand things there. My daddy worked in de field, but my mammy worked in de big house, helpin' to cook.

"There was pretty good order on de plantation, generally at de time in 1856, when I was 'bout seven years old. Most of de slaves go right along doin' their chores, as expected of them, but a few was restless, and they break de rules, by runnin' 'bout without askin', and always there was one or two who tried to escape slavery by goin' far away to the North.

"I 'member seein' one big black man, who tried to steal a boat ride from Charleston. He stole away one night from Master Mobley's place and got to Charleston, befo' he was caught up with. He tell the overseer who questioned him after he was brought back: 'Sho', I try to git away from this sort of thing. I was goin' to Massachusetts, and hire out 'til I git 'nough to carry me to my home in Africa.'

"It was de rule when a trial was bein' held lak this, for all de bosses and sometimes de missus to be there to listen and to ask the run'way slave some questions. After this one talked, it was Missus Mobley herself who said; 'Put yourself in this slave's shoes, and what would you do? Just such as he has. The best way to treat such a slave is to be so kind and patient with him, that he will forget his old home.'

"He was led away and I never did hear if he was whipped. He lak a Cherokee Indian, he never whimper if he should be whipped 'til de blood stream from him; but I do know he never got away again. He was de first one to pick up his hat and laugh loud, when President Lincoln set all slaves free in January, 1863. He say: 'Now I go, thank de Lord, and he strike right out, but he not git much beyond de barn, when he turn and come back. He walked in de yard of de big house, and he see Missus Mobley lookin' out at him. He take off his hat and bow low and say:

"Missus, I so happy to be free, that I forgits myself but I not go 'til you say so. I not leave you when you needs a hand, 'less de master and all de white folks gits home to look after you.

"De missus look down at her feet end she see de black man, so big and strong, sheddin' tears. She say to him: 'You is a good nigger and you has suffered much; make yourself at home, just as you have been doin' and when you want to go far away, come to me and I'll see that you git 'nough money to pay your way to Boston and maybe to Africa.' And that is what happen' a year or two later.

"My daddy go 'way to de war 'bout this time, and my mammy and me stay in our cabin alone. She cry and wonder where he be, if he is well, or he be killed, and one day we hear he is dead. My mammy, too, pass in a short time. I was sixteen when Sherman's army come through Fairfield County. I see them ridin' by for hours, some of them laughin' and many of them has big balls in their hands, which they throw against de house and it explode and burn de house.

"I have always 'spected that am just de way they set de houses when Columbia was burned in a single night. Some of de houses in Fairfield was burned, some in Winnsboro, and others in de country, but Columbia was de only place that was wiped out. As de army pass, we all stand by de side of de road and cry and ask them not to burn our white folks' house, and they didn't.

"I came to Columbia in 1868, and for a time I cooked in one or two of de hotels, then running in Columbia. About 1878, I was employed as cook in de home of de late W.A. Clark, and I stayed there, in de servant's quarters, on de place 'til I became too feeble to continue.

"It has been one of de big pleasures of my life that I has so many fine white friends, and so far as I knows, de good will of all de black folks as well. While workin' at Mr. Clark's home, which stood in a fine grove of magnolias at the corner of Elmwood Avenue and Park Street I never thought I should live to see it fade away. But you know it did, since de big stone mansion was torn away and de Junior High School now stands in that grove.

"While there, I think it was about thirty years service, I saw many of de leading white folks of de city and state, as guests there; they, at least many of them, still befriend me. De remnants of de Clark family treat me fine when they see me, and sometimes they drive by to see me. Of course, I had a pretty nice little roll of money when I got too old to work reg'larly but it has all been spent since. One day I's thinkin' 'bout it and I recalls de sayin' of my Missus Mobley. She say: 'Money has wings and it soon fly away.'

"For de last twelve years now, I has been de guest of Missus Ruth Neal, a fine Christian woman and a teacher in de public schools. She always treat me just as though I be her mother. My white friends have not forgot me to date and they enable me to live, without too much aid from my present benefactor. Her chillun, all in school now, call me 'Auntie.' Lookin' over my life it seems to me, I has done de best I could to live right and I have a hope that when de summons comes my Lord will say: 'Well done, Amie.'"

BALLAM LYLES

> Interview with "Uncle" Ballam Lyles (74)
> Carlisle, S.C.
> —Caldwell Sims, Union, S.C.

"Likker puts de wrong ideas in people's haids. I see dat ever since de time I shed my shirt tail. When dey gits likker in dem, dey thinks dey is important as de president. All o' 'em wants to act like millionairs. And if de truth be known, ain't narry one uv 'em worth killing. Likker jes' brings 'em down to dat. It'll do anybody like dat. It don't make no difference how rich dey is nor how white dey is. It'll sho' ruin 'em. And de niggers, it does dem de same way, 'cept dey don't have as far down to come as de white folks does. And dat's de reason I ain't got no use fer no likker.

"When I was a lil shirt-tail boy, I recollects our soldiers gwine from house to house wid packs on dere backs. Dey was de awfullest looking white folks dat us had ever seed. Dat picture still stay right clear in my mind, even if I is a old man wid everything a growing dim. Dey sot up a camp at Marse's Bill Oxner's place—dat in Goshen Hill and ain't nothing much left dar fer you to see now. Dem soldiers never had nothing in dere packs but a few old rags and maybe a lil keepsake from de women folks back home what dey loved. Dere hair was dat long and stringy dat it was all matted around de face and neck. 'Cause in dem days, all de fine white mens wore beards, kaise dat was de fashion. But dem soldiers' beards looked wusser dan dere hair. Dere faces carried de awfullest look what you is ever seed on any man's face. Dere clothes looked wusser dan any darky's clothes had looked 'fo de war. None o' dem never had no garments a fittin 'em. Us'd look out and say, 'Yonder comes some mo' o' dem old lousy soldiers.'

"Wheeler's soldiers come to Mr. Oxner's place and burnt de crib and tuck all our corn and jes' wasted it. Den dey tuck our meat and carried on something scandalous. Dey stayed a day or two and when dey had 'stroyed everything and scared us all half to death, dey went on somewheres else."

EISON LYLES

Interview with Eison Lyles (73)
Santuc, S.C.
—Caldwell Sims, Union, S.C.

REMINISCENCES

"Dey comes slow—dem things you calls recollects, or whatever it is; but I knows what I is talking about, dat I does. My daddy named Aaron Lyles. Him and Betsy Lyles was my parents. She come from Virginia. Deir white folks, de Lyles, brought dem from Virginia to Maybinton, S.C.

"I was too little to know much of de old war, but jes' can remember living wid Mr. Alf Wright when de horn blow, saying dat de war was done over. I thought Jedg'ment Day done come!

"I soon learn't to put up 'hopper'. Dat was hanging up strong ash wood and hickory ashes in a bag dat was wet, so dat de lye would drip out in a box whar soap was made. When de moon got right, de grease was biled off de bones and put in de lye; den it was cooked up into soap. It was done on de increase of de moon and only a sassafras stick was used for stirring. De soap maker stirred from her all de time. When a real hopper was made, it was in a V shape, wid a trough underneath for de drippings. Dat is all of de kind of soap folks had in dem hard times. If it was too strong when you took a bath, de skin would come off. Hard soap was used for washing, and soft soap for clothes. Another thing we did wid lye, was to shell corn and put de grains in lye and clean it. When it come white, we called it 'hominy'.

"Things slip me sometimes, dat is, dey slips my memb'ance. I reckons dat old Gordam Mill was run by water, down yonder on Tyger River. Tyger separates Maybinton from Goshen Hill. Mr. Bill Oxner had de post office, and he lived up in a big grove whar de squirrels was real tame and loved to play.

"When we lived on de old Lyons place I got acquainted wid Mr. Bob Lyons. His family refuged from Charleston to Maybinton during de war, and dey stayed dar until he died; den his folks went back to Charleston. I know'd Mr. Jim Thomas, den.

"My father went from dat to Herbert's. We had it hard dar. Had so many ups and downs, and de overseer was hard on us, too. As to age, I ain't so sho about my right age, but I been old enough to sleep by myself for a long time. Folks knows me well and I stands well wid dem, and I tries to stand well wid God. My name was down in de old Lyles Bible, but it done burn't now. Miss Ellen done dead and ain't none of my set of Lyles living dat I knows de wharabouts of. I was born over on de Newberry side, so dey says; but dat don't matter, I knows de Union side jes' as well.

"I lived wid Mr. Byars at Herbert's on a big plantation. Oh, Lawdy, I couldn't remember how many plows dey run down dar. I was gitting big enough to go to see de gals, and I sho had to walk a fur ways to see 'em. De first buggy in dat country belonged to Mr. Epps Tucker. He had a net to go on de horse to keep de flies off'n him.

Dat's de first horse wid a net on him to come to Gilliam's Chapel.

"I run around four or five years for nature and for fun. Had in mind picking a wife, and I got one dat I like de looks of in about four years. Us up and married. I know'd Dr. Cofield, Dr. Geo. Douglas, Dr. Peak Gilliam and men like dat. Things run along all right till de night of August 31, 1886. Dat night dis old man prayed, 'O Lawd, come down, we need You. We need You and we need You bad. Ain't no time for chillun's foolishness, so don't send your Son, Jesus Christ, kaise it's You we needs. Dat earth sho was shaking everywhars, and things was falling. De Lawd or something had things by de hand dat night. Next day de Lawd heard folks prayers and stopped dat earth's gwines on. Of all de ups and downs, I spec dat was de worst scared I ever was.

"Atter dat us built St. Luke, and we had logs for seats. We marched together and sung: 'Let's go down to de water and be baptized. I promised de Lawd dat I'd be baptized when St. Luke was finished. 'Ligion is so sweet, 'ligion is so sweet.'

"Little boys watched us while us was building St. Luke's. Dey would play in de branch and sing: 'Little boy wouldn't swim, kaise leather tacked to his shoe'. Den dey would catch hands and jump up and down on de bank and sing: 'Loop de la—loop de loop de la; Deacon coming out, deacon coming out.'

"Den all would run to de shade trees and put on deir clothes. And when us finished St. Lukes, such a baptizing as us had! All of us marched down to de pool while we sung:

Let's go down to de water and be baptized.
'Ligion is so sweet, I's promised de Lawd I'd be baptized;
'Ligion is so sweet, and I's promised de Lawd I'd be baptized."

MOSES LYLES

Interview with Moses Lyles, 81 years old
—W.W. Dixon, Winnsboro, S.C.

Moses Lyles lives in the section of Fairfield County that borders on Broad River. He lives in a two-room house, of the 'saddlebag' type, with his wife, Carrie, and his daughter, Carita. The home is the ordinary tenant house of a Negro in the South. Pictures, cut out of the illustrated Sunday editions of newspapers, are used to decorate the inside walls of the rooms. There are two windows to each room, which are closed with plank shutters. The floors are clean and yellowed from much scouring and sweeping. On the outside is a tiny walk to the house, bordered on either side by rows of jonquils. And about the yard are 'butter and egg' flowers, that were so much in vogue in slavery times.

"Yes sir, I was a slave. I b'long to Dr. John J. McMahon, dat is, my mammy was his cook. My father b'long to Marse Thomas Lyles. Deir plantations jined and folks could see 'cross de fields from one house to another. I never hear 'bout any trouble dat was caused by pappy comin' every so often to see and be wid my mammy.

"My mistress name Sarah. Her and Marster John was de father and mother of young Marster John J. McMahon, a lawyer. My old marster and mistress have two girls, Miss Annie and Miss Lillie, dat was livin' when Marster die. Just a few weeks after he die, here come young Marse John into a troubled land, in de last year of de war, '65.

What you think of dat? Niggers 'low dat's what give him de power dat him have. You never hear 'bout dat? Well, they do say, when a male child come after de father's death, dat male child gwine to be a big man in all sorts of ways. How was him great? What did him do? Why everything. Widout a daddy and widout money, him got to be a 'fessor in de college and a lawyer. He tell de judge what's what in dat very court house over yonder. Git to be de head of all de teachers in de State and show them how to learn de chillun. He come back sometimes and show farmers how to farm. Know how to cure my dog of de mange, show my wife how to cure her chickens dat had de 'pip', and tell us what to do if ever a cow git sick wid de hollow horn or de hollow tail. Why, Marse John could count all de stars in de sky, tell you deir names while settin' on de top rail of de lot fence at night; git up de nex' mornin', look 'round and say whether it gonna rain or not, dat day. He not tell by de sky, but just go out, run his fingers through de grass, and dat grass tell him, somehow, it gonna rain or it not gonna rain. How him love dat old place, and de Salem cross road and Monticello. Him was riding high in de saddle of might and power down dere in Columbia. Him come home and say to me and Carrie: 'I love dis old place, wid its red hills and gullies, its pine trees, ash trees, hickory trees and scaly bark trees, de berry weeds and thistles 'bout de barnyard fence and I want to be buried up here, not in Columbia, so dat de weeds and grasses, dat I walk on when a boy, might grow over me when I's dead.' Then him say: 'Mose does you know how to castrate and spay pigs?' I say: 'I does not.' Him say: 'Time for you to learn.' Us and de hands go out to de lot and wid de guff, guff, guff and guffin' of de old hogs and de squealin' of de pigs, him take all patience and learn me spayance and castration.

"My pappy, as I might have told you, was Henry Lyles and my mammy, Mary Woodward. My brudders and sisters was John, Henry, Martha, Sallie, Jim, and de baby of all, Bill. Bill and me is de only ones livin'.

"One day I was plowin' 'long and a thinkin' a whole lot of foolishness 'bout social 'quality dat was bein' preached to us by de leaders of de Radical 'Publican party, which I b'longed to. Nigger men lak dat kinda talk, nigger women didn't lak it so much. They fear dat if nigger man have a chance to git a white wife, they would have no chance wid de nigger men. They was sure dat no white man would take a black wife, 'ceptin' it be a poor white trash man and then if they git one of them, him would beat her and work her harder than in slavery time.

"When I git to de end of de row, I say: 'Whoa!' I turns my back to de plowstock, ketches my hands on de handles and say to myself: 'De great Moses in de Bible have a black wife. What is good 'nough for him is just too good for me.' Then Carrie flit through my mind, as I see her de last time in a red pokeberry dyed dress, a singin': 'Swing Low Sweet Chariot, Jesus Gonna Carry Me Home'. Then I think 'bout dat word 'carry' in de tune and dat word 'home' in de song and dat word 'me' twist and 'tween them two words 'carry' and 'home', I says: 'Come 'round here, mule. Dat sun soon go down; ain't got long here for to stay. You got to eat and you's got to trot and I's got to ride. You's got to carry me to see Carrie.' I went dat night and ask her for to be my wife. Her say: 'Dis is mighty sudden, Mose. When de idea fust come to you?' Then I tell her and she laugh. What she laugh 'bout? Laugh at de fool things I tell her and de very joy of de moment.

"Us marry dat fall and have had nine chillun. Who they? Dere's Henry, Tozier, Lydia, McGee, Nancy, Tolliver, Bessie, May, and Carita. Carita name Carrie for her mammy but her loll it 'bout her tongue and change it to Carita.

"Old Marse Dr. John McMahon was of de buckra type. Freedom come too soon. De nigger was de right arm of de buckra class. De buckra was de horn of plenty for de nigger. Both suffer in consequence of freedom."

GEORGE MCALILLEY

> Interview with George McAlilley, 84 years old
> —W.W. Dixon, Winnsboro, S.C.

George McAlilley lives with his son-in-law, daughter, and small grandchildren, in a one-room frame house, with a lean-to shed room annex. The annex has no fireplace, no window, is ten feet by eight feet in dimension and it is in this pen that George and the two small children sleep. The house is three miles north of the town of Winnsboro, set back in a cotton field, 500 yards east of US #21.

George gathers the firewood from the neighboring woods, picks blackberries in summer, and assists in the harvesting of cotton from the fields in September.

"You think I feeble? Looks is 'ceivin' sometimes. Dere is some stren'th in me yet. Just set a nice dish of collards, fat back, corn bread, and buttermilk befo' dis old nigger and you can see what dese old gums can do wid them. 'Spects I can make 'way wid a plate of fried chicken, too, quick as de nex' one. If you don't believe it, try me dis day, at dinner time!

"I was born in slavery time, on Mr. Jno. S. Douglas's plantation, close to Little River. I b'long to him. He told me I was born in 1853. Had it wrote down in a book. When I was birthed, de master set de date down in a book, wid de name of my pappy, Joe and my mammy, Rachael. Bless de Lord! They b'long to de same master and live on de same place, in a teency log house. I 'members it. I sho' does. De roof leaked and us had a time when it rain.

"My mistress name Miss Maggie; she was a fine woman. Come from de Boyce stock, a buckra. I tells you dere was no finer mistress in de land, than she was. She was good to her little niggers; special, I 'low! I was one of them.

"Us had a white overseer, Mr. Erwin. If it hadn't been for my mistress, 'spect he'd a wore de hide off me one time when he ketched me in de watermelon patch.

"What kind of work I do? Hoe cotton, pick cotton, pick peas, mind de cows and keep de calf off at milkin' time. I plowed some de last year of de war, '65 it was.

"My marster and mistress was very 'ligious in deir 'suasions. They was Seceders and 'tended Hew Hope Church. When us went dere, us went up in de gallery. No piano nor organ was 'lowed in de church them days. I set up dere many a Sabbath and see Marse Robin Stinson knock his fork on de bench, hold it to his ear, and h'ist de tune. Then all jine in and let me tell you it had to be one of de Bible psalms, by de sweet singer of Israel, and no common glory hallelujah hymn. No sir, they didn't tolerate deir chillun engagin' in breakin' de Sabbath in dat way!

"It sorta comes to my mind dat in de summer time after crops was lay by, us went to hear one of our color expound de word in a brush harbor, nigh Feasterville. His name was Alfred Moore, de pappy of Isaiah and Phillip Moore. You sho' knows them two. 'Member us had to git a pass to go to dat meetin'. Patarollers (patrollers) was dere, and if you didn't have a pass you got a whippin' and was sent home. Can I tell you some of de tales dat Isaiah and Phillip Moore used to tell? Yes sir! When you gits through wid me, I'll tell you one or two.

"No sir, I never marry durin' slavery time. I was just a boy; wasn't too young to like de gal's company, though. Marse John was a rich man; had two plantations. One was de home place and de other de river place, where de corn, oats, and hay was raised. He had a flock of sheep, too.

"All of our clothes was made from wool and cotton dat was made right dere on de plantation. Wool was sheared from de sheep. Cotton was picked from de field. De cotton was hand-carded, took to de spinnin' wheels, made into thread, loomed into cloth, sewed into clothes, or knitted into socks and stockin's.

"Marster had a hoss-gin and a screw-pit, to git de seed out de cotton and pack de lint into bales. My brothers was Vince, Bill, Sam, and John. My sisters was Mary and Liza.

"Does I recollect de Yankees? I sho' does. They burnt de gin-house and school house. Took de mules, hosses, chickens, and eggs. Marster was sharp 'nough to bury de meat in de woods, 'long wid other things they didn't git. They set de house afire at de last, and rode off. Us put de fire out and save de mansion for Marse John.

"I didn't jine de church in slavery time; lak to dance then. Our fiddler was Buck Manigo, de best fiddler, black or white, in de State, so white folks say.

"Ku Klux didn't come 'round our parts. My ma stay on as cook, after freedom. I stay for $5.00 a month and eat at de kitchen. I was always a democrat and weared a red shirt in de Hampton parades.

"I marry Patsy Jenkins. She live twenty years and us had seven chillun. Did you know, boss, after Patsy dead and buried, I got to be a old fool 'bout women again? Dat I did. De devil put it into dis old gray head to marry a young gal; Mary Douglas was her name. Joy come dat fust night and misery popped in de door de very nex' mornin'. Us couldn't 'G' 'bout nothin'. She, at de last, left me for 'nother man over on de Broad River side. I's steered my course clear of de women's skirts ever since. I's now livin' wid my grand-daughter, Irene Wilson, 'bove town.

"'Bout de tale you want to hear. Well, Preacher Alfred Moore, a colored slave, search de scripture for names for his chillun. One boy him name Isaiah and one name Phillip. They both was mighty good slaves of Dr. Walter Brice, our doctor. My marster and Dr. Price's son, Marse Thomas, marry sisters and I see a heat of Isaiah and Phillip. Isaiah had a tale 'bout Niggerdemos (Nicodemus) and Phil had a tale 'bout a eunuch. Which one you want to hear? Both? I's gittin' tired. I'll just tell Isaiah's tale 'bout Niggerdemos. You has seen de blisters on sycamore trees? I knows you have. Well, Isaiah 'low they come 'bout in dis way: In de days of de disciples dere was a small colored man named Niggerdemos (Nicodemus), dat was a republican and run a eatin' house in Jerusalem. He done his own cookin' and servin' at de tables. He heard de tramp, tramp, tramp of de multitude a comin', and he asked: 'What dat goin' on outside?'" They told him de disciples done borrowed a colt and was havin' a parade over de city. Niggerdemos thought de good Lord would cure him of de lumbago in his back. Hearin' folks a shoutin', he throwed down his dish rag, jerked off his apron, and run for to see all dat was gwine on, but havin' short legs he couldn't see nothing'. A big sycamore tree stood in de line of de parade, so Niggerdemos climbed up it, goin' high 'nough for to see all. De Savior tell him: 'Come down; we gwine to eat at your house, Niggerdemos'. Niggerdemos come down so fast, when he hear dat, he scrape de bark off de tree in many places. Niggerdemos was sho' cured of de lumbago but sycamores been blistered ever since. Nex' time you pass a sycamore tree, look how it is blistered. Isaiah is asleep now, in de white folks graveyard at Concord Church. I's seen his tombstone. On it is wrote his age and day of his death. B'low dat, is just dis: 'As good as ever fluttered'. His young Marster Tommie put it dere."

ED MCCROREY (MACK)

> Interview with Ed McCrorey (Mack), 82 years old
> —W.W. Dixon, Winnsboro, S.C.

"Yas sah, I was born in slavery time, on de Lord's Day. I 'members mammy tellin' me, but just which month, I disremembers dat. De year done gone out my 'membrance, but I is eighty-two. You'll have to help figger dat year out for me. It was befo' de Yankees come, 'cause I see them then. I good size chap, I was dat day.

"My marster was Wateree Jim McCrorey. My mistress name Miss Sara. Sure she de wife of Marster Jim. Does I recollect de chillun? 'Spect I can name most of them. Young Marster Bill marry a Miss Harper kin to de old Jedge Harper. Miss Sara, her marry a Beaty, a buckra, and Marster John got killed in de war.

"My father was name Washington, after General George Washington, though he got nothin' but 'Wash' in de handlin' of his name. My mammy name Dolly, after de President's wife 'Dolly'. De white folks tell mammy dat her was name for a very great lady. You ask me why I say father and not say mother? Well boss, let me see; maybe I regard father, but I loves mammy. My white folks say father but I learnt on de breast and knees of mammy to say mammy, and dat's a sweet name to dis old nigger, which and how I ain't gonna change 'less her changes it when I git to heaven bye and bye.

"Marster Jim live on Wateree Creek. Had big plantation and a heap of slaves. Maybe you knows de place. Marster Troy own it, after de war. De Yankees never burn up de house. It catch afire from a spark out de chimney of de house dat Marster Troy was habitatin' then. Yas sah, Yankees took all they could carry way, but didn't touch de house. Marster Troy kept a bar and lots of poor white trash continually 'round dere smokin'. 'Spect some of them no 'count folks caused de fire.

"Lord bless you! Yas sah, us had plenty to eat and wear; wore shoes in winter, though they were sorta stiff, de wooden bottoms make them dat way. Us boys run 'round in our shirt tails in summer time. Us lak dat!

"What I lak best to eat in them times? 'Lasses and pone bread for breakfast; roastin' ears, string beans, hog jowls, bread and buttermilk for dinner; and clabber and blackberry cobbler for supper. Them's good eatin's I tell you!

Did I ever git a whippin'? Lordy, Lordy! did I? Once I 'members one moonlight night 'bout midnight, a gettin' up off my pallet on de floor, goin' out in de sugar cane patch and gittin' a big stalk of de cane. When I gits back to our house, young Marster Jim ketch me and say: 'Dat you Ed?' I'd lak to deny it was me, but dere I was, ketch wid de cane on me. What could I say? I just say: 'Please Marster Jim, don't tell old marster, just do wid me what you laks'. He make his face grim and sentence come from his mouth: 'Ten lashes and privilege of eatin' de cane, or five lashes and de cane be given de pigs in de pen; lashes 'plied wid a hame string on de bare back and rump'. Dat last word seem to tickle him and he laugh. Dat brightened me some. 'Which you goin' to take', say young marster.

I say, 'I wants de sugar cane, Marster Jimmy, but please make de lashes soft as you can'. Then he git stern again, took me by de hand, lead me to de harness house, got a hame string and say, 'Now don't you bellow, might wake mother'. Then he give me de ten lashes and they wasn't soft a-tall. I didn't cry out on de night wind though. Dat ended it.

"My white folks 'tended Wateree Church. I never went to church in time of slavery, though. I now b'longs to de Big Zion African Methodist Church in Chester, S.C. What I feel lak when I jine? I felt turnt all 'round, new all over. It was lak I never had been, never was, but always is to be 'til I see Him who clean my heart. Now you is teched on sumpin' dat I better be quiet 'bout.

"I marry Emily Watson, sumpin' 'bout her attractive to all men, white men in particular. After I got four chillun by her, one of de big white men of de county have a ruction wid his widow-wife and step chillun. They left him. Emily was a cookin' for him. It wasn't long befo' she quit comin' home at night. I leaves de place. Emily have four chillun by dat white man. One of my chillun by Emily, is a street sweeper for de town of Winnsboro. 'Spect he is fifty years old. Dat was our oldest child. De second one up and marry a preacher, Rev. Brown. De other two in New Jersey and they make a heap of money they say, but I never see de color of dat money.

"Our neighbors was Gen. Bratton and Capt. Ed. P. Mobley. Both powerful rich men and just 'bout set de style of polite livin'. Everybody looked up to General Bratton, expected nothin', got nothin'. Everybody dat come 'round Marster Ed. P. Mobley, expect sumpin' and went away wid sumpin'.

"After freedom, Marster Ed's son, Marster Mose, marry Miss Minnie McCrorey; her de mother of Marster Bill Mobley, County Treasurer, Richland County. She die and Marster Mose take another sister, Miss Emma. Her son big doctor at Florence, S.C.

"Does I know any funny stories? Does you want a true story? Yas? Well, all Marster Ed Mobley's niggers lak to stay wid him after freedom. They just stay on widout de whippin's. 'Stead of whippin's they just got cussin's, good ones too. Dere was two old men, Joe Raines and Joe Murray, dat he was 'ticular fond of. Maybe he more love Joe Raines de bestest. One day Joe Murray let de cows git away in de corn field. At dinner time Marster Ed cuss him befo' de whole crowd of hands, layin' 'round befo' dinner; and he cuss him powerful. After dinner Joe Murray grieve and complain much 'bout it to de crowd. Joe Raines up and allow: 'Next time he cuss you, do lak I do, just cuss him back. Dis is a free country, yas sah. Just give him as good a cussin' as he gives you'.

"Not long after dat, de boar hog git out de lot gate, when Joe Murray was leadin' his mule out. Marster Ed lit out on Joe Murray a cussin' and Joe Murray lit out on Marster Ed a cussin', and then Marster Ed ketch Joe and give him a slavery time whippin' and turn him loose. Joe Murray take his mule on to de field, where he glum wid Joe Raines. Joe Murray tell 'bout de boar hog gitting out and de cussin's and de whippin's. Joe Raines allow: 'You didn't cuss him right. You never cuss him lak I cuss him, or you'd a never got a whippin'.' Joe Murray allow: 'How you cuss him then, Joe?' Say Joe Raines very slow, 'Well when I cuss Marster Ed, I goes way down in de bottoms where de corn grow high and got a black color. I looks east and west and north and south. I see no Marster Ed. Then I pitches into him and gives him de worst cussin' a man ever give another man. Then when I goes back to de house, my feelin's is satisfied from de cussin' I have give him, and he is sure to make up wid me for Marster Ed don't bear anger in his bosom long. De next time cuss him but be sure to go way off somewhere so he can't hear you, nigger'.

"Some time I sorry I's free. I have a hard time now. If it was slavery time, I'd be better off in my body and easy in my mind. I stays wid my daughter, Emily. My old marster, Wateree Jim, is de bestest white man I has ever knowed. My race has never been very good to me.

"I was too young to work much, just 'tend to de cows, carry water in de fields, pick up chips, find de turkey and guinea nests. I's never voted in my life, never been in jail in my life. Seem lak I's just a branch or pond dryin' up on de road side, and de onliest friend I's got is de President and dat good old dog of mine.

"Goodbye and God bless you sir, 'til we meet again."

RICHARD MACK

> Interview with Richard Mack, 104 years old
> Rosemont School, Charleston, S.C.
> —Martha S. Pinckney, Charleston, S.C.

Richard Mack, a happy philosopher, 104 years old, in perfect mental and physical condition, is still working as janitor of the Rosemont school. He is of the aquiline type, with eyes bright and deep set, and a black skin with a red light shining through, showing Indian relationship.

"I was born in Limestone, Va. My first master was Green Bobo. I was sold when I was ten years old; not really sold, but sold on a paper that said if he didn't take care of me, I would come back—a paper on me—a kind of mortgage—speculators bought negroes and sell um. Missis, I never had a stripe put on me. I had a privilege of being among all people." (Richard Mack enjoyed every experience of his life and has no root of bitterness in his nature). "Then I come to South Carolina. My mother, Jane, she live to be 108; she come to South Carolina too. We got back together again," (he paused with a bright smile) "Orangeburg, at Captain Cherry's—Captain Cherry here in Charleston is related to him—Cherry Plantation is there now; Captain Cherry had plenty of money.

"Tony was my father, a carriage driver; he wore his tall hat and fine clothes (livery) and he was a musician—played the violin at the Academy on the 'old Ninety-Six Road'. All the white people educated their children there, and they had parties. Oh, the beautifulest ladies—they wore long dresses then and had long hair—the beautifulest! My father—Daddy Tony, they call him—he was a musician—always played the violin." Here he mentioned the names of songs of that day, before the War of 1861, and repeated these words with much merriment:

> Would have been married forty year ago,
> If it hadn't been for Cotton Eye Joe

"Songs—lots of um—

> Run nigger, run, de Patrol ketch you

He roared with laughter—"When de patrol come, I had my badge; I show him my paper and my badge! I got it still. I love dem days—I love dem people.

"My mother was a good woman—she used to get down on her knees, like this, and get up like this," (he knelt with agility, and rose unassisted, quickly, and without the least difficulty). "My aunt lived to be 141; she saw George Washington—she told me so.

"Cherokee—Kickapoo—I don't remember—my great grandfather was an Indian Chief—my nose is straight, see here." He went into the pocket of his overall, brought out a pair of eyeglasses, put them on the end of his nose, and looked over them.

"I loved dem days, I loved dem people. We lived better—we had no money—we had nothing to worry about—just do your task. Spin wheel and reel and reel for the yarn. I filled my arms full of quilt—hand made. Had task; I done all my task, and I help others with their task so they wouldn't get whipped; if people lazy and wont do, they got to be made to do; if children bad they get whipped—if nigger bad, they get a whipping.

"Old Satan wear a big shoe—he got one club foot. He can disguise himself—he make you think he got power, but he ain't got any power. He get you in trouble and leave you there. I always pray for wisdom and understanding like Solomon. I pray all the time to our good Father. People say—'Why you call him Good Father?'" (Quoted from the Bible) "I love everybody—'Love thy neighbor as thyself.'

"Yes Ma'am! Oh Heaven!—we got to be clean—we change out of the flesh to the spirit; a crown prepared for us; all we save and help are stars in our crown; you go from Mansion to Mansion—higher—higher." (He raised his arms with a rapt look)

Then he was told about "Green Pastures" and asked what he thought of it. "Why my Lord have Mercy! The Lord is a Spirit—we are changed.

"I roll the carpet for Missis to get in the carriage; a two-foot carpet from the house roll to the stoop for the carriage.

"My mother—yes Ma'am—108 years old—a smart woman in the house. Oh my Lord, Missis—cook! She wouldn't kill a chicken out of the yard; she had a coop to put them in, and it was cleaned out every day. My mother would fix the flowers; she would take this little flower, and that little flower, and put them together, and make up a beautiful bouquet, and hand them out to everybody.

My father knew all about planting; the people would come to ask 'Daddy Tony' how to plant this and when to plant that.

"I heard all the War talk, I saw a comet." (Indicating its position in the heavens, he seemed inspired, forgot his surroundings, looking back). "I saw the curtain-cloud—and snow clouds—rolls and rolls. In the War I was with my master, Capt. Cherry, and Dr. Knox, Captain in the Civil War, and Capt. Dick McMichael—all those fine gentlemen. They had hog-skin saddles that creaked—Crench—crench—as they rode;" (He was enthusiastic) "the way they could ride! Those hosses were as sensible as people; they could jump from side to side; they knew everything.

"Capt. Cherry said to me—'Why weren't you white! Why weren't you white! Why weren't you white!' I lost my old Captain—then I was with Gen. Frank Bamberg, and with his brother, Capt. Isaac Bamberg—I was Orderly. Sometimes in the War we had one hardtack a day, and had to drink water on 'um, to make 'um swell. We had to get out salt out of water, most anywhere."

"I saw Gen. Lee many times; I knew him; he had his close beard around his face; he looked fine and sat his horse so splendid." Mack was asked the color of the horse, and described the gray. Here he remembered the battlefield—"I did this"—he enacted silently—dexterously—the placing of the dead and wounded on the stretchers and bearing them away—worked so rapidly that his breath was labored. "I made the balloon flight—my eyes were good—they carried me because any object that I saw, I knew what it was; a rope ladder led up to the basket—the beautiful thing—we went up on the other side of Beaufain street; there were no houses there then, and we came down on the Citadel Green."

Mack had spoken several times with enthusiasm of the officer's cavalry 'pump sole boots'. After he had polished them, "Capt. Edwards (of Elloree) gave me a $500.00 bill for cleaning his 'pump sole boots'." Mack proudly enacted the Captain's jolly but pompous manner, as he gave the bill, and added, "I had thousands of dollars in Confederate money when the War broke up. If we had won I would be rich."

After War period: "The time Capt. Wade Hampton was stumping I followed him all over the State; I led 500 head; was with him to Camden, Orangeburg and all the way to Hampton County; led 500 Negroes through the County; I was Captain of them; I rode 'Nellie Ponsa' and wore my red jacket and cap and boots; I had a sword too; my 'red shirt' died year before last."

Asked if he knew 'Riley', Mack answered promptly—"'Democrat Riley', yes Ma'am, used to drive that fine carriage, and old Col. Cunningham's family." Riley was an ex-slave, a tall black man, devoted to the South, as he was, a Democrat of high principle, and respected by all—hated by many—a power in himself.

"I lose all my ancestors. I got a niece, Queenie Brown, in Orangeburg; I got a daughter in New Jersey; one in New York, married to a Clyde Line man; lost sight of both; both old.

"Bless the Lord! I got friends! Mr. Pooser came to see me yesterday; been in South America four years; just got back and hunt me up right off! Married Miss Dantzler of

Orangeburg—I raised them all"—with a benign look of love end ownership.

JAKE MCLEOD

Interview with Jake McLeod, 83 years old
Timmonsville, S.C.
—Mrs. Lucile Young and H. Grady Davis, Florence, S.C.

"You see what color I am. I born in Lynchburg, South Carolina de 13th day of November, 1854. Born on de McLeod place. Grandparents born on de McLeod place too. My white folks, dey didn' sell en buy slaves en dat how-come my grandfather Riley McLeod fell to Frank McLeod en grandmother fell to de McRaes. My boss give my grandfather to his sister, Carolina, dat had married de McRae, so dey wouldn' be separated. Dey take dem en go to Florida en when de Yankees went to Florida, dey hitched up de teams en offered to bring dem back to South Carolina. Some of my uncles en aunts come back, but my grandfather en grandmother stayed in Florida till dey died.

"De McLeods, dey was good people. Believe in plenty work, eat en wear all de time, but work us very reasonable. De overseer, he blow horn for us to go to work at sunrise. Give us task to do en if you didn' do it, dey put de little thing to you. Dat was a leather lash or some kind of a whip. Didn' have no whippin post in our neighborhood. I recollect my boss unmercifully whipped man I thought, but I found out dat it was reasonable. He (the slave) beat up my uncle (a slave) en my old boss put it on him. Striped him down en tied him wid buckskin string. Whipped him till he get tired en come back en whip him more. I looked right on at it. When he turn him loose, told him to go. See him whip my mother one time 'cause she whip me. Caught her by de hand en whip her right in de same field dat she whip me. It was so hot I dig holes en put my foot in de hole en dat de reason she whip me. Den if he find anyone steal a thing, he whip dem for dat.

"Dey didn' have no jails in dem days, but I recollects one woman hanged on de galleries (gallows). Hang dem up by harness en broke neck for wrongdoing like killin somebody or tryin to kill. Old woman cookin for de Scotts, named Peggy, tried to poison de Scotts. Mean to her, she say, en she put poison in de coffee. My mother walked 'bout 10 miles to see dat hangin' 'cause dey turn de slaves loose to go to a hangin'. Took her from de quarter in de wagon en I heard her tell dat de old lady, Peggy, was sittin on her coffin. My mother say she used to use so much witchcraft en some one whispered, 'Why don' you do somethin 'bout it?' She say, 'It too late now.' I hear tell 'bout dem hangin', but I ain' see none of it.

"My boss had four slave houses dat was three or four hundred yards from his house en I reckon he had 'bout 25 slaves. One was pole house wid brick chimney en two rooms petitioned off en de other three was clay house. Us had frame bed en slept on shucks en hay mattress. Dey didn' give us no money but had plenty to eat every day. Give us buttermilk en sweeten potatoes en meat en corn bread to eat mostly. Catch nigger wid wheat, dey give him 'wheat'. Den dey let us have a garden en extra patches of we own dat we work on Saturday evenings. En we catch much rabbits en fish as us want. Catch pikes en eels en cats. Catch fish wid hook en line in Lynches river wid Senator E.D. Smith's father. Rev. Bill Smith de father of E.D. Smith.

"De white folks, dey had a woman to each place to weave de cloth en make all us clothes. De women had to weave five cuts a week, one cut a night. Have reel in de shape of wheel en spokes turn en hold thread en turn en when it click, it a cut. Any over, keep it to de next week. Dey wore cotton clothes in de summer en wool clothes in de winter en had more den one garment too. Had different clothes to wear on Sunday 'cause de slaves go to de white folks church in dat day en time. Den dey had shoemaker to come dere en make all de colored peoples shoes. De Durant shoemaker come to de McLeod plantation en make dey shoes.

"I tellin you my boss was a good man en he had a big plantation wid six or seven hundred acres of land, but he didn' have to mind to see 'bout none of de work. De overseer name Dennis en he was de one to look out for all de plantation work. He lived on de McLeod place en he was good man to us. I had to thin cotton en drop peas en corn en I was a half [HW: hand] two years durin de war. If a whole hand hoes one acre, den a half hand hoes half a acre. Dat what a half hand is. Waited on de wounded de last year of de war.

"Wheat, peas, corn en cotton was de things dat peoples plant mostly in dem days. Dis how I see dem frail de wheat out. Put pole in hard land en drive horse in circle en let dem stamp it out. You could ride or walk. Two horses tramp en shake it out en den take straws en have somethin to catch it in en wind it out. Had to pick en thrash a bushel of peas a day.

"When corn haulin time come, every plantation haul corn en put in circle in front of de barn. Have two piles en point two captains. Dey take sides en give corn shuckin like dat. Shuck corn en throw in front of door en sometimes shuck corn all night. After dey get through wid all de shuckin, give big supper en march all round old Massa's kitchen en house. Have tin pans, buckets en canes for music en dance in front of de house in de road. Go to another place en help dem shuck corn de next time en so on dat way.

"My old Miss en Massa, dey always look after dey slaves when dey get sick. Use herbs for dey medicine. I used to know different herbs my mother would get. Boneset en life-everlastin make teas for fever en colds. When I was a boy, dey used to carry dem what have smallpox by de swamp en built a dirt house for dem. Kept dem dere en somebody carried feed to dem. People used to have holes in dey skin wid dat thing en most of dem died.

"I hear tell 'bout one man runnin away from Black Creek en gwine to Free State. Catch ride wid people dat used to travel to Charleston haulin cotton en things. He come back 'bout 15 years after de war en lived in dat place join to me. Come back wid barrels en boxes of old second hand clothes en accumulated right smart here. Talk good deal 'bout how he associated wid de whites. Don' know how-come he run away, but dey didn' catch up wid him till it was too late. De community have man den call pataroller en dey business was to catch dem dat run away. Say like you be authorized to look after my place, you catch dem dat slipped off to another man place. Couldn' leave off plantation to go to another place widout you ask for a pass en have it on you. White folks used to kill beef what dey call club beef. If you kill beef this week, you send this one en that one a piece till de beef all gone. White folks give me pass en tell me carry beef en deliver it. Next time, another man send us beef.

"I run away one time en somehow another de overseer know whe' I was. I recollects old Miss had me tied to de tester bedstead en she whip me till de whip broke. I see her gettin another arm 'bout full en I tear loose en run away. I slip home on steps at my mother's house lookin down playin wid de cat en look up in her face. She say, 'You good for nothin, you get out of here en get to dat barn en help dem shuck corn.' I go but I didn' go in 'cause I keep a watch on her. Another time boss had a horse apple tree dat just had one apple on it en he wanted to save dat apple till it get ripe enough for seed en fall. White man, I couldn' stand it. I eat dat apple. He put it on me dat time 'cause he saw my tracks en dat how he knew it was me. He know it was me en I couldn' get out of it.

"I get married in '76. My old boss, we all went gether. Red Shirt canvassed the country. People tried to get me to quit my wife 'cause dey say de Democrats would bring back slavery. Some voted 8 or 10 tickets. I was on de stand when Hampton spoke in Sumter. Chamberlain was elected on de Republican ticket. Sam Lee one of de men. He was white. I believe he was colored. Wade Hampton have him brought on de stand en ask questions. Ask what kind of Government it gwine be. Dey had tissue tickets en blindfolded man en he didn' take out tissue tickets. Name en number on de ticket.

"All I know 'bout de war dat bring freedom was dat de war was gwine on. I remember when dey couldn' get coffee, sugar or nothin like dat. You know dat was a tough time to think 'bout we couldn' get no salt. Cut up potatoes en parch to make coffee. Sweetened wid syrup en fore de war closed, made sugar from sugar cane. Boil dirt out de smoke house en put liquor in food. Eat poke berry for greens. Den one day we hear gun fire in Charleston en Miss made miration. I don' remember freedom, but I know when we signed de contract, de Yankees give us to understand dat we was free as our Massa was. Couldn' write, just had to touch de pin. Ask us what name we wanted to go in. We work on den for one third de crop de first year wid de boss furnishing everything. Soon as got little ahead went to share-cropping.

"I tell you it been a pretty hard time to be up against. I own dis here place en my nephew live here wid me. Dey give him government job wid de understandin he help me. Get $24.00 a month en live off dat. Daughters in New York pay tax. If dey carry out de President's plan, it be a good one. It been pretty tough in some instance. God sent thing. I tell you it a good thing. If carried out like de President want it carried out, it be better den slavery time. You know some slaves got along mighty bad 'cause most of de white people won' like our white folks.

"I belongs to de Methodist church en I believe it de right thing. Man ought to do as God arranged it 'cause he plan it. We know right from wrong."

BILL MCNEIL

                    Interview with Bill McNeil, 82 years old
                                          Ridgeway, S.C.
                          —W.W. Dixon, Winnsboro, S.C.

"In December 1855, de family Bible say, I was born on de McNeil Place in York County. De last person who have dat Bible was Captain Conductor True of de Southern Railroad trains. Had dis one name in dat Bible, just 'Bill' is set down on de page. I hear them say de Good Book am now in Tennessee, but I wouldn't swear to dat. I was born 'bout twelve miles from Chester Court House on a creek called Bullock or something lak dat.

"My pappy name Will; my mammy name Leah. I was put down in de Book as their child. When Miss Jane, daughter of old Marster McNeil, (I forgits his first name) marry, then my new marster was Marster Jim True. Miss Jane just up and marry Marster Jim and come wid him to Fairfield. Then old Marster McNeil give me, my mammy, and brother Eli, to Miss Jane.

"My pappy done passed out, ceased to live, befo' us come to Fairfield. Him b'long to de Rainey family of York. Had to git a pass to see his wife and chillun. Dat was one of de hard parts of slavery, I thinks. Does I 'members Conductor True's name? Sho, I does. It was Thurston True. When I git on de train him always slap me on de head and say: 'Well Bill, how your corporosity seem to sagasherate dis morning?' And I say: 'Very galopshous,

I thanks you, Captain'. Then us both laugh, and he pass on down de coach and all de people on dat car 'steem me very highly. I feel a little bigger than all de other niggers, all dat day long, I sho does.

"Does you know de Warren Castles' Place? 'Bout two miles from dere is where us lived befo' freedom. Marster Jim True was killed in de war. Us carry on then and make corn for de 'federate army. Our house had a dirt floor and a stick and mud chimney. Us slept on a pallet on de floor. In de summer time I run 'round in my shirt tail.

"De overseer, Tom True, de daddy of Marster Jim was a rough and hard task marster. After freedom I went to de Rembert Place, Wateree Creek, then to de DesPortes' Place five miles from Winnsboro, then to de Jordan Place on de Gum Tree Road, then to de Buchanan Place, then I buy seventy acres from Mr. Jim Curlee and live there every since 1905. My wife was there wid me and my daughter and her four chillun, Willie, Anne, Andy and Henrietta Jackson.

"I got a heap of whippin's in slavery time from old Marster Tom True. I see lots of de Yankees and their doings in war time. They just ride high, burn and take off everything from us, lak they did everywhere else.

"I vote de 'publican ticket, as I try to show my 'preciation, and dat gits me in bad wid de Klu Klux. They scare me, but no touch me. De red shirts try to 'suade me to vote their way. Some of de best white folks was in dat movement, but this time I 'members old Tom True beating me often for little or nothing. I sticks out to de end wid de party dat freed me.

"I find out, and you'll find out, boss, dat only de Lord is pure in de beginning and to de end, in His plans. De works of man and parties lak democrat and 'publican have their day; if they reign long enough de people will mourn so de Bible say.

"My old overseer, Marster Tom was a school teacher. I feel sorry for de chillun he teached, 'cause him whip me just when him git out of sorts. Miss Jane couldn't stop him, she just cry.

"Yas sir, I have knowed good white men. Mr. Warren Castles was a good man, and Manigault here in town is fit to go to heaven, when he die. I sure dat he is, although he is a nigger.

"My house and land worth $590.00, but I been going back'ards every year for last eight years. Can't get labor, can't work myself. Wonder if you white folks will help me get a pension. I's not going to beg. Dats my last word."

United States. Work Projects Administration

ANDY MARION

Interview with Andy Marion, 92 years
—W.W. Dixon, Winnsboro, S.C.

"Yes, sir, I was born befo' de war 'tween de white folks, on account of us niggers. They was powerful concerned 'bout it and we was not. My mammy always said she found me a babe in de chinkapin bushes, but you can leave dat out if you want to. They say I comed into de world in 1844. I sho' was a good plow-hand when de first gun was fired at some place down near Charleston; I think it was at Sumter. They say I was born where Marster Eugene Mobley lives now, but it b'longed to Marster William Brice, when I was born in 1844, bless God! My father named Aleck and my mother Mary. Us colored folks didn't git names 'til after de war. I took my name, when I went up to de 'lection box first time to vote for Gen. Grant for president. My father was from old Virginia, my mother from South Carolina. Our plantation had seventy-two slaves living about here and yon in log houses wid dirt floors. They bored auger holes in de sides of de room, stuck end of poles in dese holes. De pole reach' out into de room and rested on wooden blocks sort of hollowed out on top; then some slats of pine finish up de contraption bed. Quilts was spread on dis which was all de bed we had.

"I been married four times since de war and I'm here to tell you dat a nigger had a hell of a time gittin' a wife durin' slavery. If you didn't see one on de place to suit you and chances was you didn't suit them, why what could you do? Couldn't spring up, grab a mule and ride to de next plantation widout a written pass. S'pose you gits your marster's consent to go? Look here, de gal's marster got to consent, de gal got to consent, de gal's daddy got to consent, de gal's mammy got to consent. It was a hell of a way!

"I helped my marster 'mong de bullets out along de Mississippi River, but I's glad we didn't whip them 'cause I's had four wives and dere is de las' one settin' right over dere, a fixin' you some strawberries and a shakin' her belly at me laughin' lak Sarah in de Bible and thinkin' of namin' de child of her old age, 'Isaac'.

"What kind of work I do in slavery? I was de carriage driver. Us had a fine carriage and two high-steppin' horses, Frank and Charlie. I used to hear lots of things from behin' me, while drivin' de folks and saying nothin'. Money, did you say? We had no use for money. Kind words from de white folks was money 'nough for me. We just worked hard, eat more and slep' well. We got meat, hominy, and corn meal on Mondays and wheat bread, lard and 'lasses on Saturdays. No time for fishin' or huntin'. Married slaves was encouraged to have their own gardens. Our clothes was of wool in de winter from our own sheep, and cotton in de summer from our own fields. Had many spinnin' wheels and cards. Miss Mary, de mistress, saw to dis part.

"Our white folks was Psalm-singin', old style Presbyterians. You daresn't whistle a hymn on Sunday which they called Sabbath. Just as soon as I got free, I jined de Baptist church, hard shell. Brother Wright is my preacher at Blackstock now. My marster, William Brice, his wife,

Miss Mary, his son, Christie, and his daughters, Miss Lizzie, Miss Kitty and Miss Mary, was de ones I drove de carriage to Hopewell church on Sunday for. Dat church is flourishin' now. De pastor of dat church, Rev. John White, befo' he died I waited on him sixteen years, and in his will, he give me dis house and forty acres around it for my life. Dat's what I calls religion. My mistress was a angel, good, and big hearted. I lay my head in her lap many a time. Marster had a overseer twice. They was poor white trash, not as good as de niggers. Miss Mary run them both off and told marster what she couldn't see to when he was away, she'd pick out one of de slaves to see after. All de overseer done was to wake us up, see to feeding stock and act biggity. Us slaves worked from sun up to sun down.

"Sometime befo' de war, my marster sold out and bought a big place in Mississippi. On de way dere, de slaves (grown) was chained together. Yes sir, de chain was 'round de necks. We went by wagons and steamboats sometimes. We stayed in Mississippi 'til durin' de war we refugeed back to South Carolina. Dat's when de Yankees got possession of de river. We settled near New Hope church. It was in dis church dat I saw sprinkling wid a kind a brush when baptizin' de chillun. Over at Hopewell, you had to have a brass trinket (token) to show befo' you could take Communion of de Saints. We was always compelled to go to church. Boss like for de slaves to sing while workin'. We had a jack-leg slave preacher who'd hist de tunes. Some was spirituals; my wife and me will sing you one now, 'Got to Fight de Devil when You Come Up out de Water'." (This was well rendered by the old man and his wife). "Nothing stopped for slave funerals. De truth is, I can't 'member any dyin' on our places. None of our slaves ever run away.

"A pass was lak dis, on it was yo' name, what house you goin' to and de hour expected back. If you was cotched any other house, pataroller whip you sho'. Always give us Chris'mus Day. Dere was a number of dances dis time of de year. Got passes to different plantations. Dere would be corn shuckin' different places. Not much games or playin' in our set. Wife, let's sing another spiritual. Come on Janie, let's sing 'You Got to Lay Your Burden 'pon de Lord'.

"Sickness of slaves was quickly 'tended to by de doctor. 'Member gallopin' for old Doctor Douglas many a time.

"I went to de war from Mississippi as body guard for my marstar. I was close to de fightin' and see it. If it was hell then, it must be tarnation now wid all dese air-planes flyin' roun' droppin' booms on old people lak Janie and me, over dere fixin' them strawberries. De good Lord, save us from a war over Blackstock and my garden out dere!

"I was free three years befo' I knowed it. Worked along just de same. One day we was in de field on Mr. Chris Brice's place. Men come along on big, black horse, tail platted and tied wid a red ribbon. Stopped, waved his hands and shouted 'You is free, all of you. Go anywhere you wants to'. Us quit right then and acted de fool. We ought to have gone to de white folks 'bout it. What did de Yankees do when they come? They tied me up by my two thumbs, try to make me tell where I hided de money and gold watch and silver, but I swore I didn't know. Did

I hide it? Yes, so good it was two years befo' I could find it again. I put everything in a keg, went into de woods, spaded the dirt by a pine stump, put de keg in, covered it up wid leaves and left it. Sometime after, we looked for it, but couldn't find it. Two years later, I had a mule and cart in de woods. De mule's foot sunk down into de old stump hole and dere was de keg, de money, de silver and de watch. Marster was mighty glad dat I was a faithful servant, and not a liar and a thief lak he thought I was. My marstar was not a Ku Klux. They killed some obstreppary (obstreperous) niggers in them times.

"I first married Sara Halsey in 1875, she had three chillun. She died. Ten months after, I took Harriett Daniels; she had three chillun, then she died. Eight months after, I married Millie Gladden, no chillun. She lived seventeen years, died, and ten years ago I fooled dat good-lookin' Jane a-settin' over dere. She was a widow then, she was de widow Arthur. She was a Caldwell, when she was born. We have no chillun but she is still lookin' for a blessin'." (Here the nonagenarian broke forth in a quiet chuckle).

"There wasn't as much sin in slavery time, not as much sufferin', not as much sickness and eye-sore poverty. Dere was no peniten'try and chain gangs 'cause dere was no need for them. Cuttin' out de brutishness on some places, it was a good thing for de race."

MILTON MARSHALL

Interview with Milton Marshall, (82)
Newberry, S.C. RFD
—G.L. Summer, Newberry, S.C.

"I live in Newberry County, a few miles from town on Mr. Alan Johnstone's place. I rent and make a fair living. I have ten children now living and two dead. Dey is all on a farm. I was born in Union County, jes' across de Newberry line, near de Goshen Hill section. I was young when we moved to Newberry and I have lived dar nearly all my life. My father, Ned Worthy, was a slave of Frank Bynum's mother. My mother was Maria Worthy who was a slave of Mr. Burton Maybin. She cooked for a long time for de Maybin family.

"I was small in slavery time, and played wid de white chaps. We used to go wid Mr. Burt Maybin to see dem muster at de old Goshen Hill muster ground.

"Marse Burt Maybin owned 88 slaves, and I was one, and is de only one now living. We had no money in slavery time, jes' got food and clothes for our work; but my marster was a good feeder, always had enough to eat. Some of de marsters didn't give niggers much to eat, and dey had to slip off and steal. We had plenty of what was de rule for eating in dem days. We had home-made molasses, peas, cornbread and home raised meat sometimes. We killed rabbits and 'possums to eat, and sometimes went fishing and hunting. Marse wouldn't allow fishing and hunting on Sundays, but de chaps would slip off on Sundays sometimes and catch lots of fish.

"Our clothes was made at home, spun and wove by de women folks and made by dem. Copper straw and white cloth was used. Our shoes was made by a shoe-maker in de neighborhood who was named Liles. Dey was made wid wooden soles or bottoms. Dey tanned de leather or had it tanned in de neighborhood. It was tacked around de soles. It was raw-hide leather, and de shoes had to be soaked in warm water and greased wid tallow or meat skin so de shoes would slip on de feet.

"I married Missouri Rice at her own house. We had a big wedding and she wore a white dress wid two frills on it. I wore a dove-colored suit and a high brim hat wid a small crown. I bought de hat for $7.00 jes' to marry in, but used it for Sundays.

"We had good white neighbors in slavery time. My marster and mistress was all right. All of us had to go to work at daylight and work till dark. Dey whipped us a little and dey was strict about some things.

"Us chaps did not learn to read and write, dat is why I can't read and write today. Marse wouldn't allow us to learn. Once he saw me and some other chaps, white chaps, under a tree playing wid letter blocks. Dey had de ABC's on dem. Marse got awful mad and got off his horse and whipped me good.

"De niggers didn't have a church on de plantation but was made to go to de white folks church and set in back of de church. Dey had to git a pass to go to church same as any other place, or de patrollers would catch 'em and beat 'em.

"Atter de war was over de niggers built brush arbors for to hold meetings in. I sho' remember de old brush arbor and de glorious times den, and how de niggers used to sing and pray and shout. I am a Baptist and we baptised in de creek atter we dammed it up to hold water deep enough. Sometimes we used a waterhole in de woods. I remember one old Baptist song, it went:

> Down to de water I be baptised, for my
> Savior die;
> Down to de water, de River of Jordan,
> Where my Savior baptised.

"Some of de slaves was whipped while dey was tied to a stock. My marster was all right, but awful strict about two things, stealing and telling a lie. He sho' whipped dem if dey was caught in dem things. Some marsters didn't feed de slaves much, but my marster always had enough. Every Sunday he would give each nigger a quart of flour extra for breakfast.

"We had to work all day Saturdays, but Marse wouldn't let anybody work on Sunday. Sometimes he would give de women part of Saturday afternoons so dey could wash. He wouldn't allow fishing and hunting on Sundays either, unless it looked like rain and de fodder in de field had to be brought in. He always give us Christmas Day off, and we had lots of good eats den.

"I remember de old corn-shuckings, cotton-pickings and log-rollings. He would ask all de neighbors' hands in and dey would come by crowds. I can remember dem good. I remember de grain was put in drains and de horses was made to tramp on it to git de seed out. Den it was put in a house and poured in a big wooden fan machine which fanned out de chaff. De machine was turned by two men. Dey made molasses by taking de cane and squeezing out de juice in a big wooden machine. De machines now is different. Dey is made of cast.

"A stage dat was drawn by two horses went past our place. It carried mail and people. When Marse wanted to send word to any people in de neighborhood he sent it by somebody on a horse.

"Many of de slaves, and some old white people, too, thought dar was witches in dem days. Dey believed a witch could ride you and stop blood circulation.

"Dar was many dogs on de farms, mostly hounds and bird dogs.

"My grandfather was called 'Jack', and he was a nigger-driver. Dat was a nigger dat had to oversee de slaves when de marster was away from home. He would call de cows like dis, 'Su—wee, Su-wee' or 'Sook, Sook'. He called his dogs by whistling. He had several dogs. When grandpa died and was buried, his dogs would git out and bark and trail jes' like trailing a rabbit, and de trail always led to de graveyard. Dar dey would stand by his grave and howl for a long time, wid deir heads up in de air.

"De old folks made medicines from root herbs and tree barks. Herb tea was made to keep away fevers. Marse always called his big chaps up to de house in de mornings and made dem drink chinaberry tea to keep worms from gitting in dem.

"When freedom come, de slaves was notified dat a white man by de name Ban White would come to de plantation and make a speech to dem. He said, 'Now dat you is free, you will be wid your marster, and he is willing to give you 1/3 of what you make. You is free, and dar will be no more whippings.' Den Marse said, while he was crying, 'You stay on wid me and I'll give you food and clothes and 1/3 of what you make.

"Atter de war, de Ku Klux did bad in our neighborhood. Dey killed five or six niggers. I guess it was 'cause dey was Republicans and had trouble at voting times.

"I never did think slavery was right. I was jes' a chap den and never thought much about it till long since it was over. De carpetbaggers dat come to our place tried to make me believe dat de white man was our enemy, but I found out better. I am a Democrat and always was one. I was 40 years old when I repented of my sins and jined de church. I wanted to jine and be baptized and be saved."

United States. Work Projects Administration

Slave Narratives

CHARLIE MEADOW

> Interview with Charlie Meadow (83)
> Rt. 2, Union, S.C.
> —Caldwell Sims, Union, S.C.

"It bees so hot today dat I jes' setting here on de bank steps a-waiting fer Aaron to come. Aaron work out on de road yonder in front of Dr. S'ratt's house. De heat, it still come up out'n dis granite rock like dar was a fire under it somewhars. It feel good to me kaise my blood thin and I has on de thinnest clothes dat I's got, today. Sho' did git dis hot in slavery, but us never had to tramp 'round on no pavement and rock steps like dese. Us tromped on de ground and it take up a lot of heat.

"In dem days, Union had trees along dis Main street like dem dat grows on de forest now, (Forest Creek). Mister, dey never called dis street Main when I was little, dey called it Virgin. It was real narrow and de trees recht plumb over de street in de middle 'till de limbs touched over your head. Here whar we's setting was de opera house. Right dar whar I's a pinting my finger was a stone hitching post, and along dis side de street was whar de surreys driv up fer de folks to git out and go in de do' to de Opera.

"I don't want to see no picture shows; ain't never seed none of dem things afo' dey got to talking. It's de devil hisself and dat's all it is. Now dey says dat dey talks in de pictures. Well, dem dat wants to can go and pay dere hard earned money to see sech as dat, but Charlie ain't gwine narry a step. No, if you is got any money to give me, I take it; but I ain't gwine to no picture whar de devil hisself bees in de dark. Dat's how come dey has it dark, and dat's what I 'lows to my grandchilluns but dey is ig'nant and laughs at me. It ain't no good to all sech as dat anyway. I likes to go to picnics and barbecues fer my enjoyment. Befo' my legs give out, I cotch fish and killed birds and went to log rollings and corn-shuckings. Dem things give you something to recall. Dese chilluns comes from de picture show and den dey does not have nothing to recall, kaise dey has to go agin de very next Sad'day. Tain't no merits to no sech as dey does.

"Slavery, us wore thin home-made clothes and dey sho' was better dan what I has now, kaise us made dem on de home looms and spinning wheel, and dey was good. Cloth ain't no count, kaise it ain't made good in no mills like dat what us made at home in de time of slavery. 'Course I was too little to make dem, myself, but it was done at home 'till atter I got big enough to card and spin. Ain't never seed no garments as strong as dem we wore back dar. Every thing was made out of plaited cotton and it lasted fer years and years. Winter time, we wore all wool clothes, and when you furs' changed in de fall, how dey did scratch! Make a feller feel like he had de itch. Marster had enough sheep to give his folks wool, and den some fer all de darkies. I's 'bout ten years old when I could card and spin good, and dat was atter de war.

"I live down dar on de Forest (creek) in 'Patterac'. My house ain't fer from McBeth School. De mail box in Mr. Charlie Ray's yard, 'bout fo' miles from Patterac. I walks fer dat mail, dat ain't fer. Not long ago I walked to Union and dat twelve miles. At dat you see I doesn't consider fo' miles fer.

"And Marse Johnny Meadow was my Marse when I was five years old. From den on, I 'members fer myself and I does not have to take what old folks say, but as you knows, from dar back it is as I is heard it.

"Yankee Carpetbagger or something come 'round and 'lowed to our overseers dat us have to come to Union Courthouse on a certain day. Us went in all de wagons. From de winding stairs, a man say, 'you is free; you is free; you is free as your marsters is.' Grandma Julie grab me and say, 'Boy, you is free; you is free; clap your hands.' Dat never meant much to me and atter us got in de wagon to go home, grandma 'low dat she sorry she so free and footloose. Next day us went to work as usual. Some strange folks and trashy niggers and po' white folks dat ain't never had nothing, would come to see us and tell us to stop work, but dat never meant nothing to us. Us all stayed on and gathered de crops.

"Next year maw and her maw went to de Mabry Thomas plantation in Santuc to work fer a fourth. My pa stayed at de Meadow plantation. I went wid my maw, but I also stayed wid my pa and his ma some. Atter dat, when ma's maw died she went back to pa and dey worked fer a fourth; and de older boys hired to de big house fer wages. I come up to manhood and I been down dar on de Patterac ever since. I live near Charlie Giles, and dey done tuck his picture kaise he so old and wise.

"Paw name in full, Griffin George Meadow, and ma's is Alice Brice Meadow. She brought from de state of Delaware, and pa was brought from de state of Virginny. I's heard both say dat dere parents was brung all de way from Africa. Mr. Bonny Trippling fetched both my ma and pa to South Carolina atter dey was married. I 'member my grand-daddy, my ma's daddy. He was furs' George Brice; then Marse Meadow bought him and he was George Meadow.

"My grandpa went to Mississippi on his own expenses atter de Confederate War and took his wife wid him. Her name was Mahala; and her two girls, Sara and Jane, and two sons, Henry and George, went along. Dey went on a little train. It was new here den, and dey say dat it was de first train dat ever went through de state of Mississippi. De first train dat I ever saw, was de one on de Southern Railroad, from Spartanburg to Union. It run to Columbia den, and my first ride was from Santuc to Union. I set betwist my daddy's legs on de train and dat de best ride dat I ever had and I'll never forget it. It was de fastes' thing dat had ever gone through dis country. When it started off, I hollored as I was so scared. Atter it got its speed, I thought de woods was leaving me and I held tight to my daddy's knees, couldn't hardly get my breath. It didn't take any time to get to Union, fact, befo' I got used to it we was at de station and my daddy told me dat we had to get off. When we got off I could get my breath again, but I felt funny all de rest of de day.

"I has a brother, Luke, dat lives near Lockhart, S.C., and another brother, Jimmie, lives in New York. Dat is all dat I has living.

"All de darkies on de plantation lived a good life. De ladies had me to pick up trash for de stove and fireplaces in de winter time. Marse Bee was Miss Lizzie and Marse John's son. All de time I stayed 'round de kitchen and got water and eat from de kitchen and had a good time until Marse and Missus died. Dey give me plenty of food, clothes, a good house and good clean bed. We made our bed clothes on de home looms wid wool from our marster's sheep. De barns was always full and so was de smokehouse.

"For our summer clothes we plaited de hanks to make a mixtry of colors. De winter clothes was heavy, drab and plain. Our dyes was made from bark skinned from de maple trees. Dis was mixed with copperas for a pretty yellow. Green dye was bought from a store in Union, and de filling for de garments was also store-bought. I carded and spun and wove a many a day.

"We slept on straw ticks in summer, made from de wheat, and on feather beds in winter. De quilts was warm and made from many pretty home-made patterns. Lightwood knots give de only light at night. 'Puff' from flint rock give de first sparks. A piece of old iron or hard rock was used to strike de sparks wid, don't know why it was called 'puff'. Fire was kept in de kitchen hearth all de year as a usual thing.

"De overseer would 'hoop us up every morning, but we didn't work late at night. We went to de white folks' church at Harden's Ferry near de old Jeter graveyard. Church and ferry gone now. We also went to Sunday school. Every two or three afternoons in summer, Marster and Missus call us all on de kitchen porch and read de Bible and pray and tell us 'bout our Sunday school lesson. In winter we went in de kitchen where I built a big fire, to hear de Bible read. We was Methodist. My favorite preacher was a big black African named Williams who come to preach in de darky church for us every now and den. Dat was Jeter Chapel.

"First time dat I went to a baptizing was to see it at de white folks' church, Kelly Chapel. I went wid my ma and pa to see Mr. Cain and some Jones baptized. A box-pool had been built in de branch about half a mile from de church. De people draped in white was taken to dis pool and dipped, although it was a Methodist church. Sheets was hung up for a dressing-room. When dey come out of de pool dey dressed in regular clothes. It was warm weather and lots of folks had to be baptized and a lot of people was dere to see it done.

"Some years later, I went to see some darkies baptized for the first time. I had to walk a long ways. I don't go to church much now because my legs don't 'low me to walk to church."

ALBERT MEANS

Interview with Albert Means (91)
Union, S.C.
—Caldwell Sims, Union, S.C.

OLD CUSTOMS

"Sho' wuz' born in '46, das' whut my white folks says. I calls myself 97, but dat' don't make no'diffunt, 'bout a few years. I lives near Monarch, on whut's still called the Ben Brandon place. Mr. Ben had a sister, Mis' Polly. Deys' de aunt and uncle to Mis' Emma Brandon. Mr. Ben had two overseers, Mr. Caleb and Mr. Neal Willard, deys' both Willards. Yes suh' dey' sho' wuz'. Bofe wuz very kind mens.

"Marse' Ben nebber' 'low' much whippin', and he wuz as good a man as anybody has ever seed'. But one day us nigger' boys hopped into a fight. Marse' Ben done his own whippin' den'. And dats' de onliest' time dat' I is ever knowed' of anybody on all dem' plantations to be whipped.

"Marse Ben had a small house. Didn't nobody live dar' but him and his sister. Den' she up and went to Kennedy's on de Meansville road. Dat' place wuz' called in Dem' days 'Cedar Grove'. T'ain't much dar' now.

"I'se named Albert, 'case my pa belong to Marse Albert Means. I wuz always a field-hand. Marse Ben let me eat from his table after his sister went to 'Cedar Grove', kaze' wad'n nobody dar' in the house wid' him. 'Cindy' Brandon wuz de woman dat' cooked for us. My mother always belonged to de' Brandons, and my pa never 'longed to nobody but Marse Albert Means. My Marster' had only one body slave whose name was Keith. He was born, lived and died and was buried on the plantation. Marse Ben also had a cousin whose name was Marse Keith. When he died he gave all his slaves to Marse' Ben, and this is how Keith became my Masters' body slave. All Marse Ben had he left to his young neice Miss Emma Brandon, and to his cousins Miss Hettie, and Miss Mary Emma Foster.

"On Sunday we get the best things to eat of any day in the week. Sometimes we were allowed to go to church with our white folks at old Brown's Creek. We sit in the gallery. Dey' don't have none at all now. 'Cindy' go to church too. When 'Cindy' go to church us never had much to eat. All de' slaves is buried in de' Brandon's Graveyard and dere's a place fer me beside my first wife. Oh! Lord yes I got my second wife and she's a young gal', but she doos' whut I wants her to. My furs' wife belonged to Marse Jim Ellis. De' preacher on the Ellis plantation married me to Jane Ellis. Dem' wuz good times, 'caze' Marse had us plenty to eat, good clothes to wear, and he gave us a new log house to live in.

"Captain Foster got de' two Brandon places. He owned the Will Beaty Place and 'Cedar Grove'. He never owned slaves.

"Me and Jane cooked in our fireplace. It had a big crane fer' de' pot to hang on. We had a covered skillet to bake in, and a frying skillet. Us never cooked on Sunday, but made pones on Saturday. We made our Yeast of meal and hop-vine."

ANDREW MEANS

> Interview with Uncle Andrew Means, age 80
> Route #4; Spartanburg, S.C.
> —F.S. DuPre, Spartanburg, S.C.

Andrew Means, when approached, held a baby in his arms and moved very slowly around in his front yard. He was asked if the babe was his grandchild or his great-grandchild, as the old darky had previously stated his age as eighty. He replied that it was his own and he pointed out another child playing in the yard whom he said was his also. He stated, "I'se been married twice. I had fifteen children by my first wife, and these two are by my second wife. She is a young woman. But I'se sick now, 'cause I had two strokes of paralysis and I can't do much".

He remembered some things during slavery times. His mother belonged to Dock Murph's father. "I don't recollect his name", he said: "but I was born on a plantation down about White Stone on Mr. Murph's place". He stated his mother lived in a two-room log house with board floors. "My mother and my father separated, and he got killed in Florida. One day my father came there to take me with him, but I wouldn't go. I stayed with my mammy. She was a hoshand, and used to do washing around the house; she did some cooking, too. She used to pick cotton. We raised plenty of cotton; made good crops."

He said "I wonder what has become of the wild duck and the wild geese we used to have? I used to see them coming over de house, stretched out one right behind the other. There was plenty of duck and geese, but you don't see 'em now."

When questioned further about slavery times, he said, "I was so little, too little to work. I was playing marbles and pitching horse shoes. One day I looked up and I seed soldiers running their horses down the road in my direction and I got scared. They had on blue hats, or caps, but I don't recollect what kind of clothes they had on, but I remember the blue caps with a stiff front to it. No, Sir, they didn't do nothing at the house. Some of dem asked for something to eat, but when we didn't have anything to eat they couldn't get it, so rode on. I was so scared and my heart was beating so when I seed 'em coming I just lit out on a run." (At this point he laughed heartily to himself.) "I ran so hard and was so scared I run over and knocked down two railings on de fence, den I crawled under de bed."

When asked how the darkies got married in those days, he said: "They had to do the best they could. People didn't get married at that time like they do now."

He said he had heard of some of the slaves getting whippings, but he had a good master; he never saw a nigger get a whipping. "But I heard of it on some places".

He never went to white folks' church when he got big enough to go to church, but the first church he went to was a colored church.

"No, Sir, I never seed a ghost, but one night when me and another fellow was going 'possum hunting, I saw something, but I don't know what it was. De dogs treed a 'possum and laid down at de foot of the tree and just barked. Torectly something flew down out of the top of de tree and fought de dogs. It just tore them into shoe-strings—their ears and sides was all torn to shoe-strings. Some of de dogs didn't get back 'til next morning and they was all cut up. When dat thing came out de tree I left there. We didn't stay. It looked bigger than a bear. Maybe it was a ghost.

"The 'paterollers' didn't give us much trouble as long as we had a pass."

He stated he had never heard of Abe Lincoln or Jeff Davis but he recollected when Garfield was President.

When he was passed a little change, he said, "Thank you, Sir; come again, come to see me again."

United States. Work Projects Administration

JASON MILLER

Interview with Jason Miller
—*Stiles M. Scruggs, Columbia, S.C.*

STORY OF HIS GRANDMOTHER'S PRAYER

Jason Miller, a dark-colored Negro 77 years old, lives on a farm five and a half miles from Eastover, S.C., and claims that he is a grandson of Nancy Williams, whose prayer saved a ship at sea.

"My daddy was Thomas Miller and my mammy was Bernice Williams Miller, de youngest daughter of Nancy Williams. I was born in Orangeburg County in 1860, on de farm where we lived at dat time. My mammy die when I was 'bout turnin' into 16 years old and my daddy never marry no more.

"He owns 'bout 15 acres and de house we lives in and he rent more land close to us. We 'most always has plenty to eat and wear, 'cause we works de land and keeps it fit to produce food and money crops. When my daddy got too old to work much, me and my wife and our two chillun was livin' wid him.

"He never turn over de home nor de lands to me while he was livin' and I follow right in his tracks. I owns a house and 31 acres and my son and his wife and two chillun live wid me. My wife die nigh on to 15 years ago, but I is still single and right glad of it. I now owns de farm and is still boss dere. I has a reason for not turnin' them over while I lives.

"I has seen many cases, where de head of de house turn over all his belongin's to de son who move in. In most of dese cases, de head of de house become no more pow'ful than a child and often when he give it all out, he get sent to de poorhouse, to boot.

"So I still holds de whuphand for keepin' de peace and countin' one, besides. Tom does most of de sowin', plowin', and reapin'. I still makes a hand, choppin' or pickin' cotton and I digs de 'taters, too. And when it come to sellin', why I cracks de whup, 'stead of bein' on de beggin' side at home.

"Yes, sah, my daddy was a slave and I was born a slave. My grandmammy, Nancy Williams, was set plum free by her Marster Williams at Charleston, when she was just a little gal, lak. She still stay wid dis fine seagoin' family, and dat's why she was a stewardess on de ship, where Marster Williams was de captain.

"De ship was makin' de return trip from Wilmington, N.C. to Charleston, S.C. in 1847, when de big storm break on de sea. De biggest story 'bout what happen am told by Senator A.P. Butler, who was a passenger. My wife tell me, too. She say Senator Butler always look up and speak to my grandmammy when he come to Charleston and she say de Senator give grandmammy money, widout her askin' for it.

"My grandmammy sho' was known to white and black folks at Charleston and Wilmington as a Christian woman. She talk and pray for de seamen at both ports and when she livin' in Charleston, too old to serve de ship longer, de sailors often come to see her and fetch her presents of candy, coffee, flour, sugar, blankets and such as they thought she need. When she die, my wife say de sailors carry de coffin to de grave and weep.

"As de storm tale come to me from my wife, who git it from her mammy, Nancy Williams, it 'bout lak dis: De ship carry folks and produce from Charleston to Wilmington and git a load of folks and produce at Wilmington, for Charleston. 'Bout 100 miles south of Wilmington a big storm rage, lightin' flash and de waves roll mountain high. De ship wobble, first on one end and then on de other, a squeakin' awful. Pretty soon de fires wetted out and it was out of man control. But it still pitchin' pow'ful.

"Knowin' all dis, Marster Williams summon all on deck and tell them de ship am doomed. Then he say to them: 'All you standin' side by each, git 'quainted, so if anybody git to land, they can tell what become of us!'

"It was then dat my grandmammy, de stewardess, step fo'ward and say: 'Marster Williams, dis am no time to git 'quainted! What we all better do is to kneel down and pray.'

"'I can't pray,' say Marster Williams. 'If you can pray, Stewardess, go ahead!'

"All de passengers and crew was standin' dere silent and tremblin'. Grandmammy fall on her knees and pray: 'Oh, God! We, thy erring chillun can do nothin'. You can do ever'thing. Save us, if it be Thy will but Thy will be done, not ours! Amen!'

"Then she rise up and smile sweet lak and 'bout dat

time de light from a rescue ship, sent out from Wilmington to aid us, grandmammy say, shine in on us. All was saved. Many, white and black, sho' say grandmammy's prayer saved de ship and also say she am de only one who keep cool all de time. Senator Butler, who was a passenger, talk wid me once 'bout it. Long after he talk wid me, we git a book from Edgefield, in which Senator Butler tell de story, praising my grandmammy. We has that book at home now and no money could buy it."

LUCINDA MILLER

> Interview with "Aunt" Lucinda Miller
> 637 Cummings St., Spartanburg, S.C.
> —F.S. DuPre, Spartanburg, S.C.

Calling on an ex-slave who was visiting at a neighbor' house, the writer was surprised. She came out of the house briskly and jumped down the front steps and came to greet the writer with a smile on her face. "Aunt" Lucinda Miller stated she was between 10 and 11 years of age "when she was sot free". That would make her about 82 years old now. She was born in slavery, her mother being bought by Mat Alexander, who lived about five miles from Hill's factory on the Main Tyger River, for $900. Her father, who was a Linder, was owned by Bob Alexander, a brother of Mat. He lived two or three plantations away. She stated that Bob Alexander was known as a good master, but Mat was mean and cruel. She has seen her mother "whooped" by the latter either with a buggy or wagon trace, a piece of leather or anything her master could get his hands upon. She said that she had never seen any slaves in chains, but her master would whip the grown slaves, but never the small children. Her work was light farm work, and working around the house. She would bring water, wash the dishes, help make up the beds and such other work she could required in the house. She says her master was a hard driver for work to his slaves; that she knew nothing but work. When her master thought that a slave was not working hard enough, he would whip him to make him work much harder. All he thought of was work—work in cotton, corn, peas, wheat, oats or whatever he raised. When asked about the games she and the other children played, she replied that she didn't have a chance to play, for there was something for her to do all the time. She also said that Mat Alexander used to make his slaves work at night and on Sundays. When the day's work was over, he would come to their one-room log house and lock them up until next morning. He would also lock up the well so they could have no drinking water during the night. She had plenty to eat, such as it was, but flour was given to them once a week, also a little meat, some molasses and corn meal. They never had any sugar, and only got coffee when her father would bring it to her mother. The white folks and the negroes ate from the same garden. The slaves could not have a garden of their own. They also went to the same church, but none of the white folks taught the slaves anything about reading. She said that she saw "a pair of niggers" get married on the plantation by a white preacher. There were no negro preachers. Patrollers did not bother any of the four or five slave families on the Alexander place, for Mat Alexander was his own patroller. Patrollers from one plantation had nothing to do with the negroes from another plantation, as they could not even come on the other plantation unless they had permission. When going to church, the slaves had to have passes to attend church services.

When asked how the Yankee soldiers behaved when they came by the farm, she said, "a whole pastle of them came by the house one day. They asked the Missus if she had any white bread and some honey." Upon being told that she didn't have any of either, they asked for water. Aunt Lucinda was told to bring them a bucket. She drew the water from the well and, after filling it, she placed it on her head to carry it. The captain of the soldiers told her he could not drink the water from the bucket on her head, so made her place it on a stand. Then after the captain drank, the rest did also. They then came on into the yard and went to the stable, took a mule and rode it off, without saying anything. The missus had heard what the soldiers would do when they came to a farm, so all the valuables had been hidden. The horses were driven way back into the woods, the food stuff and clothing was hidden about the place. She said her mother was a good weaver and used to make lots of good clothes and quilts, but all this was put into a hole and covered up with dirt to keep the soldiers from taking it. Aunt Lucinda said the soldiers did not tarry there long after looking about for horses and such, and soon left. The only thing they got was the mule that was in the stable. When all the slaves were told by their master that they were free, they all wanted to get away from him, but stayed until the planted crops were harvested; then went to another place. Her father took her mother and his five children to live with him on another farm where they stayed for fourteen years. When they left, the Missus gave them 10 bushels of corn, 3 gallons of molasses etc. That was all her mother received for staying on after emancipation. Aunt Lucinda stated that she was known as Lucinda Alexander while a slave; then took her father's name until she was married, when she became a Miller. Her father used to hunt rabbits and opossums and bring them to his wife, her mother. She said that wild turkeys were plentiful, as she had often seen them flying around in the woods at the lower edge of the farm. She didn't know how many acres were in the farm, but the master worked 6 horses. She remembers that Mat Alexander was very mean, and would not get a doctor to a sick slave until he dropped in the fields. They had to work even if they were sick.

CURETON MILLING

> Interview with Cureton Milling, 80 years old
> Winnsboro, S.C.
> —*W.W. Dixon, Winnsboro, S.C.*

"I live about ten miles from dis town on de Jim Turner place; though he dead they still calls it de Jim Turner place. My pappy name Jeff, mammy name Dolly. Dat a lovely name in dis old mind yit, please God. Gran'mammy Peggy another good name I's got to recommen' to you, boss.

"Yes, us all b'longs to de same marster, Levi Bolicks. Guess you'd heard tell of dat man. Mistress named Martha, angel of light tied up to de prince of darkness, so it was. They had one child, Little Miss, who growed up and married a Stevenson.

"I was just a little shrimp durin' slavery time; tote water and ride behin' in de buggy to hold marster's hoss when he gits out. My mammy live in a one-room house; it had no flo' but de one de Lord create in de beginnin', de natural born earth, it was.

"What they give us to eat? Us got plenty, sich as it was. Marster Levi kept his niggers fat, just like he keep his hogs and hosses fat, he did. He had a passel of slaves and as his plantation was small he just run four plows, kept a ridin' hoss and a single buggy, and raise slaves to sell.

"He was sellin' de oldest ones away from de younger ones, all time goin' along, 'pears to me. Sometime I think he was de very old Nick turned loose in de earth for a season.

"How I explainin' dat? It's dis way: He take 'vantage of de young gal slaves. 'You go yonder and shell corn in de crib,' he say to one of them. He's de marster so she have to go. Then he send de others to work some other place, then he go to de crib. He did dis to my very aunt and she had a mulatto boy dat took his name and live right in dis town after freedom. Marster was doin' dis devilment all de time and gwine to Presbyterian Church at Salem every Sunday; dat make it look worse to me.

"Outside dis, and sellin' and partin' mothers and chillun, him was a pretty good slave marster. He marry Miss Martha Clark and had nice pretty home. He give us good clothes. Shoes? De shoes was made on de place; they had wooden bottoms, no spring to them. He gave us one day durin' Christmas, for a dance. Us had Doctor Martin to 'tend us. He was son-in-law to old Captain Stitt, another bad man that give trouble just like my marster.

"What about de Yankees? Two come first, and rode up to de kitchen, rode right up to de steps and say: 'Where de silver? Where de gold rings and jewelry you got hid for de white folks? Tell us or us'll beat you worse than you ever get beat from de lash of de patrollers.' They was as good as they words; they gets down and grab us and make us tell all us know.

"Where old marster? He done burnt de wind in his buggy wid de very things de Yankees asked for and refugeed somewhere away, sah. Did he go to war, my old marster? No sirree! He wasn't dat kind; him hire a substitute.

"After de war was over, freedom come, and with it de excitement of white folks comin' down here and havin' us believe us just as good as white folks. I have lived to see it was all a mistake. Then come de Ku Klux and scared some sense into my color. Then come Hampton and de Red Shirts. Had they a black shirt I don't believe niggers would ever have took to it. 'Dog for bread, nigger for red', they likes dat color.

"In them days of parades by day and torch light processions by night, when de niggers was asked to jine, offered a hoss to ride, knowed dere would be a drink of red-eye on de way, and then was handed one of them red shirts. What you 'spect dat nigger to do? I knowed. He's gwine to put on dat red shirt, dat red-eye gwine give him over to de democrats, and dis was de way dat Hampton was 'lected. But it never would have done to have a black shirt, no sir; I's sure of dat. Dat would have had no 'peal to our color. They is too black already to suit de most of them.

"When Hampton was 'lected I git an idea of settlin' down. I picks de plumpest woman I could find and her had a name dat seem music then to me. It was Roxanna. She allow I was a handsome man, and I was fool enough then to believe her. But one day she brung home a ten-cent lookin' glass from Winnsboro. I say to her when I takes a look in it, 'Who dis I see in here?' She says 'Dat's you, honey.' I say: 'No, Roxie, it can't be me. Looks like one of them apes or monkeys I see in John Robinson's circus parade last November.' Dere's been a disapp'intment 'bout my looks ever since, and when my wife die I never marry again.

"All our boys are dead 'cept Laurens. He live in Charlotte, and I got a sister dat marry Ike Austin and live on de Aiken place. I piddles along wid de white folks and live in a little house by myself, waitin' for God to call me home."

ABBEY MISHOW

> Interview with Abbey Mishow
> 9 Rose Lane, Charleston, S.C.
> —*Jessie A. Butler, Charleston, S.C.*

Among the few ex-slaves still living, irrespective of their age at the close of the War Between the States, the line is still very closely drawn between house servants and their children, and the field hands. Old white-haired Abbey Mishow has "misplaced de paper" telling her age but though she claims to have been very small when the war broke out she still maintains the dignity of a descendant of a house servant, nor will she permit her listeners to forget this fact for an instant.

When the writer called on her, unexpectedly, for an interview, she found Abbey, her house, and grandchildren very clean and neat. There was none of the musty, stale odor about the place common to Negro dwellings.

"I don't remember much 'bout de plantation," said Abbey, "'cept dat dey called it Waterford, and dey planted rice. You see I been jest uh leetle gal; I can't lie and say I remember. I been jest 'bout so high." She indicated about the size of a five or six year old child. "I ain't had no reason for study 'bout um and 'press it on my mind. My mudder died w'en I was almost uh baby; she was de tailor and seamstress for our people. De missus promise my ma to tek care of me, and she sho' did. I was raise just like a pet. De fust crack out of me dat window sash gwine to heist to find out what ail me. I hardly miss my ma, no mudder couldn't treat me better dan I treat.

"We been b'long to Miss (Mrs.) Reese Ford, what live at Waterford plantation, on the Black River," (Georgetown County) Abbey stated. As she mentioned the name of the old "missus," and enumerated the names of her erstwhile owners, Miss Sarah, Miss Clara, Miss Henney, Mr. Willie and Mr. Reesey, Abbey's old, wrinkled, black face softened with memories and her voice became gentle as she told of the care and kindness she had received.

"I don't know nothing 'bout de war", she continued. "I was purtected, and tek to de city. I didn't hab nothing to bodder my mind and mek me remember dose days. Mr. Willie lose he arm in de war. I is see de soldiers but I been tek care of. I been spoiled and didn't hab no interest in worryment.

"I don't know nothing about de street on de plantation, and what dey do dere, 'cause I ain't had no 'casion for go dere. I raise in de yard, I didn't wear de kind ob clothes de field-hand chillen wear, and I get my dinner from de kitchen. I don't know nothing 'bout crops 'cause we summered." (The family spent the summers at Plantersville, a resort frequented by the planters of the day) "You see I been leetle, dey didn't 'low me out de yard, I jest tek notes 'round sometimes. I tell you I bin spoiled, I raise onderneat' Miss Clara dem (and them). I nebber had no idea t'ings would ebber be like dis. I ain't got no man, and no boy, nor no kinnery to help me, nor to do nothing for me, only one weak daughter and she ain't much good. All de nation dead, t'ain't nobody left but me.

"Is I ebber see a ghost? No ma'am, I is hear 'bout dem

but I nebber see um. I ain't had 'casion to go out in de night time. I hear Plat-Eye dere but only dem what has to trabble round see um. I believe in my Jesus, yes ma'am, if it ain't been for Him how I lib?"

SAM MITCHELL

Interview with Sam Mitchell, age 87
—Mrs. Chlotilde R. Martin, Beaufort County

"W'en war come, I been minding cow for my master. My father been Moses Mitchell and my mother been Tyra Mitchell. We belong to John Chaplin and lib on Woodlawn plantation on Ladies Island. Mr. Chaplin had seven plantation. He lib at Brickyaa'd plantation in winter and in Beaufort in summer. He hab many slave, but I don't know how many. As near as I can remember, dey been fifteen slave on Woodlawn plantation.

"De slave lib on de Street, each cabin had two room. De Master don't gib you nutting for yo' house—you hab to git dat de best way you can. In our house was bed, table and bench to sit on. My father mek dem. My mother had fourteen chillen—us sleep on floor.

"Eb'ry Chuesday, de Master gib each slave a peck ob corn. W'en potato dug, we git potato. Two time in de year we git six yaa'd ob cloth, calico in spring and homespun in de winter. Once a year we git shoe. De slave had 'bout two task ob land to cultivate for se'f in w'at call Nigger field. Could raise one pig.

"All my mother chillen dead 'cept me and one sister Rhina, who lib wid me. She 80 year old.

"My father hab a boat and he gone fishing at night and sell fish. Master let him cut post and wood at night and sell, too. He had to do dis work at night 'cause in daytime he have to do his task. He was carpenter, but w'en dey was no carpentry work to do on de plantation, he plow. My mudder hoe. Little boy and old man mind cow. Little girl and old 'ooman mind baby.

"On Woodlawn dey was no overseer. We had nigger driver. Maussa didn't 'low mucher whipping, but slave had to do task. If didn't, den he git whipping. Driver do whipping, but if he whip too sewerely, Maussa would sometime tek field hand and mek him driver and put driver in field.

"If a slave was sick, Maussa would come and see w'at was de matter. Sometimes he would give de slave jollip to mek him womit (vomit), sometimes if he had fever, he would gib him hippo. If he was sick, the Master would tek him to Beaufort to de doctor. If a 'ooman slave sick, Big Missis would go and see dem.

"Slave had only one holiday in de year. Dat Christmas day. Maussa would kill a cow on every plantation on Christmas and gib all de slave some.

"On Maussa John Chaplin plantation slave have to tell him soon as dey begin to co't. If Maussa say 'No, you can't marry dat gal', den dat settle it, you can't marry um. He don't lak his slave to marry slave on nodder puson plantation, but if you do den you hab pass to wisit yo' wife. W'en slave marry, w'ite preacher marry um in de Maussa house, but Maussa don't gib you anyt'ing.

"Slave had dey own chu'ch on plantation wid nigger preacher, but on 'munion Sunday, you had to go to w'ite folks chu'ch in Beaufort and sit up stair.

"Dey wasn't no jailhouse on de plantation, but dey was a barn w'ere sometimes Maussa put slave w'en dey been bad. I never saw any slaves sold, but I hear tell of de banjo table.

"W'en slave die, Maussa let me berry um in de daytime, 'do some Maussa mek dem wait 'till night time. Nigger preacher preach funeral.

"I staa't for mind cow w'en I been nine year old. W'en I been twelve, I have for staa't wuk in field or cutting maash (marsh) or splitting rail. Slave chillen play mudpie, mek house out ob sand and secher t'ing.

"Slave on Maussa plantation could come to Beaufort on Sattidy night, but dey have to be back by 9 o'clock or patrol would get um.

"Maussa had nine chillen, six boy been in Rebel army. Dat Wednesday in November w'en gun fust shoot to Bay Pint (Point) I t'ought it been t'under rolling, but dey ain't no cloud. My mother say, 'son, dat ain't no t'under, dat Yankee come to gib you Freedom.' I been so glad, I jump up and down and run. My father been splitting rail and Maussa come from Beaufort in de carriage and tear by him yelling for de driver. He told de driver to git his eight-oar boat name Tarrify and carry him to Charleston. My father he run to his house and tell my mother w'at Maussa say. My mother say, 'You ain't gonna row no boat to Charleston, you go out dat back door and keep a-going. So my father he did so and w'en dey git 'nuf nigger to row boat and Maussa and his family go right away to Charleston.

"After Freedom come everybody do as he please. De Yankee open school for nigger and teacher lib in Maussa house to Brickyaa'd. My father git job as carpenter wid Yankee and buy ten acre ob land on Ladies Island.

"I been married two time. My last wife, Florence, living right here in Beaufort, but she left me long time ago. I hab two chillen, one daughter live to Philadelphy and de odder lib on Ladies Island. I got four grand-chillen, all ob dem grown.

"Did I ebber hear ob Abraham Lincoln? I got his history right here in my house. He was de president of de United States that freed four million slave. He come to Beaufort befo' de war and et dinner to Col. Paul Hamilton house at de Oaks. He left his gold-headed walking cane dere and ain't nobody know de president of de United States been to Beaufort 'till he write back and tell um to look behind de door and send um his gold-headed walking cane.

"Jefferson Davis? He been de Democrack president.

"Booker T. Washington? He wasn't no president, but he was a great man. I hear him speak once in de cemetery in Beaufort.

"What do I t'ink ob slavery? I t'ink slavery is jest a murdering of de people. I t'ink Freedom been a great gift. I lak my Maussa and I guess he was as good to his slave as he could be, but I ruther (rather) be free."

CHARITY MOORE

Interview with Charity Moore, 75 years
—W.W. Dixon, Winnsboro, S.C.

One quarter of a mile north of Woodward station and one hundred yards east of US #21, is the beautiful residence of Mr. T.W. Brice. In the back yard is a two-room frame house. In this house lives Charity Moore and another aged Negro woman, said to be an octogenarian. They occupy the house together and exist on the goodness and charity of Mr. Brice. Charity was born a slave of Mr. Brice's father and has lived all her days in his immediate family.

"Don't you 'member my pa, Isaiah Moore? Course you does! He was de Uncle Remus of all de white chillun 'round dese parts. He sho' was! I seen him a settin' wid you, Marse Johnnie, Marse Boyce, and Dickie Brice, in de back yard many a time. You all was askin' him questions 'bout de tale he was a tellin' and him shakin' his sides a laughin'. He telled all them tales 'bout de fox and de rabbit, de squirrel, brer tarrapin, and sich lak, long befo' they come out in a book. He sho' did!

"My ma name Nancy, dat was pa's wedded wife. Dere was no bigamous nor concubine business goin' on wid us. My brothers was Dave, Solomon, Fortune, Charlie, and Brice. My sisters was Haley, Fannie, Sarah, Frances, Mary, and Margaret. Hold your writin' dere a minute. Dere was thirteen. O yes, I left out Teeta. Dat rounds them up, a baker's dozen, Marse Thomas use to 'low.

"White folks, my pa had Bible tales he never told de white chillun. Did you know dat my pa know de catechism from cover to cover, and from de back end to de startin' end? Concord Church gived him a Bible for answering every question in the catechism. Here 'tis. (Producing catechism published and dated 1840). My pa maybe never telled you any Bible tales he told de colored chillun. He 'low dat de fust man, Adam, was a black man. Eve was ginger cake color, wid long black hair down to her ankles. Dat Adam had just one worriment in de garden and dat was his kinky hair. Eve hate to see him sad, 'cause her love her husband as all wives ought to do, if they don't.

"Well, Adam play wid Eve's hair; run his fingers through it and sigh. Eve couldn't do dat wid his kinky hair. De debbil set up in de plum bushes and took notice of de trouble goin' on. Every day Eve's hair growed longer and longer. Adam git sadder and sadder. De debbil in de plum bushes git gladder and gladder. Dere come a day dat Adam 'scused hisself from promenadin' in 'mong de flower beds wid his arms 'round Eve, a holding up her hair. De debbil took de shape of a serpent, glided after Eve, and stole up and twisted hisself up into dat hair far enough to whisper in one of them pretty ears: 'Somebody's got something for to tell you, dat will make Adam glad and like hisself agin! Keep your ears open all day long.' Then de serpent distangled hisself, drapped to de ground, and skeedaddled to de red apple tree, close by de fountain. He knowed dat Eve was gwine dere to bathe. He beat her dere, 'cause she was walkin' sorta slow, grievin' 'bout Adam and thinkin' 'bout how to cheer him up. When she got dere, de old debbil done changed from a snake to a angel of light, a male angel, I reckon. He took off his silk beaver hat, flourished his gold headed cane, and 'low: 'Good mornin'! Lovely day! What a beautiful apple, just in your reach too, ahem'! Eve say: 'I's not been introduced,' 'Well', said de debbil, 'My subjects call me Prince, 'cause I's de Prince of light. My given name is Lucifer. I's at your service, dear lady.' Eve 'flected: 'A prince, he'll be a king some day.' Then de debbil say: 'Of course, one of your beauty will one day be a queen. I seen a sadness on your lovely face as you come 'long. What might be your worry?' Eve told him and he 'low: 'Just git Adam to eat one bite out dat apple 'bove your head and in a night his hair will grow as long, be as black, and as straight as your'n.' She 'low: 'Us ain't 'lowed to eat of de fruit of de tree in de midst of de garden. Us dare not tech it, lest us die.' Then Satan stepped a distance dis way, then another way and come back and say: 'Gracious lady! Dis tree not in de midst of de garden. De one in de midst is dat crabapple tree over yonder. Of course de good Lord didn't want you to eat crabapples.' De debbil done got her all mixed up. De apple looked so good, she reached up, and quick as you can say 'Jack Robinson,' she bite de apple and run to Adam wid de rest of it and say: 'Husband eat quick and your hair will be as long, as black, and straight as mine, in de mornin'.' While he was eatin' it, and takin' de last swallow of de apple, he was 'minded of de disobedience and choked twice. Ever since then, a man have a 'Adam's Apple' to 'mind him of de sin of disobedience. Twasn't long befo' de Lord come alookin' for them. Adam got so scared his face turned white, right then, and next mornin' he was a white man wid long hair but worse off than when he was a nigger. Dere was more to dat tale but I disremember it now.

"I's livin' wid my young marster, Thomas, now. He took good care of my pa, when he got so old and feeble he couldn't work no more. God'll bless Marse Tommie for all his goodness. When Pa Isaiah come to die, Marse Tommie come every day. One day in leavin', he said in his gruff, kind way: 'Is dere anything I can do for you Uncle Isaiah?' Pa say: 'Take care of Charity.' 'I will,' say Marse Tommie. Then he 'low: 'Ain't dere something else?' 'Yes,' pa 'low, 'I want a white stone over de head of my grave.' 'What must I put on de stone,' asked Marse Tommie? 'Just my name and age,' said pa. 'Oh yes, dere ought to be something else,' says Marse Tommie. Pa shook his head. 'I want something else on it Uncle Isaiah,' said Marse Tommie. Wid a tear and a smile, pa raised his white head and said: 'You can put down, below de name and age, just dis: 'As good as ever fluttered.' And dat stone at Concord Cemetery 'tract more 'tention then any stone and epitaph in dat churchyard. Why, de white folks puts flowers on it sometimes.

"I wonder sometime in de winter nights, as de north wind blows 'bout de cracks in de house, if pa is warm and in Abraham's bosom. But I knows pa; he's 'umble. There's so many white folks in dat bosom he'll just be content to lie in Isaac's bosom or maybe de prophet Isaiah's, for who he was named.

"Wait dere! You have bad luck to leave by dat door. You comed in by dis door and you just leave by de same door. Some folks say nothin' to dat but I don't want you to risk dat. Glad you come. Good bye."

SENA MOORE

Interview with Sena Moore, 83 years old
—W.W. Dixon, Winnsboro, S.C.

Sena Moore lives alone, in a one-room frame house about five miles northeast of Winnsboro, S.C. She does seasonal work, such as hoeing and picking cotton, of which she is still fully capable. She pays $2.00 per month rent, for the house and vegetable garden spot.

"Sumpin' tell me to make haste and come here for to see you. How's you dis mornin'? Mustn't forgit my manners, though I's wantin' to tell you de ifs and hows and de ups and downs of dese many years dat I's been in dis land of sorrow and tribulation.

"I was born in 1854, on de Gladney plantation. Was a pretty smart gal, twelve years old, when de Yankees come through. Marse Riley have a Bible out yonder at Jackson Creek dat show's I's eighty-three years old. His aunty is a sister to my old marster, Jim Gladney. Miss Margaret married a Paul but Miss Nancy and Miss Mary Ann, them two never marry, bless God! De house out dere in Jackson Creek neighborhood.

"My pappy was George Stitt. My mammy was Phillis Gladney. My pappy was a slave of de Stitt family; had to git a pass to come to see mammy. He slipped in and out 'nough of times to have four chillun. Then de Stitts took a notion to sell him to Arkansas. My mammy weep 'bout dat but what could her do? Just nothin'. Old marster 'low:

'Plenty more good fish in de sea, Phillis. Look 'round, set your cap, and maybe you'll 'tract one dat'll give your heart comfort, bye and bye'. My full brudders was Luther Stitt, Bill Stitt, and Levi Stitt. My mammy then take up wid a no 'count nigger name Bill James and had one child, a boy, name Jim. He died long time ago.

"Us live in a log house wid a dirt floor and de cracks stop up wid mud. It had a wooden chimney. De beds was saplin' pole beds. De ticks was wheat straw, though most of de time us chillun sleep on de floor. My marster not a big buckra; he just had a handful of slaves. Us had to fight chinches, fleas, and skeeters (mosquitoes) 'most all night or 'til they fill theyselves wid our blood. Then they take a rest and us git a rest and slept. My grandpappy was one of de free niggers. Him was a Stitt family nigger, a blue-eyed nigger.

"Money? Lord help me, no! As I 'member, us had plenty to eat, sich as peas, beans, greens, lye hominy, and 'lasses but no flour bread.

"My young marster, Sam, was kilt in de war but Marse Tom went off and settle in Arkansas.

"What clothes us have? Just 'nough to hide our secret parts in summer. A shirt for de boys and a slip-over for de gals. They was made out of weave cloth, dat us spin of de cotton dat us picked out of de field. Wid all de drawbacks, us was happy more then than now.

"Us raise our own chickens and sing while us workin'. I never mind white chillun callin' me 'nigger'. Dat was a nickname they call me.

"Us was Presbyterians and b'long to de Jackson Creek

Church, Lebanon. Gallery was all 'round de up-stairs. Got a whippin' for goin' to sleep up dere, one Sunday, and snorin'. In them days de preacher was powerful. De folks mighty 'ticular when him come 'round and fill de back of his buggy wid sumpin' of everything on de place, lak ham, chickens, eggs, butter, marmalade, jelly, 'lasses, sugar, vegetables and fruit. Him put in full time on Sunday though, preach 'bout two hours befo' he put on de benediction.

"What 'bout my courtin' days? Well, I had them, too. A Yankee want me to go off wid him but I tell him no! Then when I 'fuse him, him 'suade another gal to love him and leave wid him. Her come back to de place six months later and had a baby by dat scamp man.

"When I was fifteen, I marry Bill Moore. Stood up wid him, dat day, in a blue worsted dress and a red balmoral over a white tuck petticoat, and under dat, a soft pique chemise wid no sleeves. Had on white stockin's and low quarter shoes. I had sweet shrubs all through my hair and it held them all night and de nex' night, too. Sill make a big laugh 'bout it, while nosin' in my hair and smellin' them sweet shrubs.

"Dr. Turner was de doctor dat 'tended de Gladney's and de slaves on de place.

"How us git fire? Us git two flint rocks, hold lint cotton under them, strike a spark, it drop down, set de cotton afire and then us fan it to a blaze.

"Yes sir, I see many good white men, more than I got fingers and toes, but a low down white man can git low downer than a nigger man. A good white lady telled me one time, dat a bad white woman is a sight worser and more low downer than a bad nigger woman can ever git to be in dis world. Now what you gonna day to dat, Mister? Well, if you have dat notion too, us won't argue 'bout it.

"Does I believe de Savior has a remedy for de laks of sich women? Let me think 'bout dat a little bit. De Savior has a cure for things, all things. How come he ain't? Didn't he give a woman de livin' water at de well and make her white as snow? Then he run seven devils out another woman, for just sich sins as us is talkin' 'bout, Mister!

"Ku Klux? Does I 'member them? Dis left knee 'members them! One night de big road full of us niggers was comin' from church. Just as us git to de top of de hill us see, comin' up de hill, a long line of hosses, wid riders dressed in pure white, hoods on deir heads, and painted false faces. They busted into a gallop for us. I was wid my brudders, Luther and Bill; they jump de side gully and got 'way in de woods. I jump but de jump was poor as a cow, I reckon, and dis very leg crumple up. I lay dere in my misery 'til daylight, and my brudder, Luther, come back and carry me home. Dat word 'home' 'minds me I ought to be goin' dere now. De Lord take a lakin' to you, and you to me! May you git to heaven when you die and I git dat pension befo' I die. Amen!"

SILAS NELSON

Interview with Silas Nelson (74)
R#2 Trenton, S.C., c/o Mr. Walter Marsh
—Caldwell Sims, Union, S.C.

"Fer 69 years Mis' Marsh done had me a-workin fer her roun the garden en house. Course Mr. Marsh had ter work me in de field wid my boys. Us has two mules, Joe an Delia. Dey stays in our lot. I plows a little but my time is a wearin'. But I gits long 'Oh Key'.

"Mr. George W. Wire tuk and died. I nursed him. I good to them all. I'se different from any other mens. I never eats milk and butter. Ain't tuck no medicine in thirty-five year. When sun set I is at my house every day.

"Lays down only 'bout two hours, dats nother way I is allus curious in de fac' dat at nights I allus has somethin ter do. De boys jes sits and looks at me and dey don't say nary a word, dey jes looks at me.

"Born in slavy, too little to tell much 'bout dat, cep I is different from my chilluns. Dey calls me curious. My pa riz up four boys. Us had four mules and hauled dirt to Graniteville evey day when us stayed together. Three brothers older than me. I is allus been crazy 'bout farmin, helped my paw evey day when I was young with everything.

"When I wuz young no man could turn me down

a workin. Now it ain't none that ken turn me down a 'walkin".

Slave Narratives

SUSAN NELSON

> Interview with Susan Nelson
> 9 Trapman Street, Charleston, S.C.
> Mrs. Arthur Lynah
> Ashley Avenue, Charleston, S.C.
> —*Martha S. Pinckney, Charleston, S.C.*

"FOREST", A FAITHFUL SERVANT

Susan Nelson, 9 Trapman street, about eighty years old, daughter of Paris ("Forest") and Christina Gibbs, is a fine type of trained house servant. Tall, slim, and erect, she carries herself with dignity, and curtsies with grace. Her color is dark brown, her features aquiline. She seldom smiles.

"I am the youngest of my family and they are all dead. I never had a child. I was married in the Methodist Church, but my husband married again. From the first I can remember, I lived in Charleston with my mother and father. He had his freedom before the war and worked on the Bay. When he came home from his days work he had a cot by the door where he would lay down to rest, and all the time he used to tell me about 'those happy days', as he said. Ask Mrs. Arthur Lynah about my father; she knows about him."

Susan goes on with her story:—

"My father belonged to Judge Prioleau and was trained to wait on the table from the time he was a boy; and this is how he nearly got a whippin'—his master liked 'Hoppin John' and there was some cold on the table—you know 'Hoppin John'? His master told him to 'heat it'; he thought his master said 'eat it', so he took it out and sat down and eat it. When he went back his master asked him where was the 'Hoppin John'? Paris say he eat it. His master was mad—after waitin' all that time—and say he should have a whippin'. But Mistress say 'Oh, no, he is young and didn't understand'; so he never got the whippin'.

"Later he was taken from waitin' on table to be his master's body-servant and that was when his name was changed. One of the young ladies, his master's daughter, was named Alice, and when he called 'Paris', it sounded like 'Alice', so his master named him 'Forest' and he kept the name from that time, for his first and his last name, and he always went by the name of Forest until he died."

He went abroad with Judge Pricleau as his body-servant, and traveled in Europe. (Authority—Mrs. Arthur Lynah)

"In later years, when his master was paralyzed, Forest was his attendant; and when his master died, Forest watched by him all night. He lay down under the couch—they used to lay them on couches then—and he slept there and wouldn't leave him, and stayed there all night; and his mistress came in the early morning and kissed his master, and she said 'you here, Forest' and he answered, 'yes, mistress.' After that, everything was changed. His mistress wanted to give him his freedom, but the rest of the family didn't agree to that, so he went to Savannah with 'Mas Charles'. But though he was treated well he was so homesick that he couldn't stay. He thought of his mistress and of the old home, and of his mother, and he ran away and came back to the Plantation. Mas Charles was so mad when he came after him that he was ready to whip him; but when he saw how happy they were he agreed to give Forest his freedom."

Before the War Between the States Forest was married, living in Charleston, and working on the Bay. Susan remembers her terror when the shells of the Federal bombardment were bursting over the city, and recalls holding out her arms for someone to hold her. Her father had returned home one afternoon and was resting from a hard days work, when a shell crashed through the walls of their little home on Tradd street, and passed immediately over him as he lay on his cot. The neighbors came rushing in thinking that everybody had been killed, but the shell had passed through, shattering the house but leaving Forest unharmed. He lived to the age of ninety-seven, valued and respected; his daughter carries on his good reputation, and is known by the name of SUSAN "FOREST."

United States. Work Projects Administration

WILLIAM OLIVER

Interview given by Uncle William Oliver, a boy in slavery time
Murrells Inlet, S.C.
—Genevieve W. Chandler, Murrells Inlet, Georgetown County, S.C.

"Underground Railway? They give it that name being they had this way to transfer the slaves. T.O. Jones was one of the officers. Growed up in Illinois.

"I was born in Horry—eight miles this side of Conway. The old Oliver place. Father Caesar Oliver; Mother Janie. Mother born near Little River—Jewitt place. Joe Jewitt raise my father. Had four brother, twelve sister:

> One Trizvan
> Two Sarah
> Three Martha
> Four William
> Five Mary, the fifth
> Six Lizzie, the sixth
> Seven Emma, the seven
> Eighth Alice, the eighth
> Nine Joanna
> Ten Havilla
> Eleven Ella
> Twelve Redonia
> Thirteen Caesar
> Fourteen Zackie
> Fifteen Eddie
> Sixteen (He could not remember)

"Three boys so scattered about you can't tell anything about them. All chimney, clay. All chimneys that day, clay. Moved right away soon as Freedom came. Women done cooking and washing same as now. Shuck mattress. My mother was a weaver. Old timey loom. Cotton and wool. Sheckel (Shuttle?)

"I remember one song my mother sang:

>Do, Lord, remember me!
>Remember me when the year go round!
>Do, Lord, remember me!
>Why can't you die
>Like Jesus died?
>He laid in His grave!
>He crippled some.
>Some He saved.

"I can't get it all.

"My father head man on the plantation. Indigo? Cut the bush down. Put it in sacks. Let it drip out. Call that indigo mud. Raise cattle and hogs loose over the County. No cash money was give to slave. Had to get a ticket. Hire they self out as stevedore—anywhere they could—and pay Massa so much for the time. Smart slave do that. Oh, yes, my father do that. If they keep themselves alive after freedom, they doing well.

"Schooling? Only by night. And that couldn't be known. When he could get any body to teach him 'ABC' but wasn't allowed to go to any school.

"We'd eat peas, rice, cornbread, rye bread, sweetbread. Most molasses. Game was all over the woods. Everybody could hunt everybody land those days. Hunting was free. When I come along had to work too hard to hunt. Could get pike out the lakes. Go fishing Sabbath. That was day off. Sunday free day. Wild turkey. 'Possum. Don't bother with no coon much. 'Possum and squirrel all we could get. Had our garden. Different bean and collard. Turnip.

"Clothes? Regular wool and cotton. Maple dye and indigo. Red, blue, gray. Lot of gray. Big slave owners had a shoemaker. Plenty of hides. Cow hides, deer hides.

"When I married, was working turpentine. Rent timber and cut boxes.

"The cruelest treatment I know of in the United States and all the other states was done in the Southwestern states. Take New Orleans. Galveston? Was fixing to get to Texas. Texas beat the country for cruelty. They tell me when your Master and Missus in this country want to make you do your task, they threaten to sell you to Texas. Had a regular 'Vanger Range' in New Orleans. Place they keep the slaves and auction them off. Man by the name of Perry Ann Marshall. He was sold out there. He told my father he'd be out in the field in the morning—hoe in hand. Had to get out there 'fore it was light, hoe in hand. Boss man there with whip. When light enough to hoe, give order, 'Heads up!' Then lots of women fell dead over the hoe. Give order. 'Heads up!' you chop! Breakfast bring to you in the field. Set right there by you hoe and eat till he say, 'Heads up!' When women fell dead, lie right there till night where the body drop—till you knock off. That's Texas! I call Texas 'Hell.' Even today black man can't get no first class ticket Texas!

"When you come right down to the truth, we always

got up fore day most of time. You could go visiting other plantation, but must have you a ticket. Patrol catch you they whip you."

Slave Narratives

ALBERT OXNER

Interview with Albert Oxner (75)
Newberry, S.C. RFD
—*G.L. Summer, Newberry, S.C.*

"I was raised in Newberry County, S.C. on de place of Mr. Chesley Davis, near Indian Creek. I now live in a rented house in 'Helena'. My grandmother come from Virginia. Old man Tom Davis who lived near Indian Creek was a grandson of Chesley Davis. My daddy was Oxner, his first name was Wash. My mother was named Sidney Davis. My first wife was Polly Miller and de second was Mary Mangum.

"Marse would whip his niggers, but he wasn't a hard man. I peeped around de house once when I was a little boy and saw him whipping a slave.

"We got our vegetables from de white folks garden. We never had any of our own. We had plenty home-raised meats and flour. We made our own clothes at home by carding, spinning and weaving. We dyed dem by making dyes from de barks of trees or red clay.

"Marse had a big plantation, and 75 to 100 slaves. My mother was de house-maid. She never learned to read and write, and none of us did, either.

"We use to hunt rabbits, 'possums, wild turkeys and squirrels, and we went fishing, too. We never had to work on Saturday afternoons or Sundays unless we had to take fodder or straw to de barn to keep it from getting wet.

"Corn-shuckings and log-rollings was common in dem days. De workers had supper when dey got through. Niggers went to white folks' churches and set in de back or in de gallery. A few years atter de war, de niggers made brush arbors to use for preaching.

"Old man Chesley Davis and two of his boys sho liked to drink liquor. His baby boy was bad to drink. We had barbecues in dem days and nearly every man would get drunk.

"Later on, old man Davis tried to preach. He preached some at de Baptist church at Bush River, and at Fairview Baptist church, about four miles above where he lived.

"I don't remember much about de Ku Klux. I never saw any of dem. I remember a little about de Red Shirts. I don't remember anything about slaves getting forty acres of land and a mule when freedom come. Since de war, de niggers have worked on farms and done odd jobs in town."

ANN PALMER

> Interview with Ann Palmer (90)
> 120 N. Church St., Union, S.C.
> —*Caldwell Sims, Union, S.C.*

"De cows lowed fer days befo' Will Abrams died. Dey got wusser and wusser jes' right 'mediately befo' he died. De owls, dey had been hollering in dis here holler down behind Miss Belle's house fer mo' dan a month. One day Miss Belle, she 'lowed she ain't never heard so many screech owls befo' dis in her life. I had done fetched her one of my collards. We was a-talking out on de back porch.

"I took and told her 'bout how Will had done got his finger infected fooling wid dem dead folks. Miss Belle, she say dat ain't got nothing to do wid Will being sick. She also 'lowed dat dat wasn't any reason fer dem owls a-screeching and gwine on so. Den I told her, I says, 'Miss Belle, ain't you heard de cows, how dey lows at night here recently? Yes'm, all dese is death signs; it ain't gwine be long neither befo' we hears 'bout somebody a-dying in dese here parts.' Miss Belle, she look at me sort of furious like, but she never say nothing dat time.

"Dat night de beastes was a-taking on so dat I had to hold my pulse. Fust (first), real tight like dis; den I presses harder and harder till I jes' natchelly squeeze all de blood out of my wristes. Dat is one of de best signs I knows fer making dem owls and cows git quiet. Yes sir, you has to hold your pulse fer five whole minutes, tight. When you does dis, de owl's voice, he git lower and lower as your pulse git weaker and weaker. Look, honey chile, all dese other niggers, dey had been a-tying up a sheet or a-putting de shovel in de fire, and a-turning over de nasty old shoes; but de owls, dey kept right on a-screeching. But dis old darky, she de one what know'd how to weaken 'em down by holding her pulse. Now, I doesn't tell dese young niggers 'round here; neither does I tell many white folks 'bout de wisdom I is learn't 'bout such things.

"Will Abrams, he been ailing fer I [TR: disremembers] how many weeks. He couldn't eat nothing but beans. I had beans in my bottom corn. Catherine, she axed me fer some and I give 'em to her. Will, he eat 'em, fer dat was his craving. His finger got wusser till it nearly driv him crazy. Den he got down and took to de bed. Look like his time, it was drawing nigh.

"White folks, de Jedgement is a-coming. We's all got to face it. De folks is wicked, both black and so is de white. How dey 'spects de good Lawd to have mercy on de wicked and sinful souls de way dey does every day is mo' dan aunt Ann can see, and I is already done lived my ninety years. De Lawd, He still sees fit to bless me wid health; and de good white folks, He 'lows dem to help me.

"How could Dr. Dawkins or either Dr. Montgomery do Will any good when de Lawd, He done sot de hour? Dr. Montgomery, he 'lowed to Catherine dat Will had two chances to die and one to live. He also said dat he had done his best. All de darkies and white folks, too, in Union, dey come over here to see Will. Lots of 'em fetched 'em some things along to give to Will. He was a good man 'cause he had done been born again, and he followed 'de straight and narrow path'. Dat's de reason dey liked him, 'cause his deeds, dey up and spoke fer him. Well, so many folks was a-gwine in dat room dat Dr. Montgomery, he say Catherine have to keep dem out. Will, he kept a-gitting weaker and weaker. De ailing in his finger had done spread all over his chest. Dr. Montgomery and Dr. Dawkins, dey held a consulation. When dey come out dey told Catherine and dem others dat Will had done took and got pneumonia from dat finger. So dat night, even de dogs, dey took to howling and gwine on. 'Tain't no use to set dar and laugh when de owls screeched and de cows lowed and de dogs howled. It sho am de death sign.

"Hard work, trouble, and a-fooling wid dem dead folks, dem de things what make Will go away so easy. He was always a-running 'round a-gitting sorry niggers out of scrapes, and a-making 'greements wid de white folks fer 'em; and dey never thanked him half de time. Us old folks, us told him to stop fooling wid dem dead niggers and all such as de like, 'cause he gwine to kill his-self. I is most blind, but de darkies, dey told me how Will fooled 'round a-doing things fer so many sorry folks.

"But den, God plucks his flowers. De night of de eighth day dem doctors had done 'lowed dat Will had pneumonia. Will look up at his wife and say, 'Git dese folks out of here so I can die by myself'.

"It was 'leven o'clock in de morning when dey come and told me. Susie Eubanks, she 'lowed dat de screeching of de owls wake her up dat morning 'bout 3 o'clock. I 'lowed dat a dog a-howling was what riz me up. Catherine 'lowed dat she hadn't laid down no time till she heard Gus's cow a-lowing. All de signs took and failed den, as dey will do on such occasions."

United States. Work Projects Administration

GEORGE PATTERSON

I

Interview with George Patterson
653 Peachtree St., Spartanburg, S.C.
—F.S. DuPre, Spartanburg, S.C.

While seeking an interview with an ex-slave today, the writer was directed to a certain house where an old man lived. Entering the premises by the rear, he observed an old man helping a woman who was washing some clothes. He was stepping around quite lively, carrying water and emptying one pot after another of the dirty water already used by the woman. After he had sufficient water for his wife's needs, he asked the writer to go with him to the front porch where he could be quiet and talk.

He stated that he was large enough during the Civil War to wait on the soldiers when they would come to his master's home for something to eat, which was at Kilgore's Bridge on Enoree River, said that his job during the slavery days was to wait on the white folks and watch the plantation.

He also stated that his father was a full-blooded Indian who was sold to his master by Joe Crews, the biggest slave trader in the country. His father was stolen somewhere in Mississippi, along with other Indians, and sold into slavery with the "niggers." He said his father told him he was stolen by Joe Crews when he was a young buck. At that time, his father went by the name of "Pink

Crews," but after he was purchased by Mr. Joe Patterson, his name became "Pink Patterson." He stated that his mother was a white woman who came from Ireland and was working on the Patterson farm. She was not a slave, but was married to his father by his "Marster."

They lived in a one-story, one-room log cabin which had a dirt floor. The whole family of 18 children and parents lived in this small house. They were comfortable, however, and all had good health. He stated that he had not been sick for fifty years, and that the only trouble with him now was a broken foot, the result of a railroad wreck about forty years ago. He said his foot still gave him trouble in bad weather.

He said that he had not been conjured at all, but had just gotten his foot broken. "Conjuring and ghosts are all foolishness anyhow." The nearest he ever come to seeing a ghost was one night when he observed a "white thing moving back and forth across the branch." He had with him his brother's cap and ball pistol, and he shot at the object two or three times, knowing that his dogs would come to him if they heard the shots. Two or three dogs came up and recognized him. He told one bull dog to go to the white thing and see what it was. After the dog had been all around the place where the thing was moving, he knew there was nothing there to frighten him. Next morning, he went out to see the object and found it to be a small tree with white leaves waving in the breeze.

Going back to slavery times, he said that on most plantations were kept squirrel dogs, 'possum dogs, snake dogs, rabbit dogs and "nigger" dogs. Each dog was trained for a certain kind of tracking. He used to train the "nigger" dogs which were used to track slaves who had run away from the plantation. He said he had two dogs that were sure never to lose the scent when they had taken it up. "If I put them on your track here and you went to Greenville, they would track you right to Greenville."

He said his master did not allow his slaves to be whipped but he had seen slaves on other plantations wearing chains to keep them from running away.

"People don't work like they used to, and this thing of higher education is ruining niggers. All their learning teaches them is how to beat a man out of a dollar and how to get out of work. It teaches them to cus, and it teaches these young girls how to make easy money. As old as I am, I've been approached by girls I didn't know and asked for a dollar. Now that thing won't do. I believe in teaching children how to read and write; but don't go any further than that. I've never seen a moving picture. Once a man offered to give me a ticket to a movie, but I told him to give me a plug of tobacco instead." When asked if he thought colored preachers should be educated, he replied that when they are educated they learn how to steal everything a man has, if they can.

"You remember reading about Joe Crews and Jim Young—what they did in this state? Well, they tried to lead all the niggers after the war was over. I was the one who got Jim Young away from the whites. I carried him to Greenville, but he got back somehow, and was killed. Joe Crews was killed, too. The Ku Klux was after them hot, but I carried Jim Young away from them. You know, the Yankees was after getting all the gold and money in the South. After the war, some Yankee soldiers would come along and sell anybody, niggers or whites, a gun. They were trying to get on to where the white people kept their money. If they caught on, they would go there and steal it. You know, there wasn't any banks, so people had to keep their money and gold in somebody's safe on some big man's place. These men in selling guns was trying to find out where the money was hid."

When asked about hunting, he said that hunting in slavery days was not like it is now, for a man could hunt on his own place then and get plenty of game. There were plenty of wild hogs in those days, as well as wild turkeys, rabbits and squirrels. Some of the hogs were so wild that no one dared to go into a pack of them, for they had tusks six inches long, and could tear a man to pieces. A man could shoot a wild hog and have no trouble over it. Cattle, he said, ran wild and were dangerous at all times.

"When you buy something now, you haven't got much. I bought a cake of soap for my wife but it was a small thing. When we used to make our own soap on the plantation, we had plenty of good soap."

He said his father followed his master and others to the war, and he drove artillery wagons at times. At Appomattox, his father told him that he drove wagons over dead soldiers piled in ditches. His father lived to be 111 years old. After he and his father were set free, they remained with Mr. Joe Patterson to help him make that year's crops; then they moved to another place.

He heard that work was plentiful in Spartanburg, and he moved here and did various kinds of work. He said that he was not as strong as he used to be, but that he could still do a full day's work except when his foot troubled him.

Uncle George was quite polite and seemed glad to talk of old times. He observed, though, that in old times people would speak to him. "You go up to a crowd now, and they won't speak. They won't notice you."

United States. Work Projects Administration

II

**Interview with George Patterson
653 Peachtree St., Spartanburg, S.C.**
—F.S. DuPre, Spartanburg, S.C.

George Patterson, ex-slave, says that during the Civil War and afterwards, when the owners of plantations in the Enoree River section had a surplus of peaches and apples, they made apple and peach brandy; and after they had filled kegs with it, rolled the kegs into a pond to keep them from leaking until they were either sold or taken out for personal use. Corn and rye whiskey were also stored in the water to keep the kegs from leaking. In those days, he stated, good whiskey sold for 40 cents a gallon. Butter sold for five cents a pound; eggs six cents a dozen, and hens that now cost 75 cents a piece, sold for ten cents. But stated George, salt was very dear and hard to get; a barrel costing as much as $50.

George also stated there were plenty of wild turkeys, ducks and wild geese on the Enoree River. The turkeys would ravage a garden or scratch up the planted seed on the plantation. He has often been sent out to frighten the wild turkeys away from the crops. He said plenty of meat could be secured by shooting the wild hogs that roamed the woods, that anybody was at liberty to kill a hog. Of course, some once tame hogs mingled with the droves of wild hogs but the tame hogs had the owner's name on them; so one had to be very careful that he did not shoot a marked hog. He said that when his father, an Indian, was stolen by Joe Crews, from the woods of Mississippi, he marched them with niggers he had also stolen, or traded for, into different sections of the country, selling them as slaves and speculating on them. He drove them just like cattle and would stop at various plantations and sell the Indians and niggers into slavery.

Slave Narratives

SALLIE PAUL

I

Interview with Sallie Paul, 79 years
Marion, S.C., Fairlee Street
—*Annie Ruth Davis*

"I remember we colored people belong to de white folks in slavery time. Remember when de war was gwine on 'cause we hear de guns shoot en we chillun jump up en holler. Yes, mam, I remember dat. Remember de 30th of dis October, I was 79 years old.

"No, mam, I ain' got no kin people. You see I been born in North Carolina. Government lady get Lindy Henderson to stay here en look out for me 'cause it be like dis, I can' see out my eyes one speck. Can' tell de night from de day. Don' discover daylight no time, child. We rents dis here house from Miss (Mrs.) Wheeler en Lindy treats me mighty good."

(Lindy: "Well, we gets along nicely. I done feed her up en she get back in bed, it be so cold en ain' got no coal to heat her. Yes, mam, has to wait on de Salvation of de Lord. Government gives us a little small salary, but we has to live mighty small, mighty small. Honey, it takes a right sharp to live on dese days. If dey wasn' helpin me, I just don' know, be as I ain' much dese days. Got dis high blood so worser en den I has such a achin in my joints en throat dat does worry me right smart too.")

"My white folks, dey was de Williamsons dere in North

Carolina. Yes, mam, dey was good to dey colored people. We lived right in dey yard or dat what you may say in de yard. All de colored people lived dere side de yard whe' dey be close enough to holler if anything get de matter. You see, I wasn' big enough to do no work much den only as we chillun tote up wood for de white folks en piddle 'bout de yard. I know I won' big enough to do nothin but jump up en keep fuss gwine all round de yard dere. I remembers dey used to get a handful of switches en stand us chillun up in a long row en give us all a lick 'bout de legs. You see, dey didn' work de chillun when dey was little bit of things en stunt dem up. Chillun grow to be 'bout 12 or 13 years old fore dey work dem in dat day en time.

"My white folks was well off peoples, honey. My Massa, he run three plantations en he had a heap of colored peoples dere. You see, people didn' run over de ground in dat day en time like dey do now. De men lift up every piece de dirt in de ground en get all de roots out it. My mother, she was one of de plow hands dere en when time come to lay off de ground, she force to work out. Dat de reason we chillun be up in de yard twixt meals. Den when breakfast en supper come, we eat to we house. Live close enough to de white folks house dat de nigger chillun could go to de house en get dey hominy en clabber 'tween meals. Oh, dey have dese here long wooden trays set up somewhe' under de tree dere in de yard dat dey would full up wid hominy en clabber for we chillun. Give some spoon en dem others never had none. Dat it, all eat out de same tray right side together. Yes, mam, when I was raise up, have plenty to eat en chillun never fail to get it."

(Lindy: "Oh, child, we was bred en born in a fat kitchen in dat day en time. We was well taken care of. People say I don' look like it 'cause I here gwine 'bout wid stick in my hand. Sho was raise up in a fat kitchen. Yes, mam, I was raise to do all de cookin en de nursin for de white folks. Ain' never see no kitchen yet dat dey could lost me in 'cause I was trained myself. Never had no chance to go to school no time. You see, if it wasn' cookin, it was chillun. 'Bout time new baby come, dat first baby be knee child en so on like dat. Well, let me hush now, honey, en let Sallie tell you dat what in her mind. She de one what you come to get speech from.")

"Yes, mam, de people ate like dey eats now, but dey didn' never know what a stove was in dem days. Some of de kitchen fireplace, you could put a whole railin in it to hang de pots on. Den dey had dem big old clay chimneys wid dirt ovens dat would hold a bushel of tatoes to a time. Just was a brick chimney now en den in slavery time. Bake all de cakes en de bread right dere on de fireplace. Child, dere sho been more to eat in slavery time den dere be now en I know dat all right. Dere been more sheep en hogs en cows en goats. No, mam, I don' think I like goat. I don' think so. I recollects I tried to eat some goat one time en it swell in my mouth. Know I wouldn' eat sheep neither. It a sin. Seem like dey so humble.

"White folks didn' give de niggers no money no time, but dey had money in slavery time much so as dey does now. You see, all de white folks wasn' equal. Some was poor en de colored people sell dem things dey white folks never want. Oh, dey take anything you carry dem.

"I don' know nothin 'bout de Yankees only I see dem come through dere de day we was freed, but won' no great heap of dem come. Coase dey was passin through dat country all durin de war en come to de colored people's house en get somethin to eat. Yes, mam, colored people feed dem en give dem somethin to travel on. It just like dis, de Yankees would give de colored people dey good clothes en take dey rags. You see, dey was desertin. Was runnin away en gettin back home. I don' know whe' if de white folks know 'bout dey dere or not, but I know one thing, Massa didn' see dem.

"Yankees didn' do no harm nowhe' in dat country to nobody, white nor colored. Never hear tell of dat, but white people was scared of de Yankees as dey was of a rattlesnake. Yankees tell de colored people dey was free as dey was, but just didn' know it. I know dey said dat 'cause I was standin up listenin to dem just like any other child be standin dere lookin up in your mouth. Den when de colored people was freed, heap of de white folks died 'cause dey grieve demselves to death over de loss of dey property. Sho know dat 'cause I see dem en hear tell 'bout it plenty times.

"Dere been plenty white folks dat wouldn' never fight against de Yankees widout dey couldn' get out of it. Dey slip off en hide in pits dey dig in de woods en in de bays. Some of dem say dey didn' have no slaves en dey won' gwine fight. Dat de way it be, if dey didn' fight, dey had to run away en stay in de woods. Dat point me to think 'bout how young Massa would slip off wid de colored boys on a Sunday to play like white people will do en would learn dem to read. Carry old Webster's Blue Back wid dem en when dey been way off yonder, young Massa would learn dem to read. My father could read, but he couldn' never write.

"Yes, mam, white folks get handful of switches en whip de nigger chillun round de legs, but wouldn' never whip none of de grown 'omans 'cause dey was breedin. Didn' kill niggers whe' I was born."

(Lindy; "My Lord, child, reckon dey would 'bout beat me to death if I been livin den 'cause I done had two husbands en ain' never bear no child yet. Doctor tell me if I want a child, I would have to go to de hospital en be operated on en I wouldn' never get my mind fixed to do dat. Honey, I lies down in dat bed dere at night en thanks my God dat I ain' never had dat operation. I know I been bless 'cause dis de time of Revelations de people livin in. Don' want no child my God gwine hold me responsible for at de Jedgment. Sho bless 'cause like I see de world gwine, people ain' got no time to be gettin ready to meet dey God. Tell my God dat I thank he a thousand times again dat I been make like I is. It a blessin, honey, a blessin.")

"Yes, mam, de white folks make dey own cloth right dere on de plantation in dem days. Dey had a loom house, but my mother had a loom right to her own door. Sometimes, she would weave piece for de white folks en den she weave for herself. White folks find all de colored people's clothes en see to have all dey weavin done in dat day en time. Dey had certain one of de colored people to do all de common weavin, but dey couldn' do dem three en four treadle till dey Missus learn dem how. My old Missus could weave any kind of cloth or blankets or anything like dat.

"Oh, de white folks be right dere to look after dey colored people if dey get sick. Coase dey gwine take care of dey niggers. Gwine save dem just as long as dey got breath in dey body. Won' no niggers gwine suffer if dey need doctor neither. Heap of dem was cared for more better in slavery time den dey is now 'cause dey had somebody dat had to care for dem or lose dem one. Ain' no white folks want to lose dey niggers.

"No, God! no, God! I hear talk 'bout it, but I don' know whe' dey can do it or not. If dey can conjure, dey keep it to demselves. Dey never tell me. I hear tell of dem things call ghosts, but I ain' never see none of dem en ain' never see no hant neither. I has see a spirit though. Peoples dat been dead, dey appears fore you en vanishes. Seen dem all right. Dem things call ghosts en things, I don' wanna see none 'cause I don' know 'bout dem. Hear talk of dem, but ain' seen nothin like dat.

"Well, it like I tellin you, everybody didn' hate dey white folks. Dat how-come some niggers stayed right on dere wid dey white people after freedom en farmed for half what dey made on de crop. You see, dey didn' have nothin to work wid so dey stayed on dere en farmed on shares.

"I couldn' exactly tell you which de better times dese days or in slavery time. I know heap of de colored people fared better when dey belonged to de white folks 'cause dey had good owners. Didn' have to worry 'bout huntin dey clothes en somethin to eat in dat day en time. Just had to work. Now dey have to hunt it en get it together de best way dey can. Oh, honey, peoples has so much worraytions dese days. Dat how-come dey ain' live a long time like dey used to."

II

Interview with Sallie Paul, age 79
Marion, S.C.
—Annie Ruth Davis

"No, mam, I ain' able to see none tall no time. Dis here one of my eye is weaken from dat other one. Cose I can tell de day from night, but say see somethin, I couldn' never do dat.

"Well, I don' know nothin more to speak 'bout den dat I been tell you dem other times you come here. It just like I tell you, we nigger chillun would look to de white folks yard in de day, but we stayed to us house in de quarter on a night. Oh, we lived close enough to de white folks yard to know dere was cookin gwine on in de Missus kitchen. No, child, we never eat us meals to de white folks house. You see, all de niggers on de plantation would draw rations den just like heap of dese people 'bout here draw rations dese days. I mean dey would draw so much of ration from dey Massa to last dem a week at a time just like de people draw government ration right 'bout here now. Dere was sho a plenty to eat in dat day en time, too, 'cause I know whe' I come up, I was raise on a plenty. Dere was abundance of meat en bread en milk all de time. Yes, mam, cows won' lackin no time whe' I was raise. I remember dey would give us chillun all de milk en hominy us could eat twixt meals. Always fed de nigger chillun to de white folks yard twixt meals. You see, dey was mighty particular 'bout how dey would raise en feed de little niggers in dem days. Been more particular den you would be particular wid a ten dollar bill dis day en time. Would keep dey little belly stuff wid plenty hominy en milk same as dey was pigs. Dey do dat to make dem hurry en grow 'cause dey would want to hurry en increase dey property. De white folks never didn' despise to see a big crop of nigger chillun comin on. Hear tell dat some of de white folks would be mean to dey colored people, but never did see nothin of dat kind 'bout my white folks' plantation. Cose de colored people would be let loose to get together on a night en when Sunday come. Dat all de time dey ever had to visit 'cause dey been force to work from sunup on de hill till sundown over de swamp.

"Oh, de colored people had plenty song in slavery time, but I ain' studyin nothin 'bout dat now. My 'membrance short dese days, child. Yes, mam, de colored people had so many song in slavery time, I can' remember de first word. Dey would sing anything dey could make a noise wid. Some of dem could read out de hymn book en some of dem couldn' tell one word from de other. Yes, mam, some of de young Massa would steal off to de woods wid dey colored mate on a Sunday evenin' en learn dem to read. No, Lord, dere won' no schools nowhe' for de colored people in dem days. White folks catch nigger wid a book, nigger sho know he gwine get a whippin soon as dat tale let loose. Now en den dey young Massa would learn dem, but dey wouldn' never let dey fore-mammy know 'bout it. Cose dey couldn' never write, but some of dem could read. Massa en Missus never know 'bout it though.

"Now, it de Lord truth, honey, I ain' want to mislead you noway. Wouldn' do dat for nothin. Don' lay no mind to heap of dis talk I hear some people speak 'bout. I gwine talk 'bout what I been touch wid. Some of de colored people fared good en some of dem fared bad in slavery time. Some of dem had good owners en some of dem had bad ones. Thank de Lord, I didn' get much of it 'cause I won' but nine years old when freedom come. (Whe' de lady? Gone?). (The old woman is totally blind and remains in bed all the time). Some of de white folks had dese here overseers en dey was rough owners. Thank God, I was little en dey never didn' whip me exceptin little bit 'bout de legs dere in old Massa yard. Remember dey cut we chillun round de legs wid a switch sometimes when dey would want to punish us en learn us better sense. Honey, us had a good old Massa. Won' no cuttin en slashin gwine on round us like dere was on dem other plantations round dere. My blessed a mercy, lady, some of dem grown niggers mighty as well been dead in dat day en time, de overseers been so mean. De little chillun wouldn' never be force to work like dey is now. Dey would just be playin 'bout dere in old Massa yard en totin wood for dey Missus. Wouldn' have to work in slavery time 'cause dey had somebody to feed dem. Dat de difference, dey have to work for what dey get dis day en time en ain' be satisfied wid it neither.

"Well, I don' know nothin 'bout dem cornshuckin dey used to have only as dey would gather de crop in dem days en haul it up to de white folks big old farm barn. Den dey would ax all de white folks 'bout dere to send dey hands dere to shuck corn one night. En pray, dey would have such a whoopin en a hollerin en de like of a big supper dere dat night. My blessed Lord, dat was a big time for we chillun. One man would have corn shuck to his barn one night en dey would all help shuck corn to another man barn de next night. You see, people was more mindful to bless one another in dat day den dey be dese days. Yes, mam, neighbor been please to turn good hand to neighbor den.

"Oh, dere ain' been no end to fine victuals in dat day en time. You know dere was a plenty to eat in slavery time 'cause de people made somethin to eat den, but ain' nothin now hardly. Child, dis a tight time we gwine through dese days. I remember dey used to have plenty 'tatoes en bread en fresh meat every day en have heap of sheep en cows en goats all 'bout de woods den, but dere ain' nothin growin in de woods dese days. Now, if a man got a hog, he got it by de tail in de pen. No, mam, de most of de people ain' got nothin now en dey ain' got nothin to buy somethin wid neither.

"I don' know, child. I settin here in dis bed day in en day out wid dese old bare eye en I don' know how de people gwine. I don' study nothin 'bout dem. I know I don' care how or which a way dey gwine 'cause I studyin 'bout most all my days behind me now. Plenty people ain' livin good as dey used to live long time ago. Seems like de times is tighter en worser den what dey used to be. Reckon de reason be dere was more made to eat den. Pa always tell we chillun dat it a sign de times gettin better when dere more made to eat, child."

III

Interview with Sallie Paul, age 79
Marion, S.C.
—Annie Ruth Davis

"I ain' tryin to remember nothin 'bout my mammy when she was a girl. I know I hear dem speak 'bout old Massa bought her en my grandmammy from off de block en raised dem to a good livin. Hear talk dat some of de colored people 'bout dere would catch old Harry in slavery time, but dere won' nothin snatchin noways 'bout my white folks. I mean some of de colored people would catch de devil in dat day en time 'cause dey come up under a rough boss. Just had half enough to eat en had to stir 'bout half naked most all de time. Not been took care of as dey should have been.

"Cose when we was chillun, de grown people would be force to punish us some of de time. Yes, mam, I do know what would happen to me, if I been get in devilment. I would get a whippin right den en dere. Nobody wouldn' never whip me, but old Massa en my mammy 'cause people won' no more allowed to whip anybody child den dey is dese days. My child done anything wrong den, you had to come to me 'bout it. I recollects, dey would whip us chillun wid tree switches round us legs. Den if dey would want to spare de punishment, dey would try to scare us out de mischief. Tell us Bloody Bones would jump out dat corner at us, if we never do what dey say do.

"Oh, I here to tell you, dey had de finest kind of enjoyments in dem days. It was sho a time, to speak 'bout, when dey had one of dem quiltings on de plantation. Didn' do nothin but quilt quilts en dance en play some sort of somethin after dey would get done. Colored people would have quiltings to one of dey own house, up in de quarter, heap of de nights en dey would frolic en play en dance dere till late up in de night. Would enjoy demselves better den de peoples do dese days 'cause when dey would get together den, dey would be glad to get together. Oh, my Lord, dey would dance en carry on all kind of fuss. Yes, mam, blow quills en knock bones together dat would make good a music as anybody would want to dance by. Child, dey had plenty scraps to make dey bed clothes wid, 'cause dey Missus would save scraps for dem.

"Yes, mam, de white folks would furnish de colored people wid clothes for true in dat day en time. Dey couldn' let dem go naked. How dey gwine work wid bare back? Cose dey fine clothes, dey managed to get dat demselves. You see, white folks wouldn' give dem no Sunday frock, but one. I tell you, de cloth was better wearin' den. Dis here cloth dese days, wear it two or three times, de wind could 'bout blow through it. Oh, dey had de finest kind of silk in slavery time. Don' hear no silk rattlin' 'bout here dese days, but would hear silk rattle in slavery time just as same as would hear paper rattlin'. Colored people wore just as much silk in dem days as dey do now 'cause when dey had a silk dress den, it been a silk dress. Won' no half cotton en half silk. Goods was sho better den, child, I say. Like I tell you, when a man had a broadcloth suit den, it won' no half jeanes. All de colored people, dat been stay on my white folks plantation, had dey own little crop of corn en fodder 'bout dey house en when a peddler come along, dey would sell dey crop en buy silk from de peddler. Dey been sell dey crop to anybody dey could. Dere was always a poor one somewhe' dat been need corn en fodder.

"No, mam, colored people didn' have no church of dey own in slavery time 'cause dey went to de white folks church. All I can tell you, we went to buckra's church en dey set in one part de church en us set in de gallery. Yes, mam, de white folks would see to it dat all dey niggers never chance to miss church service no time. En de slave owners would bury dey plantation niggers right dere to de colored people graveyard behind de church, dat was settin right side de white people graveyard.

"I won' married till long time after freedom come here en when I get married, de colored people had dese here bresh (brush) shelters for dey church en dey had dey own colored preacher, too. Honey, I marry a Paul, a slavery one, but I didn' have no big weddin. Didn' want none. Just married dere to my father's house en I had a white dress dat was made out of cotton, all I can tell. Know it won' no silk. I don' know nothin more den dat to tell you. Dat de mighty truth, all I know, I had me a husband en dat won' no great blessin, to speak 'bout.

"Don' ax me, child. Ax somebody dat know somethin 'bout dem things people say is a charm. I say, dey is ignorant people what believe in dem. I know I ain' never wear nothin round my foot 'cause I ain' got no dime to spend, much less to be puttin it round my foot. I calls dat nothin but a foolish person dat would do dat, ain' you say so? I see a woman once wear a twenty-five cents piece tie round her ankle en I ax her what she do dat for. She tell me she had de rheumatism en she hear dat would cure it. I tell her I ain' had no mind to have no faith in all dat what I hear people speak 'bout. Dat won' nothin but a devil been talkin to dat woman, I say.

"My God a mercy, I tell you, slavery time was somethin. Dat been a day. Colored people didn' have no privileges den only as dey Massa would let dem loose on a Saturday evenin' en on a Sunday. But, child, dey was just as proud of dat as people is proud of a month dese days. Didn' have no more privileges in slavery time den dese people got now in dis here chain gang. No, mam, niggers belong to dey owner in slavery just like you got a puppy belong to you. Make dem go so far en den stop.

"What I think 'bout Abraham Lincoln? I ain' took time to have no thoughts 'bout him. Hear so much talk 'bout him till I don' know what he done. Hear talk dat he been de one dat free de slaves, but whe' de power? De power been behind de throne, I say. God set de slaves free. De Lord do it. Abraham Lincoln couldn' do no more den what God give de power to do. It just like dis, I believes it was intended from God for de slaves to be free en Abraham Lincoln was just de one what present de speech. It was revealed to him en God was de one dat stepped in en fight de battle."

LINA ANNE PENDERGRASS

> Interview with Lina Anne Pendergrass
> Union, S.C., Rt. 1
> —*Caldwell Sims, Union, S.C.*

"I'se born 10 years befo' Freedom on a Christmas day. Marse Tom Sanders, whose place I'se born on, lived in Chester County. One of my first 'memberances is a dream. I though' I saw my little sister, Sars, laying on a cooling board. I was five years old at dat time. I woke my mother up and tole her 'bout it, but it was jus' a dream an' wasn't nothin' to it.

"I never had no schooling and the Ku Klux sho scairt me. They took my daddy; my brother was too young. It was on Sat'day night. Next day was Sunday, and dey didn't fix de doors what de Ku Klux broke down. Us nebber did see pa no mo'.

"As it was in de day of Noah, so shall it be in de coming of de days of Jesus Christ. Peoples fitting and a-killin' and a-scrappin' all de time now, kaize dey don't take no time to go to prayer meeting. My grandfather had a prayer-meeting house. All de niggers on de plantation went to it ever Sat'day night. Dey sot on benches, and den dey would git down on dere knees and pray. I was a little gal, and me and de other gals would fetch water for dem to drink. Us toted pine when it was cole, and us'd take coals 'round fer de ole folks to light dere pipes wid. Atter while, dey git to singin' and shoutin'. Den de Spirit done come down and tuck hole of dem. Dat would be when everybody would get happy. De ole rafters creak and shake as de Spirit of de Lord sink deeper and deeper in de hearts of the prayin' folks. Tate Sanders, de preacher from Lowryville, would come in 'bout dat time and raise his hands 'bove de congregation and plead wid de Lawd to open de hearts of de wicked so dat de Holy Spirit could come in. Wasn't no killin' and scratchin' going on in dem days. De ole folks tell us chillun dat if we do wrong, de Lawd gwine come down in His wrath and punish us on dis earth. Sides dat, He gwine send us to torment whar we's live in 'ternal hell fire. De worl' is so wicked now dat I'se looking fer de locust to come and stay five months and sting everybody in de fo'head dat ain't got religion. Den people will be so 'shame of deself fer dere wickedness dat dey will seek death, and dey won't be able to get no death.

"De Lawd, He is a-pressin' me on up. Yes, Lawd, Revelation is wonderful. De comin' out of smoke, dem's de devil's angels. When you reads de Word of de Lawd, take an interes' in it. De people dat I knows is so wicked dat my heart keeps anguished.

"I learnt myself how to read. My pa brought a Bible from de war. I has dat and I reads it. My pa got shot comin' from Mississippi. Marse Sanders hear about it and he sont and brung him home. Den us lived 15 miles from Chester on Broad River. My pappy was named Henry Dorsey. When he was young, he was Marse Sander's butler boy. He got well from de shot. Den de Ku Klux got him for something. I ain't never knowed what. I don't know what dey done when I was a baby.

"I'se nussed since I was a little gal. My ma made me make teas to cure folks' colds and ailments. She made me fetch her water and towels and other things while she wait on de sick folks. Dat's de way I was broke into nussing. Nineteen-eighteen laid out folks at Monarch. I started right after breakfas' wid two dollars. Git home at night with narry a penny. Git folks soup and milk. Everybody dat didn't get sick worked hard. De folks died anyway like flies. De Lawd give me strength to stand up through de whole time. When de flu pass on and de folks get well, den dey pay me for my services.

"Millie Nash, Andy's wife, she look atter me since I'se got ole. She gooder to me dan anybody I know, but at de same time, she's aggravation to me kaise she drink likker. Millie sho does git drunk, but I keeps on prayin' fer her. Dis mawnin she's gwine to a funeral. She was poling 'long 'hind me and drapped her pocketbook. When us git ready to go into de church, she stopped and grabbed hol' of me and say, 'Lina, whar my pocketbook?' I looks at her and say, 'Nigger, how does I know whar'bouts you throw dat thing down? You stayed 'hind me all de way from de ice house. Didn't I tell you to let dat dram alone befo' you left de house?' I sot down in front of de church and Millie turned around and went down de street toward de ice house. She seed her pocketbook where she drapped it, 'bout half way twixt de ice house and de church. When she come 'long whar I was sitting, I 'lowed to her dat I'se gwine up to de relief office. I lef' her and here I is. Won't be long befo' Millie be here, too. De funeral done marched on when Millie got back to de church."

AMY PERRY

Interview with Amy Perry (82)
—Jessie A. Butler, Charleston, S.C.

Amy (Chavis) Perry is eighty-two years old. She is strong for her age and lives alone in an old building at the rear of 21 Pitt street where she supports herself by taking in washing. She is a self-respecting old negress, with a reputation for honesty among the "white folks" whom she considers her friends.

Amy has two names, "like de people in doze times"— Amy Rebecca. She "adopted the Rebecca." Her father was John Minser Chavis, a slave in the McClure family, who, she claims, lived to be 116 years old, and "who wukked up to de las'," and Sarah (Thompson) Chavis, who belonged to Mrs. William Keller, an ancestor of the Cogswell family of Charleston. Amy says she was given to Miss Julia Cogswell as a "daily gift," Miss Julia having been a child at the same time that she was. In reply to a few leading questions Amy gave the following story.

"We is live in de country, near Orangeburg, and I remembers berry little 'bout de war and de time befo' de war. You see I bin berry little, I bin only seben year old. Some ole people mek out like dey remembers a lot ob t'ings." Here she gave the writer a quizzical look. "You know imagination is a great t'ing. Dey eider mek all dat up or dey tell you what bin tell dem. I got to stick to de trut', I 'members berry little, berry little. I don't 'member much 'bout what we did in de country befo' de war, nor what we eat, nor no games and such. I don't know what de big people wear. De cullered people mek dey own cloth, and call um cotton osnaburg. Dey mek banyans for de chillen. Sleebe bin cut in de cloth, and dey draw it up at de neck, and call um banyan. Dey is wear some kind ob slip under um but dat all. Dey ain't know nutting 'bout drawers nor nutting like dat.

"De medicine I remember was castor oil, and dogwood and cherry bark, which dey put in whiskey and gib you. Dey is gib you dis to keep your blood good. Dogwood will bitter yo' blood, it good medicine, I know.

"I 'member de people hab to git ticket for go out at night. W'en dey is gone to prayer meeting I is see dem drag bresh back dem to outen dey step. If de patrol ketch you wid out ticket dey beat you.

"I 'members w'en de Yankee come tru, and Wheeler a'my come after um. Doze bin dreadful times. De Yankees massicued de people, and burn dere houses, and stole de meat and eberyting dey could find. De white folks hab to live wherebber dey kin, and dey didn't hab enough to eat. I know whole families live on one goose a week, cook in greens. Sometimes they hab punkin and corn, red corn at dat. Times was haard, haard. De cullered people dodn't hab nutting to eat neider. Dat why my auntie bring me to Charleston to lib.

"De fust year atter freedom I gone to school on Mr. John Townsend place, down to Rockville. After peace declare de cullered people lib on cornmeal mush and salt water in de week and mush and vinegar for Sunday. Mine you, dat for Sunday. I don't see how we lib, yet we is. About eight year after de war we use to go down to de dairy for clabber. Dey give you so much for each one in de fambly, two tablespoon full for de grown people and one tablespoon for de chilluns. We add water to dat and mek a meal. In de country de cullered people lib on uh third (crop) but of course at de end of de year dey didn't hab nutting, yet dey has libed. I 'member w'en de Ku Klux was out too, de people bin scared 'cause dey is beat some and kill some."

When asked which she thought best, slavery or freedom, her answer was: "Better stay free if you can stay straight. Slabery time was tough, it like looking back into de dark, like looking into de night."

Feeling that as she remembered so little of plantation life her opinion was based on hearsay or her memories of war times, the writer told her of the answer of another old Negro woman: "No matter what slabery bring, if it hadn't been for slabery I nebber would hab met my Jesus." It seemed to make a strong impression on Amy who threw up her hands in the typical African gesture, and said "Praise de Lawd, w'en yo talk 'bout Jesus you is got me coming and going."

Amy is deeply religious. She owns four of Judge Rutherford's books which she claims to have read "from cubber to cubber" many times. "Some people b'lieve in dreams," she said, "but I don't hab no faith in dem. Lot ob people b'lieve in root and sich but dey can't scare me wid root. I roll ober dem from yuh to Jericho and dey wouldn't bodder me. A man died bad right in dat house yonder, and I went wid de doctor and close his sight and sich, and I come right home and gone to bed and sleep. He ain't bodder me and I ain't see um since. I don't believe in ghosts, nor dreams, nor conjuh, dat de worse. John de

Baptist and dem dream dreams, and de Lawd show dem vision, but dat diffrunt." With another comical look at the writer, she continued; "You can eat yo' stomach full and you'll dream. I b'lieve in some kind ob vision. You doze off, and you hab a good dream. I b'lieve dat. People get converted in dreams. I was twelve year ole when I get converted. I dreamed I was in a field, a large green field. A girl was dere dat I didn't had no use for. I had a bundle on my back. I honey de girl up and love um and de bundle fall on de ground. Dey put me in de church den.

"Some people say dey kin see ghost but you can't see ghost and lib. De Bible say if you kin see de wind you kin see spirit. If you kin see ghost you can see Gawd, and I know you can't see Gawd and lib. De Bible say so. I don't b'lieve in um, no ghost, and no cunjuh tho' my uncle Cotton Judson and my aunt Nassie both b'lieve in dem. Uncle Cotton could do most as much as de debbul (devil) hesself, he could most fly, but I nebber b'lieve in um no matter what he kin do."

In order to get her to talk the writer told her of a few of the accomplishments of the East Indians. She said, "Yes, Gawd got some people mek berry wise. Dey can't say dey mek demself wise. What race dese Indian come from, anyway, I know dem come from Indiana, but what race, Ham, Seth, Japheth or what. I hear de Indian hab some wise ways, and my people b'lieve in all kind ob ghost, and spirit an t'ing but I don't. I don't eben let um talk to me 'bout dem, w'en det start I say 'gone gome wid dat.' I can't counteract de Bible and I can't counteract Gawd, I don't b'lieve in um. Dat what I don't visit round. My people lub (love) too much idle discourse, and idle discourse is 'gainst de Bible. I nebber trapsy round w'en

I young and I don't now. Day why I don't hab no company. As long as ole people lib dey going to tell de young ones 'bout ghost an t'ing, and dey going to pass it on, and w'en dey die dey going to leab dat foolishness right yuh. No I don't b'lieve in no conjuh and no root. If dey gib me poison den dey got me."

ROB PERRY

Interview with Uncle Rob Perry & Aunt Della Britton
Trenton, S.C.
—Caldwell Sims, Union, S.C.

"Aunt Della born in 1863. He in 1864. He drove cows fer Marse Squire Jim Perry, who lived on the line of Edgefield and Newberry Counties. Mos de time dey traded in Newberry County, 'cause it nearer town. All road wuz bad in dem days, even in summer dey wuz allus rough.

"Uncle Rob toted water, picked up chips and carried rations fum kitchen to dinin room. Often Messrs. Jim Long, Sam, Jake and Bob Smith, (3 brothers) came to our big house fer dinner and to dance afterward.

"Plenty water to tote and fires to build den. Go out an git pine and cedar limbs to put over de picturs and 'roun de mantle boards' Fix up de table wid trimmins, git mo candles and put all roun. Mak egg-nog in de winter and mint juleps in de summer. Some time dar wuz sillabub, it ain't so good tho. De young mens dat I mentioned befo have me ter pick out pretty girls fer dem ter dance wid. I drap a curtsey an han' dem de name. If dey want ter dance wid him they look at him and flick dey fan an if dey didn't den dey never give him no mind.

"Dat done all pass by as evry thing does. Now I thanks God and looks to de Savior. Ef dar is success ter ye dat is what you has to do all de time. Della and I done had fifteen chilluns. Us is so lonesome as we has jes one a livin.

"Mr. Campbell, a Yankee man married Miss Joanna Perry. Her paw wuz Mr. Oliver Perry of Bouknight's Ferry on de Saluda River. In dat famly wuz Miss Isabelle and Messrs. John, Milledge, Jake and Tom. Miss Joanna marry on Friday in de parlor all fixed up wid cedar ropes a-hangin' fum de ceilin an de mo-es candles what a body ever did see. She made us buil' her a arch and kivver hit wid vines. It sot before de mantle and a white bell hung fum de middle uv it. White cloth wuz stretched over eveything and dey never let nobuddy walk in dat room cep in dey bare feet fer fear dey dirty all dat cloth.

"Miss Isabella sho picked de pianny fer Miss Joanna. A Young lady fum anuther plantation sang two songs. All pur white ladies wore dey pretties' white dresses wid flowers in dey hair. Miss Joanna had her face all kivvered up wid er thin white cloth dat fell off'n her and laid all back uv her on de floor. An de white ladies had dey white dresses a layin over de floor but didn't none uv dem have dey faces kivvered cept Miss Joanna, you see she wuz de bride.

"My ole 'oman wuz rigged in white herself. Evvything in dat house wuz fixed up extry fer da ceremony. I wo' one de men's black coats and black pants and a white shirt wid a ves' an tie. I had on a fine pair black shoes. Dey give all dat ter me en I kep it adder de weddin. Dat suit I wore ter church fer de nex ten years.

"Nex day, Saturday, come de big 'infair'. A double table wuz set up in de dinin room. Ham, turkey en chicken wuz put on dat table dat wussent teched. Dey jes stay dere along wid de fixins. All de victuals wuz placed on de plates in de kitchen and fetched to de table. Five darkies wuz kep busy refreshin de weddin diners.

"Miss Joanna an de Yankee man what she done married de day befo dat, her sister, de lady what sing en her maw an paw an de parson set at de table what they calls de bridal table. Dat table had de mo-es trimmins on hit of bows an ribbens and de like ob dat. I still sees Miss Joanna a settin dare. She wo' her weddin dress jes zactly lak she did de day befo. She never had her face kivvered up wuz de onliest change I seed. De weddin dinner musta lasted two hours'. Atter dat de carriage came roun en evvybody lined up along de front door by de cape jessamines ter throw rice an ole shoes at de bride when she come outside de big house ter git in de carrage. Evvybody wuz mighty spry to be done danced all de night befo til de sun had showed red in de Eas' dat Sadday mornin.

"Atter she gone off I jes' cud'n figger' out how Marse' had got so much together fer dat weddin', kaise hit had'n been no time since de Yankee so'ders had carried off ev'y thing and left us dat po'. But den sum years has slipped by since dat.

"When I turn back to go in de big house, I see de peafowls a sneakin' off to de river rale 'shame 'kase dey never had er sign uv a tail. All dey tail feathers wuz plucked ter make de weddin fans en ter go in de Mistus an de gals hats. Dat sho wuz er big drove en dey is de petties' fowl whut dere is, an folks doesn't give dem no mine dese days."

VICTORIA PERRY

> Interview with Victoria Perry
> 167 Golding St., Spartanburg, S.C.
> —*F.S. DuPre, Spartanburg, S.C.*

Victoria Perry, who lives in Spartanburg, says that she was just a small child when slavery times were "in vogue," being eight years old when the "negroes were set free in 1865." Her mother, she said, was Rosanna Kelly, and had lived in Virginia before she was bought by Bert Mabin, who owned a farm near Newberry. She says that she was often awakened at night by her mother who would be crying and praying. When she would ask her why she was crying, her mother would tell her that her back was sore from the beating that her master had given her that day. She would often be told by her mother: "Some day we are going to be free; the Good Lord won't let this thing go on all the time." Victoria said she was as scared of her master as she was of a mad dog. She said her master used to tie her mother to a post, strip the clothes from her back, and whip her until the blood came. She said that her mother's clothes would stick to her back after she had been whipped because she "bleed" so much. She said that she wanted to cry while her mother was being whipped, but that she was afraid that she would get whipped if she cried.

"Whenever my master got mad at any of the niggers on the place, he would whip them all. He would tie them to a post or to a tree, strip off their clothes to the waist, and whip them till he got tired. He was a mean master, and I was scared of him. I got out of his sight when he came along.

"My father was a white man, one of the overseers on the farm. I don't know anything about him or who he was. I never saw him that I knowed of. But the way Bert Mabin beat my mother was cruel.

"One day a Yankee come by the house and told my master to get all the colored people together; that a certain Yankee general would come by and would tell them that they were free. So one day the niggers gathered together at the house, and the Yankee general was there with some soldiers. They formed a circle around the niggers and the general stood in the middle and told us all we were free. My mother shouted, 'The Lord be praised.' There was a general rejoicing among the niggers and then we backed away and went home. My mother told me she knew the Lord would answer her prayers to set her free.

"I went hungry many days, even when I was a slave. Sometimes I would have to pick up discarded corn on the cob, wipe the dirt off and eat it. Sometimes during slavery, though, we had plenty to eat, but my master would give us just anything to eat. He didn't care what we got to eat.

"After we were set free, I went with my mother to the Gist plantation down in Union. My mother always wanted to go back to her home at Bradford, Virginia, but she had no way to go back except to walk. Work was mighty scarce after slavery was over, and we had to pick up just what we could get. My mother got a job on the Gist plantation, and somehow I got up here to Spartanburg.

"I married Tom Perry, and I have been here ever since, although he is dead now. He was a brick-mason.

"I sure was scared of my master, he treated us niggers just like we was dogs. He had all our ages in a big Bible at the house, but I never went there to see my age. My mother told me always to say I was eight years old when I was set free. I am eighty now, according to that."

United States. Work Projects Administration

JOHN PETTY

Interview with John Petty (87)
Hill Street, Gaffney, S.C.
—*Caldwell Sims, Union, S.C.*

"I was born on the Jim Petty place in what was then Spartanburg County.

"Marse raised all his darkies to ride young. I no more 'members when I learned to ride than I 'members when I come into the world. Marse had his stables built three logs high from the outside of the lot. When the horse step down into the lot, then I jump on his back from the third log. So little that I never could have got on no other way without help.

"The horse what I rid had a broad fat back and he trot so fast that sometimes I fall off, but I hang on to the mane and swing back on his back and he never break his gait. Then again if I didn't swing right back up he take and stop till I git landed on his back once more.

"One horse called Butler, farm horse named Tom, mule called Jack, slave horse called Stoneman, then one called Cheny, one Jane, one Thicketty and the studhorse named Max. I allus play with him, but my folks was ig'nant to that fact. I lay down and he jump straight up over me. I git corn and he eat it from my hand. There was apples and salt that he loved [HW: to eat] from my palm. He throw his fore legs plumb over my head, and never touch me at all. All this gwine on in Max's stable. It big enough for a dozen or more horses, 'cause it hardly ever beed that Max git out and his stable had to be big so as he could exercise in it. So I slip in there and we play unbeknownst to the old folks, white or black. The door slided open. When I git tired and ready to go out then I slide the door open. Maxie knowed that I was gwine and he had the most sense. He watch till I git the door slid open and if he could he run by me and jump out. I never could git him back in and he race 'round that lot till the hands come in from the field at dark. He have a good time and git all sweaty.

"When he jump over me out'n the sliding door, then I hide under the feed house till Mammy holler, 'Lawdy, fore the living, yonder is Max a-ripping hisself plumb to he death in that lot.' Then they send for some the mens to git him back. Atter they done that then I crawl out, climb the lot fence and run through the field home. When I sets down Maw 'lows, 'Does you know it's real curious thing how that old stud-horse git his door open and come out'n that stable. It must be haints creeping 'bout right here in the broad open daylight!' At that I draw up real near the fire and say, 'Maw, does you reckon that the haints is gwine to come and open our door some time?'

"On t'other hand, if I be real quick a-gitting out of the stable door before Max turn and see me, when then he couldn't git out. None of them never knowed 'bout the good times that me and Max used to did have. And it 'pears real strange to me now that he never did hit me with his foots nor nothing. That horse sure 'nough did love me and that's jest all what it is to that. I also used to slip in the extra feed house and fetch him oats and the like 'twixt and 'tween times. He stay that fat and slick. But it wouldn't nary lil' darky would go near that studhorse but me. They's all skeered to death when he git in the lot and when they seed him in there they would run and git in the house and slam the door plumb shut.

"When I done come up nigh 18 or something like that, the big freedom come 'round. Marse Jim say us could all go and see the world as we'uns was free niggers. Us jump up and shout Glory and sing, but us never sassed our white folks like it 'pears to be the knowledge up North. I'd done been there and they thinks us turned our backs on our white folks, but I never seed nothing but scalawag niggers and poor white trash a-doing that, that I ain't. One nigger went from the plantation to the north as they called it.

"When he had done stayed there fer five years then he come back and hired out to Marse Jim. He looked real lanky, but I never paid that no mind then. He was older than I was and he always 'lowing, 'John, up in Winston all the niggers makes five dollar a day; how come you don't go up there and git rich like I is'. Some of the older ones laugh when he talk to me like that and he lean to my ear and say real low, 'They's ig'nant.'

"One day when the crops done laid by I told Marse Jim, as I allus call him that, I 'lows, 'Marse, dis fall I gwine north to git rich, but I sure is gwine to bring you folks something when I comes south again'.

"So Marse give me my money and I set out for the north. I got to Winston-Salem and got me a job. But it was that hard a-cleaning and a-washing all the time. 'Cause I never knowed nothing 'bout no 'baccy and there wasn't nothing that I could turn off real quick that would bring me no big money. It got cold and I never had no big oak logs to burn in my fireplace and I set and shivered till I lay down. Then it wasn't no kivver like I had at Marse Jim's. Up there they never had 'nough wood to keep no fire all night.

"Next thing I knowed I was down with the grip and it took all the money dat I had and then I borrowed some to pay the doctor. So I up and come back home. It took me a long time to reach Spartanburg and from there I struck up with the first home niggers I seed since I left in the fall. That make me more better than I feel since the first day what I 'rive at Winston. Long afore I 'rive at home, I knowed that I done been a fool to ever leave the plantation.

"When I git home all the darkies that glad to offer me the 'glad hand'. I ax where that nigger what 'ticed me off to the north and they all 'low that he done took the consumption and died soon after I done gone from home. I never had no consumption, but it took me long time to git over the grippe. I goes to old Marse and hires myself out and I never left him no more till the Lawd took him away.

"God knows that the slaves fared better than these free niggers is. Us had wool clothes in the winter and us had fire and plenty wood and plenty to eat and good houses to keep out the rain and cold. In the summer us had cool clabber milk and bread and meat and spring water and now us don't have all them things and us can't keep up no houses like our log houses was kept.

"Why, Charlie Petty, Marse's son, wore home made clothes at home jest as us did. He was dat proud that he 'come editor or something of a Spartanburg paper."

SARAH POINDEXTER

> Interview with Sarah Poindexter, 87 years old
> 800 Lady Street (in the rear), Columbia, S.C.
> —*Stiles M. Scruggs, Columbia, S.C.*

"My name is Sarah Poindexter. I was born in 1850, on de plantation of Jacob Poindexter, 'bout ten miles beyond Lexington court house. These old eyes of mine has seen a mighty lot of things here'bouts durin' de eighty-seven years I been 'round here.

"De first time I see Columbia, it de powerfulest lot of big wood houses and muddy streets I ever see in my life. De Poindexter wagon dat carry my daddy and my mammy and me to de big town, pretty often mire in mudholes all 'long de big road from de plantation to de court house. Dat trip was made 'bout 1857, 'cause I was seven years old when I made dat trip.

"Since that first trip I has lived in sight of Columbia, 'most all my life. My daddy, my mammy and me lived on de plantation of Master Poindexter until 1863. We might a lived there longer, if things had not been so upset. I sho' recall de excitement in de neighborhood when roving crowds of niggers come 'long de big road, shoutin' and singin' dat all niggers am free. Snow was on de ground, but de spirits of de niggers was sho' plenty hot.

"De Poindexter plantation was one big place of excitement them days. De slaves work some, all durin' de war, sometimes I now 'spects it was for de sake of de missus.

All of us loved her, 'cause she was so kind and good to us. She was cryin' and worryin' all de time 'bout her man-folks, who was away fightin' damn Yankees, she say. She sho' had plenty of backbone or spunk, when stragglers show up, they always hungry and always ready to take what they want to eat, until the missus come on de scene with her trusty shotgun. It seem like de war last forever to me, 'stead of 'bout five years. To a child, Lordy, how long de years hang on, and when we get past fifty, oh, how fast de time runs.

"One day mammy stay in bed, too sick to go to de big house to cook, and befo' noon, who should come to our cabin but Missus Poindexter herself, carryin' a basket. She set it down and say to mammy: 'Lawzy Sadie, I not leave you here to starve; then she uncover de basket and set out a big plate of chicken and dumplin', hot biscuits, coffee, and a lot of other good things.

"When she gone, mammy eat some and give me some, and mammy git up next mornin' and say: 'Sis, my white folks' missus am so good and kind, I am goin' to work for her today, best I can'. She went but she wasn't good well yet. Missus Poindexter many times fetch me a piece of candy or somethin' when she go to town and back.

"No, I never see Columbia burn in 1865, but we reckon that it was burnin' that night in February, 1865, 'cause we smell it and de whole east look lak some extra light is shinin' and pretty soon, some folks come ridin' by and tell us the whole city in flames. De next time I see it, I guess there wasn't fifty houses standin'. Chimneys standin' 'round, is about all there was where most of de city was standin' befo'.

"My daddy was killed down 'bout Aiken, shortly after 1865. Me and mammy come to Columbia and live in a cabin in de alley back of Senate Street, where mammy take in washin' and cook for some white folks, who know her; I helped her. She die in 1868, and I goes 'way with four other nigger gals to Durham to work in a tobacco factory. Both white and nigger women work there, but de nigger women do most of de hard work, strippin' de leaves, stemmin' them, and placin' them to dry. White women finish them for de trade.

"In 1870 when I comes back to Columbia de city am acomin' back. Big buildin's up along de streets, but most of them was made of wood. Soon after that I gets work in a hotel, but Columbia at that time was not so big and Durham was smaller still, although Durham had more brick houses. I was happier on de Poindexter plantation and had fewer things to worry 'bout than when I was as-cratchin' 'round for myself.

"You ask has I been married? Yes, I marry a dandy lookin' young man, 'bout my own age, 'bout a year after I comes back to Columbia. His name, so he say, is Sam Allen. He make fun of some other niggers who work at one thing or another to live. One day he come to where I work and say he bound to raise ten dollars. I hands him de cash, and he gives me a good kiss right there befo' de folks, but I never see him again. I hear, after he gone, that he win some more money at a gamblin' place on Assembly street, and reckon he decided to blow 'way, while blowin' was good.

"De folks who know me always call me Sarah Poindexter and I got it honestly, like other honest slaves who never know what their real name was, and so I keeps it to the end of the road.

"I am now livin' with a distant relative and firmly trustin' in Jesus, as I have done for more than fifty years, that he will keep me to the end of the trail here and greet me when I pass on 'way up Yonder'."

SAM POLITE

Interview with Sam Polite, age 93
—Mrs. Chlotilde R. Martin, Beaufort County

"W'en gun shoot on Bay Pint (Bay Point) for freedom, I been sebenteen year old wuking slabe. I born on B. Fripp Plantation on St. Helena Island. My fadder been Sam Polite and my mudder been Mol Polite. My fadder b'long to Mister Marion Fripp and my mudder b'long to Mister Old B. Fripp. I don't know how mucher land, neider how much slabe he hab, but he hab two big plantation, and many slabe—more'n a hundred slabe.

"Slabe lib on Street—two row ob house wid two room to de house. I hab t'ree sister name, Silvy Polite, Rose Polite and Minda Polite. Hab brudder, too, but he die.

"My fadder and mudder ain't marry. Slabe don't marry—dey jest lib togedder. All slabe hab for stay on plantation in day time but w'en wuk done, kin wisit wife on odder plantation. Hab pass, so Patrol won't git um.

"W'en I been leetle boy, I play en Street—shoot marble play aa'my and sech t'ing. W'en hawn blow and mawning star rise, slabe' hab for git up and cook. W'en day clean, dey gone to field. 'Ooman too old for wuk in field hab for stay on Street and mind baby. Old mens follow cow. Chillen don't wuk in field 'till twelve or t'irteen year old. You carry dinner to field in your can and leabe um at de heading (end of row). W'en you feel hongry, you eat. Ebery slabe hab tas' (task) to do. Sometime one task (quarter acre), sometime two tas', and sometime t'ree. You haf for wuk 'til tas' t'ru (through). W'en cotton done mek, you hab odder tas'. Haffa cut cord ob maash (marsh) grass maybe. Tas' ob maash been eight feet long and four feet high. Den sometime you haffa (have to) roll cord ob mud in cowpen. 'Ooman haffa rake leaf from wood into cowpen. (This was used for fertilizer.)

"W'en you knock off wuk, you kin wuk on your land. Maybe you might hab two or t'ree tas' ob land 'round your cabin what Maussa gib you for plant. You kin hab chicken, maybe hawg. You kin sell aig (egg) and chicken to store and Maussa will buy your hawg. In dat way slabe kin hab money for buy t'ing lak fish and w'atebber he want. We don't git much fish in slabery 'cause we nebber hab boat. But sometime you kin t'row out net en ketch shrimp. You kin also ketch 'possum and raccoon wid your dawg.

"On Sattidy night ebery slabe dat wuks gits peck ob corn and pea, and sometime meat and clabber. You nebber see any sugar neider coffee in slabery. You has straw in your mattress but dey gib you blanket. Ebery year in Christmas month you gits four or eider fibe yaa'd cloth 'cording to how you is. Out ob dat, you haffa mek your clote (clothes). You wears dat same clote till de next year. You wears hit winter en summer, Sunday en ebery day. You don't git no coat, but dey gib you shoe. In slabery, you don't know nutting 'bout sheets for your bed. Us nebber know nutting 'bout Santa Claus 'till Freedom, but on Christmas Maussa gib you meat and syrup and maybe t'ree day widout wuk. Slabe wuk 'till daa'k on Sattidy jest lak any odder day—I still does wuk 'till daa'k on Sattidy.

But on Sunday slabe don't wuk. On Fourth ob July, slabe wuk 'till twelbe o'clock and den knocks off. On Sunday slabe kin wisit back and fort' (forth) on de plantations.

"Slabe don't do mucher frolic. W'en 'ooman hab baby he hab mid-wife for nine day and sometime don't haffa wuk for month w'en baby born, Missis send clote (clothes) from Big House. W'en nigger sick, Maussa sen' doctor. If you been berry sick, doctor gib you calomus (calomel) or castor oil. Sometime he gib you Dead-Shot for worms, or Puke (powder) to mek you heave. If I jest hab a pain in muh stummick, my mudder gib me Juse-e-moke w'at he git outen de wood." (I was unable to get any definite idea of what 'Dead-Shot', 'Puke' or 'Juse-e-moke' were.)

"If slabe don't do tas', de git licking wid lash on naked back. Driver nigger gib licking, but Maussa 'most always been dere. Sometime maybe nigger steal hawg or run 'way to de wood, den he git licking too. Can't be no trouble 'tween white folks and nigger in slabery time for dey do as dey choose wid you. But Maussa good to slabe If dey done day's tas' and don't be up to no meanness. Missis don't hab nutting to do wid nigger.

"In slabery, nigger go to white folks chu'ch. Slabe don't know nutting 'bout baptizing. W'en nigger dead, you can't knock off wuk for berry um. You haffa wait 'till night time to put um in de graabe (grave). You berry um by de light ob torch. Old Man Tony Ford bin de man w'at 'tend to funerals. Dey wasn't no nigger preacher on de plantation but dey been people to hold praise (prayers).

"I nebber see nigger in chain, but I shum (see them) in stock. I see plenty nigger sell on banjo table. Dey put you up on flatform (platform) en dey buy you. I see my uncle sell he brung one hundred dollar. 'Ooman don't sell widout he chillen.

"Mister Johnnie Fripp been my n'oung Maussa. W'en he chillen git marry, Old Maussa diwide de nigger. He gib Maussa Johnnie t'irty slabe and I been one ob dem. Maussa buy plantation on de Main (mainland). He build big house. He hab four boy and two gal. He hab five hundred acre. He ain't hab no oberseer, jest driver. We don't know no poor white trash on de Main, neider on St. Helena Islant.

"I wuk in field on Maussa Johnnie Fripp plantation. Sometime we sing w'en us wuk. One song we sing been go lak dis:

> Go way, Ole Man
> Go way, Ole Man
> W'ere you bin all day
> If you treat me good
> I'll stay 'till de Judgment day,
> But if you treat me bad,
> I'll sho' to run away.

"W'en war come, Missis tek me and two more niggers, put we and chillen in two wagon and go to Baarnwell (Barnwell). My mudder been one ob de nigger. We stay in Baarnwell all enduring (during) de war. My fadder he been wid de Rebel—been wid Mr. Marion Chaplin. W'en Freedom come, Missis didn't say nutting, she jest cry. But she gib we uh wagon and we press (stole) a horse and us come back to St. Helena Islant. It tek t'ree day to git home. W'en we git home, we fine de rest ob de nigger yere been hab Freedom four year befo' we! I wuk for uh nigger name Peter White. Muh fadder come back, and buy 20 acre ob land and we all lib togedder. I gone to school one or two year, but I ain't larn (learn) much. Four year after war, I buy fifteen acre ob land. Dat was dis yere same place w'ere I libs now. After w'ile I goes to wuk in rock (phosphate mines). I hears 'bout Ku Klux. Dey been bad people. Dey will kill you. Been marry to four wife. Dis yere last one, he been born in slabery too, but he don't 'members much 'bout um. He been leetle gal so high jest big 'nuf for open gate for white folks. I hab t'ree chillen, two libbing. I hear tell my boy William been marry to a w'ite 'ooman in England and hab t'ree chillen. My gal Alice lib in New Yawk. Sometime she send me money. I hab two great-gran.

"Abraham Lincoln? He de one w'at gib we liberty for wuk for we se'f. He come to Beaufort 'fore de war. He come as uh rail-splitter and spy 'round. He gone back w'ere he come from and say: 'You eider got to gib dese nigger t'ree day for deyse'f or dere will be blood-shed.' And he been right. I would be glad for shum (see him) but I nebber shum.

"I don't know nutting 'bout dat genman Mister Davis, neider Mister Washington—you say he been a nigger, too?

"Wat I t'ink 'bout slabery? I t'ink it been good t'ing. It larn nigger to wuk. If it ain't mek nigger wuk, he wouldn't do nutting but tief (thief). You don't find nigger wuk for slabery running 'round looking for ready money—dat been all dese yere n'oung nigger want. Me—I slabing for self right now. I don't want nobody for mek me wuk, but slabery larn me for wuk. I hab wuk five hundred head ob man in rock and today ain't one can come to me and say: 'Sam Polite, you beat me out ob one penny.'

"Slabery done uh good t'ing for me, 'cause if he ain't larn me to wuk, today I wouldn't know how to wuk."

WILLIAM PRATT

> Interview with William Pratt (77)
> Newberry, S.C. RFD
> —G.L. Summer, Newberry, S.C.

"I live with my children on a farm in Newberry County. I have a good place to live and plenty to eat. I work on the farm. I moved from Chester County in the year 1898, the year the Spanish-American War started.

"I was born in Chester County in April 1860. My parents belonged to the Pratts, but my mother belonged to the Kennedys before she married. They went to Robert K. Kennedy and was with him as his slaves. He was a good man but his wife was mean. She sure could 'cuss out slaves if they made her mad. She whipped me once when I was a small boy. I couldn't do much with her. My daddy's family belonged to the Pratts who lived seven miles from Chester. They was good folks to slaves. They always had lots to eat from their big garden. The white folks went hunting, and it was said some wild turkeys was around Price's Mountain, about nine miles south of Chester.

"We got up before day and went to work and worked till sundown. My mammy cooked for the family; and one day the mistress got mad at her and hit her on the head with a coffee paddle. We worked all day on Saturdays but didn't work on Sundays. On Christmas we had a holliday and had frolics and big eats.

"The patrollers once caught my daddy out at night

without a pass and whipped him a little, just for mischief. He was always allowed to go about where he wanted to go without a pass, but next time he asked Miss Polly for a paper to take out with him.

"After the war the Ku Klux didn't bother us but the Red Shirts come and wanted us to join them, that is they wanted my brother to join. He wouldn't join though. My brother-in-law joined and wore one of the shirts with them. He wanted Wade Hampton elected as he believed it was best for us. He was a Democrat and said they all ought to wear them. Once some mischief was played on a Negro who was a Republican and voted for Chamberlain. He was given a card and told to go to a certain merchant and show the card to him, that the merchant was a Chamberlain man and would give him supplies. He showed the card to the merchant who got mad and told the Negro if he didn't get out of his store he would kill him.

"Some of the old folks sometimes saw ghosts. A negro went to church one night on a horse, and somebody slipped up behind and spurred the horse. The Negro went home as fast as he could, saying that he had seen a ghost.

"When Freedom come, Old Man Kennedy took it well and said we was all free, but his wife just cursed us and said, 'Damn you, you are free now'. Old Marse Kennedy had some sons killed in the war. James and Douglas Kennedy lived in Chester County after the war.

"We used to dance jigs by ourself, and we danced the 'hack-back', skipping backwards and forwards facing each other. When one danced a jig he would sing, 'Juber this, Juber that, Juber kills a yellow cat'. My brother used to sing a cotton picking song: 'My mammy got meat skin laid away; grease my belly three times a day'.

"We was Baptist and baptized by immersion. An old Baptist song that was sung at the baptism was: 'Trouble water today, trouble water today, trouble water today. He will save you, He will save you; come to Jesus today, come to Jesus today, come to Jesus today. He will save you, He will save you, just now.'

"An old wood-chopping song which is yet sung by negroes is:

> Come on baby, let us go down;
> Come on baby, let us go down;
> Ten-pounder hammer stove my head;
> 'nough to kill my body dead.

"I married Rosy Kennedy, a daughter of Mose Kennedy, and had five children, but only two are now living. I have several grandchildren living in Chester County. I worked first on the Kennedy place. Their daughter, Miss Julie, was good to us. She married Robert Orr of Chester. She didn't have many beaux before because her mother was so mean nobody wanted to come around her. Miss Julie helped at my wedding. When my wife wasn't able to get breakfast so I could go to work, Miss Julie would tell me to come to her house and eat. That was after her mother died.

"I think Abraham Lincoln didn't do just right, 'cause he threw all the negroes on the world without any way of getting along. They was helpless. He ought to have done it gradually and give them a chance to get on their own. I think Booker Washington is a great man and has done great work, because he says negroes must have education and learn to work, too, and not sit down and expect more because he is educated.

"I joined the church because I believe there is a 'here-after', and I wanted to learn more about Jesus and get His forgiveness for what I had done wrong. We need Him always, because St. Matthews says the last state of man is worse than the first."

Slave Narratives

HENRY PRISTELL

> Interview with Henry Pristell, 83 year old
> Estill, S.C.
> —Phoebe Faucette, Hampton County

'Uncle Henry' Pristell and his wife, Lucina, live in the town of Estill in the usual type of small negro cabin. 'Uncle Henry' has a record of his age that shows that he is eighty-three years old but he is so well preserved that it is hard to believe. Although he is very bald, and his closely cut hair is nearly white, he gets about so easily and talks with such vigor he seems much younger.

"Oh, yes ma'am, I kin tell you 'bout de war times. I seen lots of dat, ma'am. I seen lots: I couldn't tell you all 'bout it—it been so distressful—but I kin tell some. When de Yankees come, at first sight of dem dey was string right 'long as far back as Luray. And string out crossways all over everywhere. Dey was jes' as thick together as de panels in dis fence. Dey was thousands of 'em! It was in de afternoon, an' dey was over everywhere—over de woods, over de fields, an' through de swamps, thick as dem weeds out dere! Dey didn't leave anything! Dey burn de fences down, shoot de cows, de hogs, de turkeys an' ducks an geese, de chickens an' everything. Dey didn't stay no time—didn't spend de night—jes' pass through. I see some of 'em set a fence afire an' stop dere an' cook. Dere was rail fences of fat pinewood in dem days.

"For de plantation use, dey didn't burn none of de

colored folks' houses nor de old boss' house. An' as for anybody being injured when dey pass through I didn't see none of dat. I must speak de truth, ma'am I didn't see anything out of the way. Jes' burn things an' take things to eat. Dere was Mr. Thomas' place, an' Mr. David Horton's place, den Mr. Wallace' place. Dey didn't burn any of 'em. I was on de Wallace place. My old boss been Mr. Sam Wallace. De house been up dere till 'bout thirty year ago. Dat been a fine place. Oh, yes ma'am. De house was built up high off de ground—as high as de top of dat room dere. I don't know why dey didn't burn de house. Now dat's all I kin tell you 'bout dat. In all other little doings, I didn't so much as realize it 'cause dey been little scattering doings. I do remember dat dere was a camp at Lawtonville for a while. Dey built a place for de prisoners, of mud. Dey dug a pit down in de ground 'bout three feet deep, den made de walls of mud. I'm satisfied 'bout dat. Dey didn't stay long. It was de Southern soldiers had de camp.

"After de war, we stay dere on de place. Stay dere for years. My father been Abram Pristell, my mother Lucy Pristell. 'Fore de war, I been jes' a little boy. Didn't have no special work to do. I penetrates 'round de yard dere by de kitchen. My mother would cook for de folks. Penetrate several days an' several night. De kitchen was off from de house. It had a big fireplace in it. Didn't have no stove. I'll be honest wid you. I'm satisfied 'bout dat! Had a loom in it an' a spinnin' wheel. I seen dem a many a time spinnin' an' weavin'. Oh, yes ma'am, I'm satisfied 'bout dat! An' dey had plenty of good things to eat. Oh, dey was well secured. You'll never see dat no more—not on dis side! But dey had plenty of people to feed an' to take care of. 'Course we don't want dose times no more, 'cause while some of de boss been good to 'em some of 'em been bad. What little time we got here we wants to take it easy an' quiet."

United States. Work Projects Administration

JUNIUS QUATTLEBAUM

> Interview with Junius Quattlebaum, 84 years old
> —Henry Grant, Columbia, S.C.

Junius Quattlebaum lives with his grandson, a short distance south of the Guignard Brick Factory, in the town of New Brookland, S.C. He is partially capable of self-support from what work and produce he is able to pick up around the City Market in Columbia.

"Well, sir, you want to talk to me 'bout them good old days back yonder in slavery time, does you? I call them good old days, 'cause I has never had as much since. I has worked harder since de war betwixt de North and de South than I ever worked under my marster and missus. I was just a small boy while de war was gwine on, but I was big 'nough to see and know what went on dere on de plantation all right.

"I was born on Marster Jim Quattlebaum's plantation over dere in Saluda County. He had 'bout sixty-five slaves in all, countin' de chillun. My marster wouldn't have no overseer, 'cause he say overseers would whip his niggers and he didn't 'low nobody, white or black, to do dat. If his niggers had to be whipped, he was gwine to do dat hisself and then they wouldn't be hurt much. Marster lak to see his slaves happy and singin' 'bout de place. If he ever heard any of them quarrelin' wid each other, he would holler at them and say: 'Sing! Us ain't got no time to fuss on dis place.'

"Marster lak he dram, 'specially in de fall of de year when it fust git cool. Us used to have big corn shuckin's on de plantation at night, 'long 'bout de fust of November of every year. All de corn was hauled from de fields and put in two or three big piles in de barnyard and de slaves would git 'round them, sing and shuck de corn. De slave women would hang buckets of raw tar afire on staves drove in de ground 'round de crowd, to give light. Them was sho' happy times.

"Marster would give all de grown slaves a dram or two of pure apple brandy, on them corn shuckin' nights, and take several smiles (drinks) hisself. I 'members so well, one of them nights, dat marster come to de barnyard, where us was all lit up, a singin' fit to kill hisself. Us was s'prised to see marster settin' down wid us niggers and shuckin' corn as fas' as us was. After a spell, him stood up and took 'nother smile, then say: 'Pass de jug 'round and let's all take a drink.' Wid dat, one of de niggers grab de jug of liquor and passed it 'round to all de shuckers. Then marster say: 'Everybody sing.' Some of de niggers 'quire: 'What you gwine to sing?' He say:—'Sing dis song: Pass 'round de bottle and we'll all take a drink.' Some of them in de crowd 'jected to dat song, 'cause they had 'nough liquor in them to 'ject to anything. Marster kinda scratch he head and say: 'Well, let me git a pole and you all is gwine to sing.' And singin' dere was, as sho' as you's born. Them niggers 'round de corn piles dat night h'isted dat song right now; dere was no waitin' for de pole or nothin' else. They wanted to sing, bad.

"De next mornin', after dis night I's talkin' 'bout, Miss Martha, our good missus come 'round to de slave houses and 'quire how they all felt. She say: 'You all can rest today and do what you want to do, 'cause Marster Jim ain't feelin' so well dis mornin'.' She knowed what was gwine on at de corn shuckin' de night befo' but she ain't said nothin' 'bout it. Mammy said many times dat de missus didn't lak dat whiskey drinkin' business in nobody. She was a pure and 'ligious woman if dere ever was one in dis world. Dere ain't no wonder dat de marster was foolish 'bout her. Mammy say de onliest way for both white and black to keep from lovin' Miss Martha, was to git away from her and not be so you could see her.

"Dis is de way our marsters treated deir slaves. I don't care what de world does write and say 'bout slave owners; I knows dis. Us slaves dat b'long on marster's plantation had de best folks to live and work wid I has ever seen or knowed. Dere is no sich kindness dese days betwixt de boss and them dat does de work. All de slaves worked pretty hard sometimes but never too hard. They worked wid light and happy hearts, 'cause they knowed dat marster would take good care of them; give them a plenty of good vittles, warm clothes, and warm houses to sleep in, when de cold weather come. They sho' had nothin' to worry 'bout and no overseer to drive them to work, lak some slaves on other plantations had. Easy livin' is 'bout half of life to white folks but it is all of life to most niggers. It sho' is.

"No, sir, de patarollers (patrollers) didn't bother none of marster's slaves. I has done told you he wouldn't let nobody, white or black, whip his niggers, 'cause he thought too much of them and de work they could do on de plantation when they was well and healthy. Yes, sir, I 'members, lak yistiddy, when Columbia was burned by de Yankees in 1865. All dat happened in de month of February, I thinks. Some of de niggers on de plantation said they seen de smoke from dat big fire, but I has my doubts 'bout de truth of dat.

"When Christmas come, all de slaves on de plantation had three days give to them, to rest and enjoy themselves. Missus and de two little misses fixed up a big Christmas tree. It was a big holly bush wid red berries all over it. It sho' was a picture of beautifulness. I can see missus so plain now, on Christmas mornin', a flirtin' 'round de Christmas trees, commandin' de little misses to put de names of each slave on a package and hang it on de tree for them. She was always pleased, smilin' and happy, 'cause she knowed dat she was doin' somethin' dat would make somebody else happy. She tried as hard to make de slaves happy as she did to make her own white friends happy, it seem lak to me. Close to de tree was a basket and in dat basket was put in a bag of candy, apples, raisins and nuts for all de chillun. Nobody was left out.

"Christmas mornin', marster would call all de slaves to come to de Christmas tree. He made all de chillun set down close to de tree and de grown slaves jined hands and make a circle 'round all. Then marster and missus would give de chillun deir gifts, fust, then they would take presents from de tree and call one slave at a time to step out and git deirs. After all de presents was give out, missus would stand in de middle of de ring and raise her hand and bow her head in silent thanks to God. All de slaves done lak her done. After all dis, everybbdy was happy, singin', and laughin' all over de place. Go 'way from here, white man! Don't tell me dat wasn't de next step to heaven to de slaves on our plantation. I sees and dreams 'bout them good old times, back yonder, to dis day."

Transcriber's Note

Original spelling has been maintained; e.g. "stob—a short straight piece of wood, such as a stake" (American Heritage Dictionary).—The Works Progress Administration was renamed during 1939 as the Work Projects Administration (WPA).

Slave Narratives

www.ingramcontent.com/pod-product-compliance
Lightning Source LLC
Chambersburg PA
CBHW071651160426
43195CB00012B/1425